P. VERGILI MARONIS

AENEIDOS

LIBER QVARTVS

P. VERGILI MARONIS

AENEIDOS

LIBER QVARTVS

EDITED WITH A COMMENTARY

BY

R. G. AUSTIN

OXFORD
AT THE CLARENDON PRESS

Oxford University Press, Walton Street, Oxford OX2 6DP
London Glasgow New York Toronto
Delhi Bombay Calcutta Madras Karachi
Kuala Lumpur Singapore Hong Kong Tokyo
Nairobi Dar es Salaam Cape Town
Melbourne Auckland
and associates in
Beirut Berlin Ibadan Mexico City Nicosia

First published 1955
Reprinted 1960, 1963 (with corrections)
1966, 1973, 1979
First issued as Paperback 1982

British Library Cataloguing in Publication Data
Virgil
    [Aeneid. Book 4]. P. Vergili Maronis Aeneidos,
    liber quartus.
    1. Virgil   2. Latin poetry
    I. Title   II. Austin, R.G.
    873′.01   PA6801.A5/
    ISBN 0–19–872111–0

Printed in Great Britain
at the University Press, Oxford
by Eric Buckley
Printer to the University

PREFACE

THE plan of this edition originated in a course of lectures which I gave to pass-degree students at University College, Cardiff, in 1948. I felt then that there was room for a commentary which should try to show something of Virgil's method, thought, and art to a type of student for which the existing editions were not designed. Modern conditions are so different from the old that a fresh approach seems needed in many matters that once were taken for granted; in particular, the classical background of such students' reading is now much more limited, and as a rule they know little Greek, often none at all; they understand but little of the music of the Latin hexameter, regarding 'scansion' as a higher mystery, largely because they have never had the opportunity of constructing verses, however unpoetic; and they have often been taught by those who are similarly handicapped. They need to be reminded that Latin literature is not something hermetically sealed, but is related to other literatures that form part of many degree courses. They need to be shown Virgil as a poet, with a poet's mind, not as a mere quarry for examiners. On the other hand, so much loving care has been spent in recent years on the study of Latin usage in general and of Virgilian style in particular, that in many ways something new is needed also by the young university student who is eager and able to read Virgil with real scholarship and discrimination. In this edition, I have tried to be useful to both classes, and I hope that in attempting this I have not fallen between two stools.

The difficulty that confronts a commentator on Virgil is as much that of what to omit as of what to include: as the wise Quintilian remarks, 'inter virtutes grammatici habebitur aliqua nescire'. I have tried not to overload this book with detail, and have preferred to indicate where discussion of minutiae may be found rather than to list and evaluate other people's views, except where it seemed to me really necessary to do so. Everyone will notice omissions of this and that point, or of reference to this or that book. Again, on some matters a definite opinion is impossible: Virgil looks so different as our moods change. Anatole France did well to remark that nothing is less probable than that two men in the same country have an absolutely similar impression of a line of Virgil. If some rather elementary points of metre or prosody appear to have been stressed too much, or to be over-simplified, it is because I know something of the difficulties that the modern student finds in such things; but I have dealt also with certain subtleties of Virgilian metric for those more advanced readers who may care for them.

I owe a very special debt of thanks to Mr. G. W. Williams, Fellow of Balliol, for constant stimulating criticism and for bringing to my notice much that would otherwise have escaped me. Professor W. S. Watt, of the University of Aberdeen, has given me valuable help on many points. The patience of Miss Elizabeth Thomas, of University College, Cardiff, has saved me from many careless references. But without the receptive minds of my Cardiff students this edition would never have been begun.

R. G. A.

CARDIFF
August 1954

CONTENTS

CONTENTS

INTRODUCTION

Maist reuerend Virgil, of latine poetis prince,
Gem of ingyne, and flude of eloquence,
Thou peirles peirle, patron of poetry,
Rois, register, palme, laurere, and glory,
Chosin charbukill, cheif floure and Cedir tre,
Lanterne, lade sterne, myrour, and a per se
Maister of maisteris, swete sours and springand well,
Wide quhare ouer all ringis thyne heuinly bell.

GAVIN DOUGLAS, Preface to the *Aeneid*

THE study of Virgil brings with it the richest of all the rewards that Latin has for its initiates, and within that study the Fourth Book of the *Aeneid* holds a special place. It might have been omitted, with no apparent lacuna in the epic theme. But if Virgil had not written it and set it where he did, the *Aeneid* would have remained for ever within the penumbra of myth; for it is in this book that he tells of the most real of human experiences, without romanticizing it or in any way hiding its painful wounds. His Dido and his Aeneas are a woman and a man in love; and long after the tragic tale has run its course, the pity of it echoes through all Aeneas' life and actions, so that it is never possible to think of him as any other but the man whom Dido had loved, and who, despite himself and despite his destiny, had loved Dido. It is a book which in the last resort must be interpreted by its readers in their secret hearts, without the chilling guide of what Dryden calls somewhere 'pedantic pains'. As one reads it and reads it again, its power and its reality grow always clearer and stronger. If Virgil had written nothing else but this tale of 'Dido of Carthage, floure and lampe of Tyre', it would have established his right to stand beside the greatest of the Greek tragedians, not only in his firm and unflinching expression of a bitter moral conflict, not only in the pity and fear with which he accomplishes his catharsis of our emotions, not only in the noble simplicity of his conception, but also in the *oeconomia* of his plot and the inexorability of its onward movement. A reader who comes to it for the first time, knowing nothing of what is to be unfolded in its pages, must be stirred as on a first reading of *Antigone* or *Othello*; and in Virgil's tale his heart is riven and his conscience torn by a situation that for all its heroic outlines is yet within the bounds of credible human experience. Thomas Hardy, in *The Woodlanders*, describes his Little Hintock as a place where, sequestered though it was, 'from time to time, dramas of a grandeur and unity truly Sophoclean are enacted in the real, by virtue of the concentrated passions and closely-knit interdependence of the lives therein'. The tragedy of Dido's passion might, in essentials, occur at any time in the Little Hintocks of today.

The book must be taken in its setting. In the First Book, Dido has succoured the shipwrecked Trojans. She has already heard of Aeneas by repute, and when at last she meets him, her heart goes out to him, for she too has been driven far from home:

> me quoque per multos similis fortuna labores
> iactatam hac demum voluit consistere terra.
> non ignara mali miseris succurrere disco.

There and then Aeneas, 'come to Paradys, out of the swolow of helle' as Chaucer puts it, tells Dido the tale of the sack of Troy, so that it is through her eyes that we see his suffering. At the opening of the Fourth Book his tale is done, and she is lost:

> Anoon her herte hath pitee of his wo
> And, with that pitee, lov com in also.

And when her passion has run its course to its end upon the pyre of her own building, and Aeneas sails away to fulfil what the gods think fit, he has had his hour of happiness with her and let it go for ever. *Dis aliter visum*: the book gives us the one glimpse that we are allowed to see of him as he might have been; a chapter in his life has closed, but his memories never leave him. In the Sixth Book, he meets her grim ghost in the *Lugentes Campi*, the 'Broken-Hearted Fields' as Flecker calls them, and there he pleads urgently with her, but she will have none of him, and he

casu concussus iniquo
prosequitur lacrimans longe et miseratur euntem.

Long afterwards it was to Dido that his thoughts turned, in the bitter moment when his friend Evander's young son Pallas lay dead in his cause, and on the boy's body he set a noble garment that she had once made for him, *laeta laborum* (xi. 73): those two words should help us to understand what Aeneas had renounced in gaining his Italy.

The opening of the book shows Dido, sleepless and agonized, seeking comfort and advice from Anna; at its end we see her dying on the pyre, with Anna at her side doing all that a sister's tenderness could do to ease the sharpness of death. Between this first scene and the last Anna takes no direct part; no human agency could save Dido from the swift current of her destiny; yet Anna's presence is felt throughout, and Dido's tragedy is shown as a family sorrow The tenseness of the opening is never far relaxed in all that follows. Dido hears from Anna the advice that she has hoped to hear, despite herself; she takes it, but she gains no peace, and it is with the knowledge of her heightened passion that we presently listen to the two mocking goddesses, Juno and Venus, agreeing not to quarrel over the victim of their sport. There follows the dazzling brilliance of the meet, a single splendid moment of unalloyed happiness as Dido and Aeneas ride out in company; and then, the storm, and the uncanny elemental witnesses to their union in the cave. The scene changes now, and we hear the gossip about them, carried by Rumour on her purposeful course until she reaches the one person who can do them both most harm, Iarbas. In all this, and in Iarbas' haughty, angry prayer to Jupiter, as well as in Jupiter's swift reaction to it in sending Mercury with a peremptory message to Aeneas (here Virgil depicts Jupiter's masculine decision as unerringly as he has shown the femininity of the two goddesses), we are made aware of the ineluctable forces that control the lives of men. We are reminded also that no man can escape responsibility for his own actions. Dido has tempted Aeneas, and Aeneas has fallen, and both must suffer the consequence. So the stage is set for the harsh conflict of will between them as they meet face to face. The tension rises as Dido speaks to Aeneas, and it is not relaxed while Aeneas replies, for beneath all his formal coldness he is repressed and strained to breaking point; and then there is a further heightening in the wild fury of Dido's second speech, with its climax as she faints and is carried away. In the rest of the book we witness the ebb and flow of her resolution: her miserable attempt to gain time to be 'schooled to sorrow', then her realization that all hope has gone, then the dim groping of the magic ritual, in which Dido has left the real world for the shadows of supernatural horror, then her weakening as she wearily argues with herself, until she comes once more to see that death alone can end her misery, irrationally blaming Anna for it all, finally returning to her consciousness of wrong done to Sychaeus. Virgil then quickly shows us Aeneas, jolted into horrified haste by a second warning from Mercury. Dido, watching his departure, rises first to a wild incoherent frenzy, then— how rapidly her moods change—she collects herself to cal-culated, purposeful utterance as she sets the curse of Car-thage upon the race of Troy. So we are brought to the death-agony on the pyre, preceded by her proud farewell to life, and to the last scene where Anna and she are together once more, until her soul slips gently away into the shelter of the winds.

Virgil planned the book on clear firm lines. He knew what he meant his Dido to be; I am sure that he was not taken by surprise and confounded by his own creation, as has been suggested. She is drawn plainly from the outset, impulsive, loving, lonely, bewildered, and always passionate. Virgil develops her character with unfaltering hand, and, as Sellar noted nearly eighty years ago, she 'grows more and more real as her passion deepens'. She is at the mercy of many changing moods,[1] with the quiet voice of conscience never wholly stilled, always half-afraid of calamity, hoping against hope that all will yet be well. She never quite casts Aeneas from her; even when she sees that he is inflexible, she makes a last bid for his pity through Anna; and when that fails, when she is driven out of her mind by strange visions of her dead husband and by terrifying dreams of her living lover, when she prepares her magic rites, so unwillingly, for Anna's deception, she still half-pretends that it is all to win him back. Even when she has resolved to die, she yet retreats, though retreat is useless, and she knows it. At the last, after all her furious anger, she still thinks of him with tenderness, in those noble moments when she is on the pyre. Virgil nowhere conceals his pity for her, and he meant his readers to share it with him: and they have always done so. 'The story of Dido has haunted the imagination of Europe, drawing tears from saints and sinners, from St. Augustine in the fourth century as from Anatole France in the twentieth.'[2] If he had really meant his contemporaries to see in her a mere picture of Cleopatra, as some hold, could he have wished this, or achieved it? Yet he does not hide Dido's faults. She breaks her word to Sychaeus, a thing which, though no fault to modern minds, was yet an offence against the older and more austere traditions of Rome. She deceives

---

[1] Cf. Dryden, *Dedication of the Aeneis* (vol. xiv of the 1808 edition, p. 173).

[2] G. S. Gordon, *Virgil in English Poetry*, in *The Discipline of Letters* (Oxford, 1946), p. 23.

her soothsayers, and the old woman who had been Sychaeus' nurse, and her sister Anna herself. She is proud in her power, and it is the blow to her pride that hurts her in Aeneas' desertion. She can see how Aeneas has shattered her whole life, but she cannot see how she has shattered his. Above all, Virgil shows her plainly as a temptress of the flesh, dominated by passion, fiercely possessive. Yet he pities her, and his sorrow transcends her weaknesses. He racks us with her misery, and we remember nothing at the last but her nobility. 'It is one of the signs of a great writer', Professor L. C. Knights once observed in a paper on *Antony and Cleopatra*,[1] 'that he can *afford* to evoke sympathy or even admiration for what, in his final judgment, is discarded or condemned.' Virgil could afford this in Dido.

But if she was clearly conceived in Virgil's mind from the first, so too was his Aeneas. We do not see him as we see Dido. Her direct presence dominates the book: his character is shown for the most part obliquely, either in some significant word (cf. 281, 291, 393), or by inference from his own repression (cf. 332, 360). For much of the time we see him through the eyes of others—through those of Dido herself, through the distorted and distorting vision of *Fama*, through the angry gibes of Iarbas, through Jupiter's curt displeasure, through the unsuccessful mission of Anna. He appears in person at the meet, in all the pride of his heroic beauty; at Carthage, happy and busy with the building of the city, when Mercury comes to shatter all his new life; in the great central scene where he answers Dido's appeal; in his hurried flight from Carthage. He does not question obedience to Mercury's command, yet his first thought is how least to hurt Dido in obeying, and in the end a second warning from heaven is needed before he carries out his resolve. Although Virgil tells us explicitly how Dido interpreted the strange marriage-ritual in the cave (172), he says nothing there of

[1] *Scrutiny*, xvi, 1949, p. 322; I owe this reference to Miss Patricia Bartlett.

Aeneas' view of it, and it is only in his single speech to
Dido (333–61) that he is permitted any direct revelation of
himself. It is from that speech alone, taken at its surface
appearance, that he is generally judged, and yet even there
his actual words do not tell us all his thoughts. I have tried
to show in my commentary something of the vibrant under-
currents of tension in this speech, which it is only wilful to
ignore. Dido never finds it difficult to let her desires overcome her conscience, but Aeneas' desires are as strong, and
his victory over them is hardly won: the speech is eloquent
of a conflict which, for him, was harder than anything that
Dido had known, and the famous words *at pius Aeneas* (393),
in which Virgil shows his victory, contain all the anguish of
his resignation to the unexplained and unexplainable bidding of God. He loved Dido, and had not been strong
enough to withstand the temptation that she brought. The
surface picture that Virgil has drawn of him cannot but
make us shocked at his conduct; and the shock is so heavy
that we forget to see that Dido's fault, in her conduct
towards him, was as grave as his. Virgil shows Aeneas as a
man puzzled and hurt by the problem of pain, not only the
pain that he suffers but the pain that he inflicts; he has
shown Anna, and even Iarbas, caught in similar bewilderment, though less pitifully. Dryden did well to write in his
grave way 'I doubt there was a fault somewhere, and
Jupiter is better able to bear the blame than either Virgil
or Aeneas'.[1] For where did the fault lie, if not with their
stars? The gods who have allowed Dido to be deceived and
betrayed are the same gods who have allowed Aeneas to be
tempted and to fall. His hurt is, in its own way, as terrible
as hers, and if Virgil awakes our pity for her, as he does, we
should let him awake pity in us for Aeneas also. We must not
forget their last meeting in the Shades. Dido had Sychaeus
there to turn to, and he 'answer'd all her cares, and equall'd
all her love'; but Aeneas had lost her as he had lost Creusa

[1] *Dedication of the Aeneis*, p. 171.

before; and, later, when Lavinia came to him, it was in sorrow that she came; he nowhere found human comfort or forgiveness in his hard and bitter path, which he had himself made the more grievous by the consequence of his own act:

> O the mind, mind has mountains; cliffs of fall
> Frightful, no-man-fathomed. Hold them cheap
> May who ne'er hung there.

The Fourth Book is all Virgil's own, in the spirit of its conception, in the problems of which it treats, and in the manner of its working out. He has taken a traditional story, of which we possess faint echoes,[1] and has removed it from the museum of myth into the living world. We may be told that Homer had thought of Calypso long before Virgil had thought of Dido. Servius may tell us that the whole tale was taken from Apollonius Rhodius, and both he and Macrobius are welcome to have believed it. ' 'Tis just as some people say, Milton hath stolen his poem, from an Italian stroller, named Andreino.'[2] We may freely conjecture what we will of Naevius' treatment of the legend.[3] We may, if we wish, see in Catullus' Ariadne a pale prototype of Dido's magnificence. Virgil had all this before him, and, what is more, he had before him the whole vast canvas of Greek tragedy, of which his grave mind took full note. But to deny him his complete and personal creation is to deny the very foundation of poetry. In the final reckoning the tale of Dido and Aeneas, as Virgil has told it, is a universal; he has told it so, because that is his poet's interpretation of an aspect of human experience which transcends all others in its meaning for man, and because the hero of his epic could not be, for him and for his purpose, an insubstantial figure remote from the imperfect world of reality,

---

[1] See Pease's edition, pp. 14 ff.

[2] Christopher Pitt, in *The Works of Virgil, in Latin and English* (London, 1753), vol. ii, p. 269; cf. Dryden, *Dedication of the Aeneis*, pp. 181 ff.

[3] See Pease, pp. 18 ff.

untouched and unperplexed and untormented by its enig-
matic gods. We can grieve for Apollonius' Medea or for
Catullus' Ariadne, as we turn the page; but Dido steps from
the page and is with us always. 'Quid enim miserius misero
non miserante se ipsum et flente Didonis mortem, quae
fiebat amando Aenean, non flente autem mortem suam,
quae fiebat non amando te, deus, lumen cordis mei et panis
oris intus animae meae et virtus maritans mentem meam et
sinum cogitationis meae?': so wept St. Augustine, more than
fifteen hundred years ago,[1] and in our own day a young
poet, Sidney Keyes, killed in the African campaign in 1943,
reinterpreted the ancient grief:[2]

> He never loved the frenzy of the sun
> Nor the clear seas.
> He came with hero's arms and bullock's eyes
> Afraid of nothing but his nagging gods.
> He never loved the hollow-sounding beaches
> Nor rested easily in carven beds.
>
> The smoke blows over the breakers, the high pyre waits.
> His mind was a blank wall throwing echoes,
> Not half so subtle as the coiling flames.
> He never loved my wild eyes nor the pigeons
> Inhabiting my gates.

In preparing this edition, I have purposely consulted few
commentaries and few books about Virgil. As Mackail well
remarks, in the preface to his edition of the *Aeneid* (Oxford,
1930), commentaries can be immoderately swollen, 'from
timidity, and because the writer is afraid of the charge of
"not seeming to be aware" of what has been written on the
point by others'. The warmth of Mackail's edition grows
constantly upon the reader, and it is rich in wisdom. I have
used Heyne-Wagner (4th edition, Leipzig and London,

[1] St. Aug. *Conf.* i. 13.
[2] From *The Collected Poems of Sidney Keyes* (Routledge, 1945),
p. 94. Printed by permission of Messrs. Routledge and Kegan Paul.

1830–41), a classic of the classics which is always a delight to handle. James Henry's *Aeneidea* (London–Dublin–Meissen, 1873–92) has been fascinating and exasperating by turns. Conington's edition nowadays is an unsympathetic book to use, owing to its depressing format and austere outlook; Page is indispensable, in spite of his imperceptive judgement of Aeneas as he appears in the Fourth Book. I owe a great debt to the vast compilation of A. S. Pease, *P. Vergili Maronis Aeneidos Liber Quartus* (Harvard, 1935), an encyclopaedia in its own right; its merits become very clear if it is set beside *Il Libro di Didone* by C. Buscaroli (Rome–Milan, 1932); but one must not go to either if one wishes to remember that Virgil was a poet. There is much freshness and discernment in the notes of A. L. Irvine, in his edition of Fanshawe's translation of 1648 (*The Loves of Dido and Aeneas*, Oxford, Blackwell, 1924); his appendix on James Henry is full of interest. I have found much guidance in R. S. Conway's edition of Book I (Cambridge, 1935). In a quite different category is the outstanding commentary on Book VI by E. Norden (2nd edition, Berlin–Leipzig, 1916; the third edition of 1927 contains a body of additional notes, but it has been less accessible to me, as I suspect it will be to many). This commentary is a scientific storehouse of Virgilian scholarship, humanely presented by a great editor, and it is essential to any study of Virgil, especially for the many-sided minutiae of style, language, and metre. I have supplemented it by frequent reference to articles in the *Archiv für lateinische Lexicographie* by various authors, notably P. Maas. Of all the literary studies of Virgil that I might name, I would single out R. Heinze, *Virgils epische Technik* (3rd edition, Leipzig–Berlin, 1928), a book which is instinct with humanity and sensitive understanding. Other books that I have often consulted are the three by Warde Fowler, *Virgil's Gathering of the Clans*, *Aeneas at the Site of Rome*, and *The Death of Turnus* (Oxford, Blackwell, 1918, 1918, 1919); C. Bailey, *Religion in Virgil*

(Oxford, 1935); J. Sparrow, *Half-Lines and Repetitions in Virgil* (Oxford, 1931). M. N. Wetmore's *Index Verborum Vergilianus* (New Haven, 1911) has given me endless help.

The text of this edition is that of the Oxford Classical Texts, edited by Sir F. A. Hirtzel (1900), the plates of which have been used by permission of the Delegates of the Clarendon Press. I have ventured to prefer an alternative reading in 54, 217, 593, 641, 646. Mackail's edition (pp. lviii ff.) has a clear account of the manuscript tradition; for a more detailed summary see Pease, pp. 71 ff.

Although I have made a special point of commenting on Virgilian metric, I have not thought it necessary to include a formal account of the structure of the hexameter; there is a very clear exposition of it in Sir Frank Fletcher's edition of Book VI (Oxford, 1941), and in W. S. Maguinness's edition of Book XII (London, Methuen, 1953); W. R. Hardie's *Res Metrica* (Oxford, 1920) is, of course, helpful at every turn. I have found much guidance on points of prosody and metrical usage in M. Platnauer's *Latin Elegiac Verse* (Cambridge, 1951).

I am grateful to Sir Basil Blackwell for allowing me to draw upon the material contained in my paper *The Fourth Book of the Aeneid*, a lecture to the Virgil Society which was published by him in 1951.

SIGLA

A = Schedae Vaticano-Berolinenses   saec. ii vel iii
F = Schedae Vaticanae   saec. iii init. vel iv
G = Schedae Sangallenses rescriptae   saec. iv
M = Codex Mediceus   saec. v
P = Codex Palatinus   saec. iv–v
R = Codex Romanus   saec. vi?
V = Schedae Veronenses rescriptae   saec. iv?
γ = Codex Gudianus   saec. ix
a = Codex Bernensis 172 et Parisinus   saec. ix
     7929
b = Codex Bernensis 165   saec. ix
c = Codex Bernensis 184   saec. ix
m = Codex Minoraugiensis   saec. xii?
π = Codex Pragensis   saec. ix
Serv. = Servii commentarii
D. Serv. = Servius Danielis (vel Deuteroservius quem
       vocat Georgii)

P. VERGILI MARONIS

AENEIDOS

LIBER IV

At regina gravi iamdudum saucia cura
vulnus alit venis et caeco carpitur igni.
multa viri virtus animo multusque recursat
gentis honos: haerent infixi pectore vultus
verbaque, nec placidam membris dat cura quietem.   5
postera Phoebea lustrabat lampade terras
umentemque Aurora polo dimoverat umbram,
cum sic unanimam adloquitur male sana sororem:
'Anna soror, quae me suspensam insomnia terrent!
quis novus hic nostris successit sedibus hospes,   10
quem sese ore ferens, quam forti pectore et armis!
credo equidem, nec vana fides, genus esse deorum.
degeneres animos timor arguit. heu, quibus ille
iactatus fatis! quae bella exhausta canebat!
si mihi non animo fixum immotumque sederet   15
ne cui me vinclo vellem sociare iugali,
postquam primus amor deceptam morte fefellit;
si non pertaesum thalami taedaeque fuisset,
huic uni forsan potui succumbere culpae.
Anna, fatebor enim, miseri post fata Sychaei   20

1–20 FGMPR   9 suspensa M^1 terret c^2 agnoscit Serv.
11 quam] quem F^1 fortis π deteriores   18 fuissent $F^2MP^1\gamma^1c^1$

coniugis et sparsos fraterna caede penatis
solus hic inflexit sensus animumque labantem
impulit. agnosco veteris vestigia flammae.
sed mihi vel tellus optem prius ima dehiscat
vel pater omnipotens abigat me fulmine ad umbras,   25
pallentis umbras Erebo noctemque profundam,
ante, pudor, quam te violo aut tua iura·resolvo.
ille meós, primus qui me sibi iunxit, amores
abstulit ; ille habeat secum servetque sepulcro.'
sic effata sinum lacrimis implevit obortis.   30

    Anna refert: 'o luce magis dilecta sorori,
solane perpetua maerens carpere iuventa
nec dulcis natos Veneris nec praemia noris ?
id cinerem aut manis credis curare sepultos ?
esto: aegram nulli quondam flexere mariti,   35
non Libyae, non ante Tyro ; despectus Iarbas
ductoresque alii, quos Africa terra triumphis
dives alit: placitone etiam pugnabis amori ?
nec venit in mentem quorum consederis arvis ?
hinc Gaetulae urbes, genus insuperabile bello,   40
et Numidae infreni cingunt et inhospita Syrtis ;
hinc deserta siti regio lateque furentes
Barcaei. quid bella Tyro surgentia dicam
germanique minas ?
dis equidem auspicibus reor et Iunone secunda   45
hunc cursum Iliacas vento tenuisse carinas.
quam tu urbem, soror, hanc cernes, quae surgere regna
coniugio tali! Teucrum comitantibus armis
Punica se quantis attollet gloria rebus!
tu modo posce deos veniam, sacrisque litatis   50

21–37 FGMPR; 38–50 FMPR   25 adigat GMPRγ²bc   26 Erebi
MP²γ²bcπ agnoscit Serv.   27 ante] sancte Markland   36 Libya
P¹ Serv.   40 insuperabile] intractabile R   41 ante v. 40
conlocat Immisch, fortasse recte   42 furentes] vagantes c deteriores
Isidorus   43 Barcaei] Vaccaei Isidorus orig. ix. 2, 107

indulge hospitio causasque innecte morandi,
dum pelago desaevit hiems et aquosus Orion,
quassataeque rates, dum non tractabile caelum.'
  His dictis impenso animum flammavit amore
spemque dedit dubiae menti solvitque pudorem.   55
principio delubra adeunt pacemque per aras
exquirunt; mactant lectas de more bidentis
legiferae Cereri Phoeboque patrique Lyaeo,
Iunoni ante omnis, cui vincla iugalia curae.
ipsa tenens dextra pateram pulcherrima Dido   60
candentis vaccae media inter cornua fundit,
aut ante ora deum pinguis spatiatur ad aras,
instauratque diem donis, pecudumque reclusis
pectoribus inhians spirantia consulit exta.
heu, vatum ignarae mentes! quid vota furentem,   65
quid delubra iuvant? est mollis flamma medullas
interea et tacitum vivit sub pectore vulnus.
uritur infelix Dido totaque vagatur
urbe furens, qualis coniecta cerva sagitta,
quam procul incautam nemora inter Cresia fixit   70
pastor agens telis liquitque volatile ferrum
nescius: illa fuga silvas saltusque peragrat
Dictaeos; haeret lateri letalis harundo.
nunc media Aenean secum per moenia ducit
Sidoniasque ostentat opes urbemque paratam,   75
incipit effari mediaque in voce resistit;
nunc eadem labente die convivia quaerit,
Iliacosque iterum demens audire labores
exposcit pendetque iterum narrantis ab ore.
post ubi digressi, lumenque obscura vicissim   80
luna premit suadentque cadentia sidera somnos,

51–81 *FMPR*   51 hospitio et causas *F*   53 dum . . .
caelum *damnat Ribbeck*   54 impenso *F*[1] *Parisinus* 7906 *agnoscit
Serv.*: penso *P*[1]: incensum *F*[2]*MP*[2]*Rγbcπ Serv.*   inflammavit *MP*[2]*γb*
58 frugiferae *F*[2]*Rγ*[2]

sola domo maeret vacua stratisque relictis
incubat. illum absens absentem auditque videtque,
aut gremio Ascanium genitoris imagine capta
detinet, infandum si fallere possit amorem.   85
non coeptae adsurgunt turres, non arma iuventus
exercet portusve aut propugnacula bello
tuta parant: pendent opera interrupta minaeque
murorum ingentes aequataque machina caelo.

  Quam simul ac tali persensit peste teneri   90
cara Iovis coniunx nec famam obstare furori,
talibus adgreditur Venerem Saturnia dictis:
'egregiam vero laudem et spolia ampla refertis
tuque puerque tuus (magnum et memorabile numen),
una dolo divum si femina victa duorum est.   95
nec me adeo fallit veritam te moenia nostra
suspectas habuisse domos Karthaginis altae.
sed quis erit modus, aut quo nunc certamine tanto?
quin potius pacem aeternam pactosque hymenaeos
exercemus? habes tota quod mente petisti: 100
ardet amans Dido traxitque per ossa furorem.
communem hunc ergo populum paribusque regamus
auspiciis; liceat Phrygio servire marito
dotalisque tuae Tyrios permittere dextrae.'

  Olli (sensit enim simulata mente locutam,   105
quo regnum Italiae Libycas averteret oras)
sic contra est ingressa Venus: 'quis talia demens
abnuat aut tecum malit contendere bello?
si modo quod memoras factum fortuna sequatur.
sed fatis incerta feror, si Iuppiter unam   110
esse velit Tyriis urbem Troiaque profectis,

82–92 *FMPR*; 93–111 *F (recentiore manu) MPR*   85 amantem *F*   91 furori] pudori *Rm*   94 nomen *Canonicianus deteriores Ribbeck*   98 certamina tanta *Heinsius*   106 Italia *Wakefield* adverteret π *libri Pierii, agnoscit Serv.*

miscerive probet populos aut foedera iungi.
tu coniunx, tibi fas animum temptare precando.
perge, sequar.' tum sic excepit regia Iuno:
'mecum erit iste labor. nunc qua ratione quod instat   115
confieri possit, paucis (adverte) docebo.
venatum Aeneas unaque miserrima Dido
in nemus ire parant, ubi primos crastinus ortus
extulerit Titan radiisque retexerit orbem.
his ego nigrantem commixta grandine nimbum,   120
dum trepidant alae saltusque indagine cingunt,
desuper infundam et tonitru caelum omne ciebo.
diffugient comites et nocte tegentur opaca:
speluncam Dido dux et Troianus eandem
devenient. adero et, tua si mihi certa voluntas,   125
conubio iungam stabili propriamque dicabo.
hic hymenaeus erit.' non adversata petenti
adnuit atque dolis risit Cytherea repertis.
   Oceanum interea surgens Aurora reliquit.
it portis iubare exorto delecta iuventus,   130
retia rara, plagae, lato venabula ferro,
Massylique ruunt equites et odora canum vis.
reginam thalamo cunctantem ad limina primi
Poenorum exspectant, ostroque insignis et auro
stat sonipes ac frena ferox spumantia mandit.   135
tandem progreditur magna stipante caterva
Sidoniam picto chlamydem circumdata limbo;
cui pharetra ex auro, crines nodantur in aurum,
aurea purpuream subnectit fibula vestem.
nec non et Phrygii comites et laetus Iulus   140

112–115 F (recentiore manu) MPR; 116–121 F (recentiore manu)
MR; 122–140 MR   112 foedere deteriores quidam, agnoscit Serv.
116 confieri $R\gamma^{1}c^{2}$ (in rasura) Serv.: comfieri M^{2}: quod fieri $M^{1}\gamma^{2}$:
ʟuo fieri $Fb^{1}\pi^{2}$ 118 primus $M^{1}R$: primum M^{2} 126 damnant
ᵖeerlkamp Ribbeck   127 aversata R agnoscit Serv.   129 re-
inquit M^{1}

incedunt. ipse ante alios pulcherrimus omnis
infert se socium Aeneas atque agmina iungit.
qualis ubi hibernam Lyciam Xanthique fluenta
deserit ac Delum maternam invisit Apollo
instauratque choros, mixtique altaria circum   145
Cretesque Dryopesque fremunt pictique Agathyrsi:
ipse iugis Cynthi graditur mollique fluentem
fronde premit crinem fingens atque implicat auro,
tela sonant umeris: haud illo segnior ibat
Aeneas, tantum egregio decus enitet ore.   150
postquam altos ventum in montis atque invia lustra,
ecce ferae saxi deiectae vertice caprae
decurrere iugis; alia de parte patentis
transmittunt cursu campos atque agmina cervi
pulverulenta fuga glomerant montisque relinquunt.   155
at puer Ascanius mediis in vallibus acri
gaudet equo iamque hos cursu, iam praeterit illos,
spumantemque dari pecora inter inertia votis
optat aprum, aut fulvum descendere monte leonem.

Interea magno misceri murmure caelum   160
incipit, insequitur commixta grandine nimbus,
et Tyrii comites passim et Troiana iuventus
Dardaniusque nepos Veneris diversa per agros
tecta metu petiere; ruunt de montibus amnes.
speluncam Dido dux et Troianus eandem   165
deveniunt. prima et Tellus et pronuba Iuno
dant signum; fulsere ignes et conscius aether
conubiis, summoque ulularunt vertice Nymphae.
ille dies primus leti primusque malorum
causa fuit; neque enim specie famave movetur   170
nec iam furtivum Dido meditatur amorem:

141–143 *MR*; 144–161 *MRV*; 162–171 *MPRV*   168 conubii
P²RVb²c²   169 malorum] laborum *P¹ Parisinus* 7906 *Philar-
gyrius*

coniugium vocat, hoc praetexit nomine culpam.

Extemplo Libyae magnas it Fama per urbes,
Fama, malum qua non aliud velocius ullum:
mobilitate viget virisque adquirit eundo,   175
parva metu primo, mox sese attollit in auras
ingrediturque solo et caput inter nubila condit.
illam Terra parens ira inritata deorum
extremam, ut perhibent, Coeo Enceladoque sororem
progenuit pedibus celerem et pernicibus alis,   180
monstrum horrendum, ingens, cui quot sunt corpore plumae,
tot vigiles oculi subter (mirabile dictu),
tot linguae, totidem ora sonant, tot subrigit auris.
nocte volat caeli medio terraeque per umbram
stridens, nec dulci declinat lumina somno;   185
luce sedet custos aut summi culmine tecti
turribus aut altis, et magnas territat urbes,
tam ficti pravique tenax quam nuntia veri.
haec tum multiplici populos sermone replebat
gaudens, et pariter facta atque infecta canebat: 190
venisse Aenean Troiano sanguine cretum,
cui se pulchra viro dignetur iungere Dido;
nunc hiemem inter se luxu, quam longa, fovere
regnorum immemores turpique cupidine captos.
haec passim dea foeda virum diffundit in ora.   195
protinus ad regem cursus detorquet Iarban
incenditque animum dictis atque aggerat iras.

Hic Hammone satus rapta Garamantide nympha
templa Iovi centum latis immania regnis,
centum aras posuit vigilemque sacraverat ignem,   200
excubias divum aeternas, pecudumque cruore
pingue solum et variis florentia limina sertis.

172-196 *MPRV*; 197-202 *MPR*   174 quo *P¹Vγ²bcπ Priscia-*
nus Serv.   179 extrema *R¹*   182 *post* oculi *interpungit Nauck*
187 magnas et *M¹*   191 a sanguine *Rγ²*   196 cursu *P²*:
cursum *γ Nonius*

isque amens animi et rumore accensus amaro
dicitur ante aras media inter numina divum
multa Iovem manibus supplex orasse supinis: 205
'Iuppiter omnipotens, cui nunc Maurusia pictis
gens epulata toris Lenaeum libat honorem,
aspicis haec? an te, genitor, cum fulmina torques
nequiquam horremus, caecique in nubibus ignes
terrificant animos et inania murmura miscent?   210
femina, quae nostris errans in finibus urbem
exiguam pretio posuit, cui litus arandum
cuique loci leges dedimus, conubia nostra
reppulit ac dominum Aenean in regna recepit.
et nunc ille Paris cum semiviro comitatu,   215
Maeonia mentum mitra crinemque madentem
subnexus, rapto potitur: nos munera templis
quippe tuis ferimus famamque fovemus inanem.'
   Talibus orantem dictis arasque tenentem
audiit Omnipotens, oculosque ad moenia torsit   220
regia et oblitos famae melioris amantis.
tum sic Mercurium adloquitur ac talia mandat:
'vade age, nate, voca Zephyros et labere pennis
Dardaniumque ducem, Tyria Karthagine qui nunc
exspectat fatisque datas non respicit urbes,   225
adloquere et celeris defer mea dicta per auras.
non illum nobis genetrix pulcherrima talem
promisit Graiumque ideo bis vindicat armis;
sed fore qui gravidam imperiis belloque frementem
Italiam regeret, genus alto a sanguine Teucri   230
proderet, ac totum sub leges mitteret orbem.
si nulla accendit tantarum gloria rerum
nec super ipse sua molitur laude laborem,

203–216 *MPR*; 217–233 *MP*   204 numina] munera *multos legisse testatur* D. Serv., *commendat Kvičala*   217 subnexus *deteriores duo*: subnixus *ceteri, testantur Nonius Serv.*   227 genetrix nobis *P*[1] *deteriores Ribbeck*   233 laborum *M*[1]*P*[2]*γ*[1]

Ascanione pater Romanas invidet arces?
quid struit? aut qua spe inimica in gente moratur   235
nec prolem Ausoniam et Lavinia respicit arva?
naviget! haec summa est, hic nostri nuntius esto.'
   Dixerat. ille patris magni parere parabat
imperio: et primum pedibus talaria nectit
aurea, quae sublimem alis sive aequora supra   240
seu terram rapido pariter cum flamine portant.
tum virgam capit: hac animas ille evocat Orco
pallentis, alias sub Tartara tristia mittit,
dat somnos adimitque, et lumina morte resignat.
illa fretus agit ventos et turbida tranat   245
nubila. iamque volans apicem et latera ardua cernit
Atlantis duri caelum qui vertice fulcit,
Atlantis, cinctum adsidue cui nubibus atris
piniferum caput et vento pulsatur et imbri,
nix umeros infusa tegit, tum flumina mento   250
praecipitant senis, et glacie riget horrida barba.
hic primum paribus nitens Cyllenius alis
constitit: hinc toto praeceps se corpore ad undas
misit avi similis, quae circum litora, circum
piscosos scopulos humilis volat aequora iuxta.   255
haud aliter terras inter caelumque volabat
litus harenosum ad Libyae, ventosque secabat
materno veniens ab avo Cyllenia proles.
ut primum alatis tetigit magalia plantis,
Aenean fundantem arces ac tecta novantem   260
conspicit. atque illi stellatus iaspide fulva
ensis erat Tyrioque ardebat murice laena
demissa ex umeris, dives quae munera Dido
fecerat, et tenui telas discreverat auro.

234–257 *FMP*; 258–264 *MP*   236 *eicit Ribbeck*   241 portent *M*¹   243 mittit] ducit *P*¹   245 vento se *Kvičala*   256–258
sunt qui hos versus damnant   256 volabat] legebat *Bentley omisso*
ad v. 257   257 ad *P²γ*¹: at *M*¹ *ut videtur*: ac *M²abcπ*: ao *P*¹

continuo invadit: 'tu nunc Karthaginis altae   265
fundamenta locas pulchramque uxorius urbem
exstruis? heu, regni rerumque oblite tuarum!
ipse deum tibi me claro demittit Olympo
regnator, caelum ac terras qui numine torquet:
ipse haec ferre iubet celeris mandata per auras: 270
quid struis? aut qua spe Libycis teris otia terris?
si te nulla movet tantarum gloria rerum
[nec super ipse tua moliris laude laborem,]
Ascanium surgentem et spes heredis Iuli
respice, cui regnum Italiae Romanaque tellus   275
debetur.' tali Cyllenius ore locutus
mortalis visus medio sermone reliquit
et procul in tenuem ex oculis evanuit auram.

At vero Aeneas aspectu obmutuit amens,
arrectaeque horrore comae et vox faucibus haesit.   280
ardet abire fuga dulcisque relinquere terras,
attonitus tanto monitu imperioque deorum.
heu quid agat? quo nunc reginam ambire furentem
audeat adfatu? quae prima exordia sumat?
atque animum nunc huc celerem nunc dividit illuc   285
in partisque rapit varias perque omnia versat.
haec alternanti potior sententia visa est:
Mnesthea Sergestumque vocat fortemque Serestum,
classem aptent taciti sociosque ad litora cogant,
arma parent et quae rebus sit causa novandis   290
dissimulent; sese interea, quando optima Dido
nesciat et tantos rumpi non speret amores,
temptaturum aditus et quae mollissima fandi

265–285 *MP*; 286–293 *FMP*   267 oblite] ignare *P¹*
268 dimittit *Pγ¹cπ*   269 ac] et *Mbc*   terram *Pγ*   273 *om.*
MPγ¹a¹b¹   276 debetur *M²Pγabc*: debentur *M¹ Serv.*   283 quo-
nam *Nonius*   285, 286 = viii. 20, 21 *non interpretatur Serv.*,
damnat Heyne: unum v. 286 (*ab F¹Pγ¹ omissum*) *uncis secludit Ribbeck*
285 atque] utque *Heinsius, fortasse recte*   288 Serestum] Cloan-
thum *π Parisinus 7906 Donatus, probat Kvičala*   289 -que *om. Pγc*

tempora, quis rebus dexter modus. ocius omnes
imperio laeti parent et iussa facessunt.   295
    At regina dolos (quis fallere possit amantem?)
praesensit, motusque excepit prima futuros
omnia tuta timens. eadem impia Fama furenti
detulit armari classem cursumque parari.
saevit inops animi totamque incensa per urbem   300
bacchatur, qualis commotis excita sacris
Thyias, ubi audito stimulant trieterica Baccho
orgia nocturnusque vocat clamore Cithaeron.
tandem his Aenean compellat vocibus ultro:
'dissimulare etiam sperasti, perfide, tantum   305
posse nefas tacitusque mea decedere terra?
nec te noster amor nec te data dextera quondam
nec moritura tenet crudeli funere Dido?
quin etiam hiberno moliris sidere classem
et mediis properas Aquilonibus ire per altum,   310
crudelis? quid, si non arva aliena domosque
ignotas peteres, et Troia antiqua maneret,
Troia per undosum peteretur classibus aequor?
mene fugis? per ego has lacrimas dextramque tuam te
(quando aliud mihi iam miserae nihil ipsa reliqui),   315
per conubia nostra, per inceptos hymenaeos,
si bene quid de te merui, fuit aut tibi quicquam
dulce meum, miserere domus labentis et istam,
oro, si quis adhuc precibus locus, exue mentem.
te propter Libycae gentes Nomadumque tyranni   320
odere, infensi Tyrii; te propter eundem
exstinctus pudor et, qua sola sidera adibam,
fama prior. cui me moribundam deseris,—hospes
(hoc solum nomen quoniam de coniuge restat)?

294-301 *FMP*; 302-305 *AFMP*; 306-310 *FMP*; 311-324 *MP*
295 et] ac *M²b*   309 moliri *FPa*   312 et] sed *P¹*: si *m Güthling*
323 morituram *Priscianus*

quid moror? an mea Pygmalion dum moenia frater   325
destruat aut captam ducat Gaetulus Iarbas?
saltem si qua mihi de te suscepta fuisset
ante fugam suboles, si quis mihi parvulus aula
luderet Aeneas, qui te tamen ore referret,
non equidem omnino capta ac deserta viderer.'   330
    Dixerat. ille Iovis monitis immota tenebat
lumina et obnixus curam sub corde premebat.
tandem pauca refert: 'ego te, quae plurima fando
enumerare vales, numquam, regina, negabo
promeritam, nec me meminisse pigebit Elissae   335
dum memor ipse mei, dum spiritus hos regit artus.
pro re pauca loquar. neque ego hanc abscondere furto
speravi (ne finge) fugam, nec coniugis umquam
praetendi taedas aut haec in foedera veni.
me si fata meis paterentur ducere vitam   340
auspiciis et sponte mea componere curas,
urbem Troianam primum dulcisque meorum
reliquias colerem, Priami tecta alta manerent,
et recidiva manu posuissem Pergama victis.
sed nunc Italiam magnam Gryneus Apollo,   345
Italiam Lyciae iussere capessere sortes;
hic amor, haec patria est. si te Karthaginis arces
Phoenissam Libycaeque aspectus detinet urbis,
quae tandem Ausonia Teucros considere terra
invidia est? et nos fas extera quaerere regna.   350
me patris Anchisae, quotiens umentibus umbris
nox operit terras, quotiens astra ignea surgunt,
admonet in somnis et turbida terret imago;
me puer Ascanius capitisque iniuria cari,
quem regno Hesperiae fraudo et fatalibus arvis.   355

325–355 *MP*   343 Priami . . . manerent *damnant Peerlkamp*
Ribbeck   348 detinet] demeret *Parisinus* 7906 *quod 'in novis et
emendatis libris' quosdam invenisse dicit D. Serv.*

nunc etiam interpres divum Iove missus ab ipso
(testor utrumque caput) celeris mandata per auras
detulit: ipse deun₁ manifesto in lumine vidi
intrantem muros vocemque his auribus hausi.
desine meque tuis incendere teque querelis;   360
Italiam non sponte sequor.'
    Talia dicentem iamdudum aversa tuetur
huc illuc volvens oculos totumque pererrat
luminibus tacitis et sic accensa profatur:
'nec tibi diva parens generis nec Dardanus auctor,   365
perfide, sed duris genuit te cautibus horrens
Caucasus Hyrcanaeque admorunt ubera tigres.
nam quid dissimulo aut quae me ad maiora reservo?
num fletu ingemuit nostro? num lumina flexit?
num lacrimas victus dedit aut miseratus amantem est? 370
quae quibus anteferam? iam iam nec maxima Iuno
nec Saturnius haec oculis pater aspicit aequis.
nusquam tuta fides. eiectum litore, egentem
excepi et regni demens in parte locavi.
amissam classem, socios a morte reduxi   375
(heu furiis incensa feror!): nunc augur Apollo,
nunc Lyciae sortes, nunc et Iove missus ab ipso
interpres divum fert horrida iussa per auras.
scilicet is superis labor est, ea cura quietos
sollicitat. neque te teneo neque dicta refello: 380
i, sequere Italiam ventis, pete regna per undas.
spero equidem mediis, si quid pia numina possunt,
supplicia hausurum scopulis et nomine Dido
saepe vocaturum. sequar atris ignibus absens
et, cum frigida mors anima seduxerit artus,   385
omnibus umbra locis adero. dabis, improbe, poenas.
audiam et haec manis veniet mihi fama sub imos.'

356-387 MP   374 suscepi *Priscianus*   375 *damnat*
Ribbeck   378 iussa] dicta *M*   381 *alii* ventis pete *coniungunt*

his medium dictis sermonem abrumpit et auras
aegra fugit seque ex oculis avertit et aufert,
linquens multa metu cunctantem et multa parantem   390
dicere. suscipiunt famulae conlapsaque membra
marmoreo referunt thalamo stratisque reponunt.
   At pius Aeneas, quamquam lenire dolentem
solando cupit et dictis avertere curas,
multa gemens magnoque animum labefactus amore   395
iussa tamen divum exsequitur classemque revisit.
tum vero Teucri incumbunt et litore celsas
deducunt toto navis. natat uncta carina,
frondentisque ferunt remos et robora silvis
infabricata fugae studio.   400
migrantis cernas totaque ex urbe ruentis.
ac velut ingentem formicae farris acervum
cum populant hiemis memores tectoque reponunt,
it nigrum campis agmen praedamque per herbas
convectant calle angusto; pars grandia trudunt   405
obnixae frumenta umeris, pars agmina cogunt
castigantque moras, opere omnis semita fervet.
quis tibi tum, Dido, cernenti talia sensus,
quosve dabas gemitus, cum litora fervere late
prospiceres arce ex summa, totumque videres   410
misceri ante oculos tantis clamoribus aequor!
improbe Amor, quid non mortalia pectora cogis!
ire iterum in lacrimas, iterum temptare precando
cogitur et supplex animos summittere amori,
ne quid inexpertum frustra moritura relinquat.   415
   'Anna, vides toto properari litore circum:
undique convenere; vocat iam carbasus auras,
puppibus et laeti nautae imposuere coronas.

388–418 MP   390 parantem] volentem Mc   395 secludit
Ribbeck   402 veluti Macπ   407 operae M¹: opera Nonius
416 post litore interpungunt Markland alii   418 post hunc versum
548, 549 inserit Ribbeck

hunc ego si potui tantum sperare dolorem,
et perferre, soror, potero. miserae hoc tamen unum   420
exsequere, Anna, mihi; solam nam perfidus ille
te colere, arcanos etiam tibi credere sensus;
sola viri mollis aditus et tempora noras:
i, soror, atque hostem supplex adfare superbum:
non ego cum Danais Troianam exscindere gentem   425
Aulide iuravi classemve ad Pergama misi,
nec patris Anchisae cineres manisve revelli:
cur mea dicta negat duras demittere in auris?
quo ruit? extremum hoc miserae det munus amanti:
exspectet facilemque fugam ventosque ferentis.   430
non iam coniugium antiquum, quod prodidit, oro,
nec pulchro ut Latio careat regnumque relinquat:
tempus inane peto, requiem spatiumque furori,
dum mea me victam doceat fortuna dolere.
extremam hanc oro veniam (miserere sororis),   435
quam mihi cum dederit cumulatam morte remittam.'
  Talibus orabat, talisque miserrima fletus
fertque refertque soror. sed nullis ille movetur
fletibus, aut voces ullas tractabilis audit;
fata obstant placidasque viri deus obstruit auris.   440
ac velut annoso validam cum robore quercum
Alpini Boreae nunc hinc nunc flatibus illinc
eruere inter se certant; it stridor, et altae
consternunt terram concusso stipite frondes;
ipsa haeret scopulis et quantum vertice ad auras   445
aetherias, tantum radice in Tartara tendit:
haud secus adsiduis hinc atque hinc vocibus heros

419-442 *MP*; 443-447 *FMP*   427 cinerem *M*   revulsi
Oblongus Pierii, agnoscit Serv.   428 neget *M²P¹ agnoscit D. Serv.*
434 dolore *M¹γ¹c¹*   436 dederis *γ²abcπ Serv.*   cumulata *M*:
dederis cumulatam *probasse Tuccam et Varium testatur Serv., qui
etiam* dederit cumulata *agnoscit*: cumulatum munere mittam *Klouček*
443 alte *b Serv.*   445 oras *Lachmann*   446 radicem *MP¹γa²*

P. VERGILI MARONIS

tunditur, et magno persentit pectore curas;
mens immota manet, lacrimae volvuntur inanes.
Tum vero infelix fatis exterrita Dido   450
mortem orat; taedet caeli convexa tueri.
quo magis inceptum peragat lucemque relinquat,
vidit, turicremis cum dona imponeret aris
(horrendum dictu), latices nigrescere sacros
fusaque in obscenum se vertere vina cruorem.   455
hoc visum nulli, non ipsi effata sorori.
praeterea fuit in tectis de marmore templum
coniugis antiqui, miro quod honore colebat,
velleribus niveis et festa fronde revinctum:
hinc exaudiri voces et verba vocantis   460
visa viri, nox cum terras obscura teneret,
solaque culminibus ferali carmine bubo
saepe queri et longas in fletum ducere voces;
multaque praeterea vatum praedicta priorum
terribili monitu horrificant. agit ipse furentem   465
in somnis ferus Aeneas, semperque relinqui
sola sibi, semper longam incomitata videtur
ire viam et Tyrios deserta quaerere terra,
Eumenidum veluti demens videt agmina Pentheus
et solem geminum et duplices se ostendere Thebas,   470
aut Agamemnonius scaenis agitatus Orestes,
armatam facibus matrem et serpentibus atris
cum fugit ultricesque sedent in limine Dirae.
Ergo ubi concepit furias evicta dolore
decrevitque mori, tempus secum ipsa modumque   475
exigit, et maestam dictis adgressa sororem
consilium vultu tegit ac spem fronte serenat:
'inveni, germana, viam (gratare sorori)

448–478 FMP   450 exercita Markland   456 sorori est F
462 solaque] seraque Nonius   464 piorum M agnoscit Serv. probat
Ribbeck   468 Tyrios] Teucros Schrader   471 scaenis] Poenis
Markland   473 divae $F^1P\gamma^1$ 476 ac M

quae mihi reddat eum vel eo me solvat amantem.
Oceani finem iuxta solemque cadentem   480
ultimus Aethiopum locus est, ubi maximus Atlas
axem umero torquet stellis ardentibus aptum:
hinc mihi Massylae gentis monstrata sacerdos,
Hesperidum templi custos, epulasque draconi
quae dabat et sacros servabat in arbore ramos,   485
spargens umida mella soporiferumque papaver.
haec se carminibus promittit solvere mentes
quas velit, ast aliis duras immittere curas,
sistere aquam fluviis et vertere sidera retro,
nocturnosque movet manis: mugire videbis   490
sub pedibus terram et descendere montibus ornos.
testor, cara, deos et te, germana, tuumque
dulce caput, magicas invitam accingier artis.
tu secreta pyram tecto interiore sub auras
erige, et arma viri thalamo quae fixa reliquit   495
impius exuviasque omnis lectumque iugalem,
quo perii, superimponas: abolere nefandi
cuncta viri monimenta iuvat monstratque sacerdos.'
haec effata silet, pallor simul occupat ora.
non tamen Anna novis praetexere funera sacris   500
germanam credit, nec tantos mente furores
concipit aut graviora timet quam morte Sychaei.
ergo iussa parat.
    At regina pyra penetrali in sede sub auras
erecta ingenti taedis atque ilice secta,   505
intenditque locum sertis et fronde coronat
funerea; super exuvias ensemque relictum
effigiemque toro locat haud ignara futuri.

479–508 *FMP*   482 attorquet *M*[1]   485 et] ut *Sabbadini*:
is *Regel, cui verba* is . . . ramos παρένθεσις *videntur*   486 *eiciunt
Schrader Deuticke*   490 movet] ciet *F*[2]*P*[2]*γabπ*   497 super-
imponant *FM*[1] agnoscit *D. Serv.*   498 iuvat *F*[2]*M*[2]*a*[1] *Serv.*: ivat *F*[1]:
iubet *M*[1]*P*[1]*γ*[2]*a*[2]*bcπ*: iubat *P*[2]*γ*[1]   500 protexere *M*[1]

P. VERGILI MARONIS

stant arae circum et crinis effusa sacerdos
ter centum tonat ore deos, Erebumque Chaosque   510
tergeminamque Hecaten, tria virginis ora Dianae.
sparserat et latices simulatos fontis Averni,
falcibus et messae ad lunam quaeruntur aënis
pubentes herbae nigri cum lacte veneni;
quaeritur et nascentis equi de fronte revulsus   515
et matri praereptus amor.
ipsa mola manibusque piis altaria iuxta
unum exuta pedem vinclis, in veste recincta,
testatur moritura deos et conscia fati
sidera; tum, si quod non aequo foedere amantis   520
curae numen habet iustumque memorque, precatur.
  Nox erat et placidum carpebant fessa soporem
corpora per terras, silvaeque et saeva quierant
aequora, cum medio volvuntur sidera lapsu,
cum tacet omnis ager, pecudes pictaeque volucres,   525
quaeque lacus late liquidos quaeque aspera dumis
rura tenent, somno positae sub nocte silenti.
[lenibant curas et corda oblita laborum.]
at non infelix animi Phoenissa neque umquam
solvitur in somnos oculisve aut pectore noctem   530
accipit: ingeminant curae rursusque resurgens
saevit amor magnoque irarum fluctuat aestu.
sic adeo insistit secumque ita corde volutat:
'en, quid ago? rursusne procos inrisa priores
experiar, Nomadumque petam conubia supplex,   535
quos ego sim totiens iam dedignata maritos?
Iliacas igitur classis atque ultima Teucrum
iussa sequar? quiane auxilio iuvat ante levatos
et bene apud memores veteris stat gratia facti?

509–521 FMP; 522–539 MP   517 molam MPγ¹c Ribbeck,
qui versum 486 post hunc transponit, ut molam e spargens pendeat
528 om. MPγ¹a¹b²c¹m, ignorat Serv. eicit Ribbeck, cf. ix. 225

quis me autem, fac velle, sinet ratibusque superbis   540
invisam accipiet? nescis heu, perdita, necdum
Laomedonteae sentis periuria gentis?
quid tum? sola fuga nautas comitabor ovantis?
an Tyriis omnique manu stipata meorum
inferar et, quos Sidonia vix urbe revelli,   545
rursus agam pelago et ventis dare vela iubebo?
quin morere ut merita es, ferroque averte dolorem.
tu lacrimis evicta meis, tu prima furentem
his, germana, malis oneras atque obicis hosti.
non licuit thalami expertem sine crimine vitam   550
degere more ferae, talis nec tangere curas;
non servata fides cineri promissa Sychaeo.'
    Tantos illa suo rumpebat pectore questus:
Aeneas celsa in puppi iam certus eundi
carpebat somnos rebus iam rite paratis.   555
huic se forma dei vultu redeuntis eodem
obtulit in somnis rursusque ita visa monere est,
omnia Mercurio similis, vocemque coloremque
et crinis flavos et membra decora iuventae:
'nate dea, potes hoc sub casu ducere somnos,   560
nec quae te circum stent deinde pericula cernis,
demens, nec Zephyros audis spirare secundos?
illa dolos dirumque nefas in pectore versat
certa mori, variosque irarum concitat aestus.
non fugis hinc praeceps, dum praecipitare potestas?   565
iam mare turbari trabibus saevasque videbis
conlucere faces, iam fervere litora flammis,
si te his attigerit terris Aurora morantem.
heia age, rumpe moras. varium et mutabile semper
femina.' sic fatus nocti se immiscuit atrae.   570

540–554 *MP*; 555–570 *FMP*   540 sinat *P*¹   541 inrisam
*M*²γ²*b*¹π   552 Sychaei *M*: Sychaeies *P*¹   559 iuventae *P*γ*a*
Serv.: iuventa *FMb*²*c*   564 varioque (*M*²*ab*¹π svarioque *M*¹) irarum
fluctuat (*M*γ²*ab*π) aestu (*FMab*¹π) *Haupt Deuticke*   565 hinc] in *F*¹

Tum vero Aeneas subitis exterritus umbris
corripit e somno corpus sociosque fatigat
praecipitis: 'vigilate, viri, et considite transtris;
solvite vela citi. deus aethere missus ab alto
festinare fugam tortosque incidere funis   575
ecce iterum instimulat. sequimur te, sancte deorum,
quisquis es, imperioque iterum paremus ovantes.
adsis o placidusque iuves et sidera caelo
dextra feras.' dixit vaginaque eripit ensem
fulmineum strictoque ferit retinacula ferro.   580
idem omnis simul ardor habet, rapiuntque ruuntque;
litora deseruere, latet sub classibus aequor,
adnixi torquent spumas et caerula verrunt.
   Et iam prima novo spargebat lumine terras
Tithoni croceum linquens Aurora cubile.   585
regina e speculis ut primam albescere lucem
vidit et aequatis classem procedere velis,
litoraque et vacuos sensit sine remige portus,
terque quaterque manu pectus percussa decorum
flaventisque abscissa comas 'pro Iuppiter! ibit   590
hic,' ait 'et nostris inluserit advena regnis?
non arma expedient totaque ex urbe sequentur,
deripientque rates alii navalibus? ite,
ferte citi flammas, date tela, impellite remos!
quid loquor? aut ubi sum? quae mentem insania mutat?   595
infelix Dido, nunc te facta impia tangunt?
tum decuit, cum sceptra dabas. en dextra fidesque,
quem secum patrios aiunt portare penatis,
quem subiisse umeris confectum aetate parentem!

   571–583 *FMP*; 584–599 *MP*   572 fatigat praecipitis *iungit
Kvičala, 'nonnullos' apud D. Serv. secutus: vulgo colon post* fatigat *ponunt*   576 stimulat *Mab Serv.*   586 primum $M\gamma^2bc\pi$
593 deripient *Heinsius*: diripient *codd.*   596 nun *P*: num *Probus
Cledonius*   598 portasse *M*: *de Servio non liquet, qui ad v.* 597 '*hic est
quem dicunt portare deos', ad v.* 598 '*sunt qui aiunt patrios penatis
portasse' interpretatur*: portarese *Parisinus* 7906   599 umero P^1

non potui abreptum divellere corpus et undis   600
spargere? non socios, non ipsum absumere ferro
Ascanium patriisque epulandum ponere mensis?
verum anceps pugnae fuerat fortuna.—fuisset:
quem metui moritura? faces in castra tulissem
implessemque foros flammis natumque patremque   605
cum genere exstinxem, memet super ipsa dedissem.
Sol, qui terrarum flammis opera omnia lustras,
tuque harum interpres curarum et conscia Iuno,
nocturnisque Hecate triviis ululata per urbes
et Dirae ultrices et di morientis Elissae,   610
accipite haec, meritumque malis advertite numen
et nostras audite preces. si tangere portus
infandum caput ac terris adnare necesse est,
et sic fata Iovis poscunt, hic terminus haeret:
at bello audacis populi vexatus et armis,   615
finibus extorris, complexu avulsus Iuli
auxilium imploret videatque indigna suorum
funera; nec, cum se sub leges pacis iniquae
tradiderit, regno aut optata luce fruatur,
sed cadat ante diem mediaque inhumatus harena.   620
haec precor, hanc vocem extremam cum sanguine fundo.
tum vos, o Tyrii, stirpem et genus omne futurum
exercete odiis, cinerique haec mittite nostro
munera. nullus amor populis nec foedera sunto.
exoriare aliquis nostris ex ossibus ultor   625
qui face Dardanios ferroque sequare colonos,
nunc, olim, quocumque dabunt se tempore vires.
litora litoribus contraria, fluctibus undas
imprecor, arma armis: pugnent ipsique nepotesque.'
    Haec ait, et partis animum versabat in omnis,   630
invisam quaerens quam primum abrumpere lucem.

600–631 *MP*   616 complexu] conspectu *Nonius*   629 nepo-
tesque] -que *om.* P²*ya*²*π*²

tum breviter Barcen nutricem adfata Sychaei,
namque suam patria antiqua cinis ater habebat:
'Annam, cara mihi nutrix, huc siste sororem:
dic corpus properet fluviali spargere lympha,   635
et pecudes secum et monstrata piacula ducat.
sic veniat, tuque ipsa pia tege tempora vitta.
sacra Iovi Stygio, quae rite incepta paravi,
perficere est animus finemque imponere curis
Dardaniique rogum capitis permittere flammae.'   640
sic ait. illa gradum studio celebrabat anili.
at trepida et coeptis immanibus effera Dido
sanguineam volvens aciem, maculisque trementis
interfusa genas et pallida morte futura,
interiora domus inrumpit limina et altos   645
conscendit furibunda gradus ensemque recludit
Dardanium, non hos quaesitum munus in usus.
hic, postquam Iliacas vestis notumque cubile
conspexit, paulum lacrimis et mente morata
incubuitque toro dixitque novissima verba: 650
'dulces exuviae, dum fata deusque sinebat,
accipite hanc animam meque his exsolvite curis.
vixi et quem dederat cursum fortuna peregi,
et nunc magna mei sub terras ibit imago.
urbem praeclaram statui, mea moenia vidi,   655
ulta virum poenas inimico a fratre recepi,
felix, heu nimium felix, si litora tantum
numquam Dardaniae tetigissent nostra carinae.'
dixit, et os impressa toro 'moriemur inultae,
sed moriamur' ait. 'sic, sic iuvat ire sub umbras.   660
hauriat hunc oculis ignem crudelis ab alto

632–650 *MP*; 651–661 *FMP*   632 Sychaei est *Mc*   640 flammis *M*   641 celerabat *M¹abcπ D. Serv.*   anilem γ²*ab¹c¹*:
inilem *P¹*   646 gradus] radus *P¹*: rogos *Mabc editores plerique*
651 sinebant *FP²*   655, 656 *transponunt codd. quidam deteriores*
660 sic ? sic *interpunxit Serv.*

Dardanus, et nostrae secum ferat omina mortis.'
dixerat, atque illam media inter talia ferro
conlapsam aspiciunt comites, ensemque cruore
spumantem sparsasque manus. it clamor ad alta   665
atria: concussam bacchatur Fama per urbem.
lamentis gemituque et femineo ululatu
tecta fremunt, resonat magnis plangoribus aether,
non aliter quam si immissis ruat hostibus omnis
Karthago aut antiqua Tyros, flammaeque furentes   670
culmina perque hominum volvantur perque deorum.
audiit exanimis trepidoque exterrita cursu
unguibus ora soror foedans et pectora pugnis
per medios ruit, ac morientem nomine clamat:
'hoc illud, germana, fuit? me fraude petebas?   675
hoc rogus iste mihi, hoc ignes araeque parabant?
quid primum deserta querar? comitemne sororem
sprevisti moriens? eadem me ad fata vocasses:
idem ambas ferro dolor atque eadem hora tulisset.
his etiam struxi manibus patriosque vocavi   680
voce deos, sic te ut posita, crudelis, abessem?
exstinxti te meque, soror, populumque patresque
Sidonios urbemque tuam. date, vulnera lymphis
abluam et, extremus si quis super halitus errat,
ore legam.' sic fata gradus evaserat altos,   685
semianimemque sinu germanam amplexa fovebat
cum gemitu atque atros siccabat veste-cruores.
illa gravis oculos conata attollere rursus
deficit; infixum stridit sub pectore vulnus.
ter sese attollens cubitoque adnixa levavit,   690
ter revoluta toro est oculisque errantibus alto
quaesivit caelo lucem ingemuitque reperta.

662–688 *FMP*; 689–692 *MP*   662 secum nostrae *M*[1]
668 clangoribus *Pa*   669 ruit *P*[1]   671 volvuntur *P*[1]γ²*c*[1]
690 attollit *P*[1]: attollet *P*[2]   692 repertam *M*[1]γ*bc*²π

Tum Iuno omnipotens longum miserata dolorem
difficilisque obitus Irim demisit Olympo
quae luctantem animam nexosque resolveret artus.   695
nam quia nec fato merita nec morte peribat,
sed misera ante diem subitoque accensa furore,
nondum illi flavum Proserpina vertice crinem
abstulerat Stygioque caput damnaverat Orco.
ergo Iris croceis per caelum roscida pennis   700
mille trahens varios adverso sole colores
devolat et supra caput astitit. 'hunc ego Diti
sacrum iussa fero teque isto corpore solvo.'
sic ait et dextra crinem secat: omnis et una
dilapsus calor atque in ventos vita recessit.   705

693-705 *MP*   698 necdum *Pγ*

COMMENTARY

(Note: abbreviated references to periodicals follow the system of *L'Année Philologique* ; *ALL = Archiv für lateinische Lexicographie*; L.-H. = Leumann-Hofmann, *Lateinische Grammatik*, Munich, 1928, the fifth edition of Stolz-Schmalz.)

A PROPER comprehension of the full sorrow of this Book cannot be gained without remembering certain lines of Book I. Dido on her first appearance is shown as *forma pulcherrima* (496), happy and animated in the building of her city. She welcomes the Trojan castaways in the words 'urbem quam statuo, vestra est; subducite navis; Tros Tyriusque mihi nullo discrimine agetur' (573 f.); Aeneas vows always to honour her, saying 'semper honos nomenque tuum laudesque manebunt, quae me cumque vocant terrae' (609 f.); and she takes him into her palace with understanding and comfort ('non ignara mali miseris succurrere disco', 630). That is the prelude to the love that so swiftly grew between these two noble and honourable beings, which was so soon to turn to the incalculable misery depicted in the Fourth Book.

1–30. *After hearing Aeneas' tale, Dido is on fire with passion, and is sleepless. In the morning she goes to her sister Anna, and confesses her love ; but she solemnly vows that she will not fail in her resolve never to marry again, nor break faith with her dead husband Sychaeus. And then she bursts into tears.*

Heyne comments: 'Splendida libri frons, et eximia gravissimi amoris declaratio.'

1. at regina: Virgil at once introduces the dominant figure of the book (cf. 296, 504, where the same words mark crises in the tragic tale). The strongly contrasting particle *at* not only shows that the story now turns from Aeneas and the Trojans to Dido, but also points the antithesis between Aeneas' sufferings that are now past, a mere tale that is told (*conticuit tandem*, iii. 718), and Dido's sufferings that are already beginning, between his composed silence and her agitation.

iamdudum: graphic and natural; Dido's love has been coming upon her 'all this long while', and by now the time when she did not love Aeneas seems far away. *Cura* bears the sense, common in poetry, of the 'pain' of passion (cf. 332, G. iv. 345), but it is more usually plural (so 394, 448, 551). Note the interwoven alliteration of *v*, *m*, *c* in these first five lines, followed by patterns with *l* and *s*; see C. E. S. Headlam, *CR* xxxiv, 1920, pp. 23 ff.

2. **vulnus . . . igni**: 'feeds the wound with her life-blood, and is wasted by a flame deep down within her.' The line shows Virgil's method of 'theme and variation': her wound causes her fever, and her fever deepens her wound. *Venis* is probably instrumental; Henry compares Soph. *Ph.* 313 κακοῖσι βόσκων τὴν ἀδηφάγον νόσον. *Caecus* is often used passively, of something not seen or deliberately concealed (cf. Eur. *HF* 199 τυφλοῖς ὁρῶντας οὐτάσας τοξεύμασιν): no one else but Dido knows of the fire in her heart, and even she, as yet, scarcely realizes its strength. *Carpere* well expresses the gradualness and the inexorability of her passion; it implies the action of taking a part from a whole, and so the completion of something by successive stages, as in *carpere viam, opus*; little by little the fire will wear her down to nothingness (cf. 32).

3 f. **multa . . . honos**: 'many a thought of the hero's high valour comes racing back to her heart, many a picture of the glories of his line'; *multus* implies both the frequency of Dido's thoughts (hence the frequentative *recursat*) and the abundance of *virtus* and *honos* in Aeneas.

viri: here the noun has its full force; but often forms of *vir* are used simply to avoid those of *is* (see on 479); Mackail has some statistics on i. 91.

recursat: not a common word; it occurs again in i. 662, xii. 802, both times with reference to *cura*.

4. **honōs**: Virgil always uses this form of the nominative, and both in Cicero and in Livy *honor* is very rare; but Horace, Ovid, and Silver Age prose writers avoid *honos* as an archaism; Silver Epic, however, uses it freely. Similarly, Virgil always has *arbōs*, never *arbŏr*, and in vi. 277 he has *labōs*. These forms in *-ōs* were the original ones, but when intervocalic *-s-* became *-r-* in the oblique cases, the nominative forms became *-ōr* by analogy, and later *-ŏr*. Such scansions as *pavōr* (ii. 369), *amōr* (*E.* x. 69, *A.* xi. 323, xii. 668), *labōr* (*G.* iii. 118), *dolōr* (xii. 422) reflect the original quantity.

vultus: 'features', a frequent plural; the way Aeneas looked, the way he spoke, is stamped upon her mind; cf. Apoll. Rhod. iii. 454 ff. (Medea thinking of Jason) αὐτός θ' οἷος ἔην, οἵοισί τε φάρεσιν ἕστο | οἷά τ' ἔειφ', ὥς θ' ἕζετ' ἐπὶ θρόνου, ὥς τε θύραζε | ἤιεν.

5. It is characteristic of Virgil that he does not elaborate the picture of Dido's sleeplessness (contrast Val. Flacc. vii. 1 ff.). Possibly *cura* here has a wider sense than in line 1, implying her general 'worry' at her situation (cf. x. 217 'neque enim membris dat cura quietem', of Aeneas at sea).

6 f. A Virgilian picture of dawn; cf. Milton, *PL* v. 1–2 'Now

Morn, her rosy steps in the eastern clime/Advancing, sowed the earth with orient pearl'. Virgil does not use fixed formulae like Homer, but varies his method (cf. 129, 584–5, iii. 588–9, v. 42, etc.; see Norden on vi. 535, and cf. Horace's parody of the style in *Sat.* i. 5. 9, ii. 6. 100), and the reader is always conscious of the recurrent miracle. An amusing passage in Seneca (*Epp.* 122. 11 f.) shows how the manner could be overdone by poetasters.

6. **Phoebea lampade**: the Sun. Note the scansion *Phoebēa*: the normal rule is that a vowel is short if another vowel follows it, but this is a Greek word transliterated into Latin, and the Greek prosody is kept (*-eus* represents -εῖος); cf. *Grynēus* (345), *Achillēus* (iii. 326), *Pallantēus* (ix. 196), and contrast *Romulĕus* (viii. 654). Similarly, *Aenēas = Αἰνείας* (but note *Aenĕades*, which follows the Latin rule), *Medēa = Μήδεια*; cf. *Cymodocēa* (x. 225), *Calliopēa* (*E.* iv. 57).

lustrabat: 'was moving over'; Virgil describes the ordered procession of the dawn (cf. i. 607 f. 'dum montibus umbrae/lustrabunt convexa'). See Warde Fowler, *The Death of Turnus* pp. 96 ff., for this word, 'one of the most beautiful and most untranslatable in the language'; it is primarily a religious term, used of a ritual purificatory procession. Here, as in 607, Lucr. v. 693, etc., the idea of illuminating is implicit: the advancing dawn purifies the world ('nox quodammodo polluit mundum', says Servius) with her spreading light. Cf. Cic. *de div.* i. 17 (from his own poem *de consulatu suo*) 'principio aetherio flammatus Iuppiter igni/ vertitur et totum conlustrat lumine mundum', where the idea of movement is made quite plain by *vertitur*. 'It is necessary to *feel* the word' (Fowler, loc. cit.)

7. **umentem . . . umbram**: note the way in which epithet and noun 'frame' the line, a symmetrical arrangement which Virgil much likes (the reverse order is rare, e.g. 165); see Norden, *Aeneis VI*, pp. 391 ff., for some statistics.

polo: a poetic word; like *axis* it is a convenient synonym for *caelum* where a spondee is not suitable. *Dimoverat* suggests the flinging back and parting of a great curtain.

This line occurs again in iii. 589 (so 129 = xi. 1); but such examples of the Homeric type of 'epic repetition' are few; see J. Sparrow, *Half-Lines and Repetitions in Virgil*, pp. 84 ff.

8. **unanimam**: 'soul of her soul'; the word is used of brothers and sisters, husbands and wives, close friends; cf. Plaut. *Stich.* 731 'ego tu sum, tu es ego, unianimi sumus'.

male sana: 'beside herself'; Dido's mind has 'lost its health' (cf. *saucia* above). *Male* has the force of a negative (cf. ii. 23 'statio male fida carinis'); it is a colloquial usage, promoted by Virgil to poetic style (see Hofmann, *Lat. Um-gangssprache,* p. 145; so French *malsain, malhonnête*; cf. Xen. *Cyr.* ii. 3. 13, where κακῶς εἰδότες = ἀγνοοῦντες). It can also be used (again colloquially, see Hofmann p. 74) to intensify what is already bad (e.g. Catull. 10. 33 'insulsa male', and cf. such phrases as *male mulcare, male perdere*).

sororem: Anna has not been mentioned before, but Dido's action in seeking her out is so natural and touching that one almost expects to find her. She is a very credible person, loving, honest, obedient, not very clever, with a real personality of her own (cf. E. Swallow, *Classical Weekly*, xliv, 1951, pp. 145 ff.); less shadowy than Chrysothemis or Ismene, and only formally resembling the Chalciope of Apollonius Rhodius (Medea's relations with her sister are very different from those of Dido with Anna—see Heinze, *Virgils epische Technik*, pp. 127 f.).

Notice the rhythm of the line; the elision at the end of the second foot, and the absence of a third-foot caesura, give a metrical picture of urgency (see note on 278, and cf. 222, x. 228; ii. 57, 203, 359).

9. **suspensam**: proleptic; her thoughts make her 'hung up' in bewilderment and fear; cf. ii. 728 f. 'nunc omnes terrent aurae, sonus excitat omnis/ suspensum' (of Aeneas escaping from Troy).

insomnia: ἐνύπνια, visions seen between sleeping and waking, which have prevented her from gaining *placida quies*. The conflict between her loyalty to her dead husband Sychaeus and her sudden passion for the living Aeneas distracts and terrifies her.

10 f. **quis . . . armis**: 'what a fine man this stranger is who has taken shelter in my home! How noble his mien and bearing! How strong his breast and shoulders!' *Armis* is a well-known ambiguity, but on the whole I would accept Henry's arguments for taking it from *armus*, not from *arma*; Aeneas is *os umerosque deo similis* (i. 589), and *quam . . . armis* is a variation of *quem . . . ferens*, both referring to physical characteristics (*armus* is more often used of animals, but see xi. 641 'ingentemque animis, ingentem corpore et armis', Val. Flacc. iv. 265 f. 'vigil ille metu cum pectore et armis/ huc alternus et huc', of a boxing-match).

12. **genus**: either 'he is the child of gods' (cf. vi. 792 'Augustus Caesar, divi genus', Catull. 61. 1 f. 'collis o Heliconii/ cultor, Uraniae genus'), or 'his lineage is divine' (cf. vi. 123 'et mi genus ab Iove summo').

13. **degeneres . . . arguit**: 'it is base-born spirits that are shown up by fear'; Dido now turns to Aeneas' bravery in adversity,

which also proves him godlike. R. L. Dunbabin (*CR* xxxix, 1925, p. 112) takes the words to refer to Dido herself, continuing the thought of *terrent* above, but this is surely too staccato.

14. **iactatus**: a characteristic Virgilian word, especially in a context such as this. *Heu* suggests *Othello* I. iii. 157 f., 'My story being done,/ She gave me for my pains a world of sighs'; Dido loves him for the dangers he has passed.

  quae ... canebat: 'what a draining of war's cup he told'; Virgil seems first to have used the participle *exhaustus* in this way, as in i. 599 'omnibus exhaustis iam casibus', x. 57, xi. 256 'ea quae muris bellando exhausta sub altis' (Servius *auct.* comments, on i. 599, 'veteres sic dicebant *clades hausi, id est pertuli*'); Ovid, Statius, and Silius followed him, and Livy introduced it to history, extending the use to the finite verb (xxvii. 39. 4 'quae ipse in transitu nunc Rhodani nunc Alpium ... per quinque menses exhausisset'; so too Pliny, *Epp.* v. 5. 7 'quantum laboris exhauserit frustra'); cf. the archaic *exanclare*, and the Greek ἐξαντλεῖν. The metaphorical use of the simple verb *haurire* is Ciceronian (*de domo* 30, *Tusc.* i. 86, etc.).

15. **fixum ... sederet**: the cumulative phrase shows how firm her resolve has been, and so her imminent desertion of it is all the more tragic in its result. The subject of *sederet* is the clause *ne ... iugali*.

16. Note the slow heavy spondees of the first three feet, marking her measured purpose. Note also the monosyllables (cf. 618, ii. 564 'respicio et quae sit me circum copia lustro', above all xii. 833 'do quod vis et me victusque volensque remitto'): they are rarer in Latin than in English, and correspondingly more noteworthy when they occur together as here (contrast, e.g., Sidney's 'My true love hath my heart and I have his', or his sonnet to Sleep beginning 'Lock up, fair lids, the treasure of my heart', or Tennyson's song 'Go not, happy day').

17. **primus amor**: 'he whom I first loved', Sychaeus.

  deceptam ... fefellit: 'cut short my hopes, and slipped away from me in death.' *Deceptus* is often used, with *spe, exspectatione*, etc., for the disappointment caused by the loss of a normal, natural hope; it is frequent in sepulchral inscriptions, e.g. *Carm. Ep.* 1150 A 1 'hunc titulum natae genetrix decepta paravi' (on a daughter who has died prematurely); see *Thes. L. L.*, s.v. *decipio*, col. 178. 66 ff.

18. **thalami taedaeque**: synonyms for 'marriage' (so too *torus*). Catullus first employs them; *nuptiae* is impossible in hexameters, and *conubium* and *coniugium* each involve certain

metrical difficulties (see note on 126, and Norden on vi. 623). With *taeda* (the torch used in the marriage-ceremony), cf. Spenser, *Epithalamion*, 'For Hymen is awake,/ And long since ready forth his mask to move,/ With his bright tead that flames with many a flake'.

What does Dido mean? She had been happy with Sychaeus, yet here she says that she is 'quite sick' of marriage. Pease suggests that she was tired of the approaches of suitors; perhaps she feels that any marriage may bring like disappointment to that of her first; perhaps the words are simply part of her own self-deception, an attempted defence against desire.

19. huic uni: with *culpae*.

forsan: almost entirely confined to poetry; its natural construction is with the subjunctive, like *forsitan*, but Virgil began to use it parenthetically with the indicative (by analogy with *fortasse*), and the usage spread among later poets. But *potui* is in any case normal in an apodosis implying possibility.

culpae: a 'fault' in love, an 'infidelity', sometimes a mere euphemism for immorality; here it is used of Dido's 'weakness' in her passion for Aeneas, which she knows is wrong—the 'tragic flaw' in her character.

20. Anna: the repetition of the name is subtle; Dido's tone becomes more urgent as she reaches her confession that she does in fact love Aeneas.

fatebor enim: 'yes, I will admit it'; *enim* is used as Plautus and Terence use it in lively conversational language, to affirm and emphasize a fact (cf. viii. 84 f. 'quam pius Aeneas tibi enim, tibi, maxima Iuno/ mactat').

fata: 'death' (cf. *fato cedere, fungi*), as Homer uses μοῖρα. The plural is regular in this sense (cf. τύχαι); Virgil has the singular *fatum* only in the sense of 'destiny'. For Sychaeus' death see i. 343 ff.: Dido's brother Pygmalion, king of Tyre, killed him 'impius ante aras, atque auri caecus amore'; he concealed the crime, but Sychaeus' ghost warned Dido to flee overseas, and so she came to Carthage.

21. coniugis: the emphatic position, and indeed the insertion of the word at all (for it is not necessary), again shows how Dido is struggling against herself: Sychaeus *is* her lawful husband still.

et . . . penatis: this clause particularizes the meaning of *fata Sychaei* (*et* is often so used by Virgil in appending an explanation or an enlargement of a theme); he was murdered on his own hearth, in the most sacred place in his own house, by his own brother-in-law. *Fraternus* is used loosely of the relationship between the two men; marriage into a Roman

family made the man or woman part of that family, and so
Sychaeus could be described as Pygmalion's *frater*. The fact
that Pompey was Caesar's son-in-law, and should have been
bound to him in family *pietas*, was a peculiarly horrible
feature of the Civil War, in Roman eyes.

22. **hĭc**: cf. vi. 791 'hic vir, hic est, tibi quem promitti saepius
audis' (see Norden); the short vowel was the original quantity, and Virgil uses it as an archaism (so too Lucr. ii. 387,
1066, vi. 9), deliberately (he might have written 'hic solus
flexit').

inflexit sensus: 'has made my feelings swerve'; cf. xii. 800
'desine iam tandem precibusque inflectere nostris'. The
verb not only marks by implication the firmness of her
previous attitude ('a rigido proposito deviavit'; Servius),
but shows also the force of the impact now made upon it;
after holding out for so long, Dido has been violently thrown
off her balance.

animumque labantem impulit: 'has shocked my heart to
a fall'; cf. Apoll. Rhod. iii. 962 (of Medea's meeting with
Jason) ἐκ δ' ἄρα οἱ κραδίη στηθέων πέσεν. *Labantem* is probably
proleptic, though not necessarily so; Virgil may intend three
stages in Dido's weakening, first the swerve from her previous firmness, then the dizziness of heart caused by the
swerve (*animum labantem*), then the final overthrow (*impulit*).
The run-on to *impulit*, followed by a strong pause, is characteristic of Virgil (cf. 72, 83, 261, 624, etc.) and very effective
(cf. Henry on ii. 247); Dido draws a deep breath before her
explicit admission that she is in love.

23. **veteris . . . flammae** : 'the imprint of that hot passion of old
days'; cf. viii. 388 f. 'ille repente/ accepit solitam flammam'.

24 ff. **sed mihi . . . resolvo**: 'but I would make this my earnest
prayer, either that earth may sooner yawn open to its depths
for me, or that the Father (who can do all things) may blast
me with his bolt and hurl me to the world of shadows, to the
pale-glimmering shadows in Hell, to the pit of night, sooner
than that I do hurt to my conscience or loose its binding
laws.' Dido, in her self-struggle, binds herself to Sychaeus'
memory in a solemn and awful prayer, again, by her own deliberate act, making the coming tragedy more dreadful.

24. **optem**: potential subjunctive of assertion, like *velim*, but a
much stronger word, for *optare* marks an ambition or an
ideal. *Dehiscat* (like *abigat* below) is a jussive dependent on
optem; its subject is placed before the verb of wishing, just as,
e.g., the normal idiom for 'I want you to do this' is 'tu velim
hoc facias'. *Prius* is taken up by *ante* in 27 (as in Greek πρότερον
is sometimes followed by πρίν). Note the quantity in *tellūs*,

and also in *dĕhiscat*: normally, a compound with *de* keeps the
long *e* of the preposition (cf. *desaevit*, 52), but here (since *h* is
not a consonant), the prefix is shortened according to the
usual rule by which a vowel is short if it is followed immediately by another vowel.

26. pallentis umbras: the repetition of *umbras* gains added awe
from the epithet; *pallens* and *pallidus* are commonly used of
phantoms, but the phrase is really a kind of oxymoron—the
ghosts are not dark shadows, but glimmer pale in the darkness.

　　Erebo: the darkness of the Underworld, here personified
(Homer's Ἔρεβος νεκύων κατατεθνηώτων, *Od.* xi. 564); cf. Milton,
PL ii. 882 f. 'Harsh thunder, that the lowest bottom shook/
Of Erebus'. For the ablative cf. vii. 140 'duplicis caeloque
Ereboque parentis', but the variant *Erebi* was known to
Servius (see Wagner's critical note in its favour).

27. pudor: a difficult word, full of shades of meaning (cf. Warde
Fowler, *The Death of Turnus*, p. 118); here it is something
like 'sensitiveness to what is right' ('sense of delicacy',
Mackail), an instinct that tells her that there is something
wrong in loving Aeneas, virtually 'conscience' (as a restrain-
ing force, like *religio*); see Mackail's note, and cf. Glover,
Virgil, p. 190.

　　Note the use of 'apostrophe', a rhetorical figure which
Virgil often employs, but never mechanically. Properly
applied, it has a strong dramatic force, but it is generally
alien to English usage to keep the figure in translation, except
where some special effect is lost by not retaining it (see some
good remarks by J. D. Duff in his preface to the Loeb Lucan,
p. vi). Apart from its dramatic aspect it is used both for
variety and for metrical convenience. Its effectiveness for
variety can be seen, e.g., in the list of vines (*G.* ii. 95, 101),
and particularly in the 'Catalogue' of Book VII (note vii.
684 f. 'quos dives Anagnia pascit,/ quos, Amasene pater'),
which is a masterpiece of Virgil's art. Metrically, the vocative
is often more mobile than an accusative form (thus, *pudorem*
could be placed only at the end of a line, whereas *pudor* offers
a number of alternative positions), and sometimes it can be
substituted for a form that will not fit dactylic metre (e.g.
Ovid, *AA* iii. 354 'ut sciat et vires, tessera missa, tuas',
where *tesserae missae* would be impossible). See Norden on
vi. 14 ff., and Bednara in *ALL* xiv, pp. 568 ff.

　　violo . . . resolvo: we might have expected the subjunctive
here, with final force, since there is a sense of prevention present. Virgil has made the pledge more vivid by substituting
the mood of fact for that of possibility (cf. Ter. *And.* 311
'omnia experiri certumst prius quam pereo'). Note that

resolvo, resolutio never bear the meaning 'resolve' in the sense of 'determination'.

28. **ille**: the juxtaposition with *meos* increases the stress on the pronoun.

amores: the plural is common, both of the affection felt and of the person for whom it is felt. Note the rare pause at the trochaic caesura in the fifth foot (cf. 193, 603); such pauses are less frequent in Virgil than in Lucretius, but more frequent than in Catullus and Cicero's poems (see Norden, *Aeneis VI*, Anh. II, p. 389).

29. **abstulit**: well chosen; Sychaeus had not only 'carried off' Dido's affections (cf. *E*. viii. 41 'ut vidi, ut perii, ut me malus abstulit error'), but he had taken them with him to the tomb. Roman sentiment was traditionally disturbed by second marriages. At a Roman wedding, the *pronubae* who attended the bride were women who had had one husband only (cf. Servius on iv. 166, and Catull. 61. 179; and sepulchral inscriptions constantly refer to women as *univirae* (cf. Prop. iv. 11. 36 'in lapide hoc uni nupta fuisse legar'). Livy tells a charming story (x. 23) of one Verginia, who, as a patrician married to a plebeian, found herself debarred from the shrine of *Pudicitia Patricia*; and so she set up her own private shrine to *Pudicitia Plebeia*, where 'nulla nisi spectatae pudicitiae matrona et quae uni viro nupta fuisset ius sacrificandi haberet'.

secum . . . sepulcro: note the alliteration of *s*, both here and in the preceding and following line. For this special type of triple initial alliteration in the second half of the line cf. iii. 183 'casus Cassandra canebat', viii. 603 'Tyrrheni tuta tenebant', ix. 635 'Rutilis responsa remittunt':· Wölfflin (*ALL* xiv, pp. 515 ff.) suggests that it is a feature that may be traced back to the Saturnian metre (as, e.g., in Naevius' epitaph), and thus be an Italian ornament of the hexameter, not a Greek one; it was adopted by Ennius ('perculsi pectora Poeni', etc.), and then passed to Virgil; Ovid has a few examples, but the Silver poets did not find it attractive.

Dido's words have a special pathos when we remember the scene in vi. 472 ff., where she meets Aeneas in the Underworld, turns from him in scorn, and is comforted by Sychaeus ('coniunx ubi pristinus illi/ respondet curis aequatque Sychaeus amorem').

30. **sic . . . obortis**: 'so she spoke her heart; and the tears flooded up and filled her bosom'; *obortis* suggests that her tears choked her speech.

This vivid, unexpected line throws a clear light on Dido's character ('hae autem *lacrimae* magnum facile poetam

arguunt', is Heyne's discerning comment); Virgil might have
left us simply with Dido's fine firm words, her weakness
seemingly overcome; but her tears show that she is unstable
and irresolute, for all her bravery—a foreshadowing of what
is to follow.

31–53. *Anna answers : Why must you live for ever alone and
childless? You have scorned others, but why fight against your
own desire? Think how you are beset by enemies : it is kind
heaven who has sent this stranger here, and by marrying him
you will raise your realm to glory. But ask the gods to forgive
you, pay sacrifice, and keep Aeneas here while the storms prevent him from sailing.*

Anna's answer shows how well she understands her sister
(cf. Heinze, op. cit., p. 419). She touches on her childlessness,
her lonely position and its dangers; and, because she knows
Dido's pride in her young city, she adds that Carthage will
grow the greater by such a marriage. It is just the answer
that Dido hoped for in spite of herself, and the meaning of
unanimam in line 8 is clearly illustrated.

31 ff. o luce . . . noris? : 'O my dear, dearer than the light to me
your sister, all alone, all the days of your young womanhood,
shall you pine in sorrow? Shall you never know the joy of
children, never the gifts of Love?' Note that Anna does not
use Dido's name (in 675 she calls her *germana*), unlike
Chalciope in Apollonius (iii. 674 ὤμοι ἐγώ, Μήδεια . . .); her
emotion is shown by the use of *o*, which is used only in passages of heightened feeling.

32. solane . . . iuventa: observe the proper use of *-ne*, which
must be attached to the word which the speaker feels to be
most important (normally the first, but note iii. 319 as Page
and Mackail punctuate it, 'Hectoris Andromache Pyrrhin'
conubia servas?'). It is Dido's loneliness that first arouses
Anna's pity, and next to this the fear that she will always be
lonely; the juxtaposition of the two adjectives is effective,
and *maerens carpere* balances them. The lovely vowel-
sounds in the line should be noted.

For the meaning of *carpēre* (future passive, note the scansion)
see on line 2. *Iuventa* is a poetic form (first found in Catullus)
for *iuventus*, which, except in the nominative, is metrically
cumbrous; on the other hand, Virgil does not use the nominative form *iuventa*, nor *senecta*, of which the oblique cases are
likewise used for the intractable forms of *senectus* (Ovid has
the nominative of both words, in pentameters—cf. Bednara,
ALL xiv, p. 346).

33. **dulcis natos**: Pease calls the words a cliché, deaf to their evocative character. Virgil had used them before, in his picture of the happy farmer (*G.* ii. 523 'interea dulces pendent circum oscula nati"), and Lucretius in his picture of the dark finality of death (iii. 895 f.) 'nec dulces occurrent oscula nati praeripere et tacita pectus dulcedine tangent'. Gray's familiar lines in the *Elegy* recall Lucretius; the idyll of the *Georgics* is reflected in Burns, *The Cottar's Saturday Night* ('Th' expectant wee-things, toddlin, stacher through/ To meet their dad, wi' flichterin noise an' glee'). Anna's eloquence is not threadbare.

Veneris nec praemia: note the postponement of *nec*, as in 365, 551, 696 (all at the same point in the line); so too *et* (124, 418, 513), *aut* (187, 317), *nam* (421), also *atque, namque, at*; see Norden, *Aeneis VI*, Anh. III, pp. 402 ff., and M. Platnauer, *Latin Elegiac Verse*, pp. 93 ff. (for a detailed analysis of the practice in elegy); Conway has an interesting note on i. 262. This mannerism, which is chiefly for metrical convenience, was introduced by the *neoterici* (the school of poets represented by Catullus), in imitation of Hellenistic usage (e.g. Callim. *Epigr.* 5. 11 Κλεινίου ἀλλὰ θυγατρὶ δίδου χάριν, Theocr. 21. 34 ἄλλως καὶ σχολά ἐστι; see references in Pfeiffer's index to Callimachus, s.vv. ἀλλά, καί, and cf. Gow on Theocr. 8. 23).

34. **id ... sepultos**: 'is *this* a concern of the dust, think you, or of the ghosts in the tomb?' The dead, says Anna, have no mind to make the living unhappy: and that Sychaeus still thinks of Dido's happiness is shown in vi. 474. Dido has her own life to lead. (For *cinerem*, see on 427.)

35. **esto**: impatiently; 'have it your own way', she argues, 'up to a point, but why fight against your own happiness?' (38).

aegram: of the misery of the mind (see Mackail on ii. 566). *Flexere* echoes *inflexit* above (22); *mariti* = 'possible husbands', i.e., 'suitors' (cf. 536). Marlowe (*Dido Queen of Carthage*, Act III) makes Dido show Aeneas the portraits of many suitors, and tell how she has rejected them.

36. **Libyae**: locative; *Tyro* is put for variety, either a local ablative or an ablative of origin ('from Tyre').

Iarbas: see on 198 ff.; Anna names him as the most persistent of Dido's suitors; *despectus* well shows the queen's grand manner in dealing with such presumption.

37. **triumphis**: with *dīvēs* (note the scansion), a reference to the victories won by the Numidians and others over their neighbours; Anna stresses the power of those whom Dido has scorned.

38. **placitone ... amori**: 'now that a love has pleased you, will you even struggle against it?'; *placito* (a passive participle of

an intransitive verb, used in an active sense, instead of a relative clause) is the important word, and so *-ne* is attached to it (see on 32). *Pugnare* with a dative (cf. μάχεσθαι) is poetic.

39. venit in mentem: this phrase is used either with a nominative of the thing which 'comes into mind', or with a genitive on the analogy of verbs of remembering; this second use is quasi-impersonal ('there comes into mind the thought' of something), and an infinitive or dependent clause may follow instead, as here ('does it not occur to you in whose lands you have settled?'). Dido had bought a strip of land from her neighbours (i. 367), perhaps from Iarbas himself (cf. 212).

41. Numidae: note the form, and cf. *Persa, poeta, nauta* (*-a* = Gk. *-ης*). The Numidians were fine horsemen and used no bridles, only a riding-switch; Virgil suggests, almost with a smile, that they 'could not bridle' themselves. *Infrenus* and *infrenis* (x. 750) were probably coined by Virgil.

Syrtis: the great sandbanks off Cyrenaica, proverbial for their dangers; the perilous sea-approach still further isolated Dido.

42. siti: ablative of cause.

furentes: not 'furious', but 'mad', 'wild'; *late furentes* is equivalent to a compound adjective ('far-raging').

43. Barcaei: the people of the famous city of Barce (from which Hamilcar and other Carthaginian leaders came). Editors are annoyed by what they call Virgil's 'loose geography' (Barce is 700 miles from Carthage); but he was not writing a guide-book.

quid . . . dicam: the rhetorical 'praeteritio', often used, as here, to vary a catalogue: the speaker mentions what he says there is no need to mention. Anna means that Dido's brother is plotting his revenge upon her.

44. This is one of the fifty-seven unfinished lines in the *Aeneid*, all of which give a complete sense, except iii. 340. They occur in all the books, and the highest number of them is in Book II, one of the most elaborate of all. They are not, however, all of the same type. (1) A few can be detached, forming notes at the beginning or end of a speech (e.g. v. 653, ix. 295); (2) a few others, though not resembling such notes, could be removed without any obvious gap resulting (e.g. 503 'ergo iussa parat'), and a somewhat greater number form part of a line and a half which could be similarly detached (e.g. 515–16); (3) the rest, by far the majority, are part of the structure and could not be removed without breaking the sense or the connexion (here, *germanique minas* is needed to explain the previous line).

These lines plainly result either from Virgil's method of composition, or from the unfinished state of the poem at his death, or from both causes together. The first group, and those in the second of the type *ergo iussa parat*, would presumably not have been left as they are if the poem had been finished. The rest present certain problems. For, resulting as they clearly do from Virgil's method of composing by paragraphs, when his thought has overflowed the line-structure and come to rest in mid-line, they are often extraordinarily effective as they stand (e.g. 361, or ix. 467 'Euryali et Nisi', where Warde Fowler observed that the ensuing pause is 'almost a sigh', or ii. 767 'stant circum', with its pitiful picture of helpless refugees). Some scholars, therefore, believe that some unfinished lines of this type were deliberately so written, either because Virgil came to realize their effect, or as a conscious metrical experiment. The case has been fully examined and argued by Sparrow in his *Half-Lines and Repetitions in Virgil*: he concludes (pp. 45 ff.) that some of the 'half-lines' may be a deliberate metrical device, as an instrument of rhetoric, but he adds 'it must be remembered that there is no need to suppose that all or any of the hemistiches were introduced intentionally; Virgil may in the course of his revision have noticed their effectiveness, and intended to make still further use of the device, or he may never have decided whether or not any of them should be eventually retained'. This caution is wise. It is easy, but dangerous, to read our own emotions into an ancient poet's technique; and although J. H. Newman's unforgettable phrase about Virgil's 'pathetic half-lines' (*Grammar of Assent*, ch. iv) shows his own sensitiveness as a critic, we cannot ever know that Virgil felt their pathos exactly in the same way as we do.

See Mackail's introduction, sections x–xi, for a discussion of the problem and its significance for textual criticism, and Warde Fowler, *Virgil's Gathering of the Clans*, pp 93 ff. One point should be borne in mind: nothing can be safely inferred, from the fact that later epic poets have no unfinished lines in their work, as to the intentional character or otherwise of the Virgilian half-lines (cf. Sparrow, p. 26), for their whole attitude towards 'effects' in the hexameter is quite different (e.g., neither Lucan nor Statius nor Silius has a single hypermetric line).

45 f. dis . . . carinas: 'to my mind, it was with the blessing of the gods, by Juno's grace, that the ships of Ilion bore their course hither on the wind.' Juno may perhaps be specifically named as the goddess who presides at marriages; but Anna

does not know how Juno hated Aeneas, and her words are
full of tragic irony. *Vento* may be either modal or causal (cf.
381); *hunc cursum* = 'cursum ad hanc terram' (cf. i. 534 'hic
cursus fuit', and Conway's note). Note that *reor* occurs six
times in Virgil, *puto* never, although with other forms of
these synonymous verbs *putare* predominates; nor is *puto* found
anywhere in Silver Epic, whereas *reor* is used by Lucan, Statius,
and Silius. Obviously *puto* was felt to be rather casual in tone
(cf. Ovid's frequent use of it, or of *at, puto*, in parenthesis, with
short final syllable).

47. **tu**: emphatic (Virgil could have written 'quam, soror, hanc
urbem'); if Dido marries Aeneas, it will be *her* act that has
brought added greatness to Carthage. *Hanc* is deictic, as
Anna sweeps her hand towards the city.

48. **coniugio**: lawful wedlock (cf. 172); there is no hint here that
Anna thought Dido not free to marry again.

49. **Punica**: note how the word balances *Teucrum* in the previous clause, and note also the interlacing of word-order in
the line. *Quantis rebus* is probably dative ('to what high
state'); Virgil's readers would surely reflect on what the
greatness of Carthage was to mean to Italy.

50. **modŏ**: this is essentially a conversational word, and is common with an imperative in lively talk. The short final vowel
shows how a pronunciation which was regular in spoken
Latin from early times had passed into the literary language;
Roman speech tended to shorten a final vowel in an iambic
word (cf. note on 4), for it was difficult in ordinary conversation to give the first syllable its necessary stress and still
make the second syllable long; and such a pronunciation as
mŏdŏ became quickly normal even in an elevated form of
writing like the hexameter, no doubt because any other
treatment of such a common word would have seemed
pedantic (*modō* is found in Plautus, Terence, and Lucretius,
but Plautus already has *modŏ* also). A half-way stage can be
seen in the group of words *mihi, tibi, sibi, ibi, ubi* (the termination of which was originally -*e*; see L.-H., p. 101, with references): ordinary speech would shorten the final vowel, and
the poets generally use this prosody, but sometimes retain the
slower and more formal pronunciation with the long vowel.
The poets' treatment of final -*o* in nouns, adverbs, and verbs
forms an interesting study; the tendency is inevitably
towards shortening (except in the dative and ablative cases of
second-declension nouns), though this happened sooner with
some forms and with some words than with others: the sheer
metrical convenience of the short final vowel gradually led
to the extension of such scansion from iambic words (which

were influenced regularly by the philological law of 'iambic shortening') to non-iambic forms. (This is, of course, a simplification of a wider technical matter: for detailed discussion see L.-H., pp. 100 ff., Kühner, *Lat. Gr.* i, pp. 108 ff., Platnauer, op. cit., pp. 50 ff.)

posce: a verb of primarily religious content (cf. i. 666 'supplex tua numina posco'); see Norden on vi. 45. By *veniam*, Anna means indulgence for Dido's forgetfulness of Sychaeus and of her pledge to him.

litatis: *litare* is a religious term, originally intransitive, 'to make a favourable sacrifice', and then transitive as here (*sacris litatis* = 'after making holy offerings'). Dido has to expiate her fault, and the words are an extension of *posce deos veniam*.

51. **causasque . . . morandi**: 'weave reason upon reason to make him dally' (cf. ix. 219 'causas nequiquam nectis inanis'), in its turn an extension of *indulge hospitio*.

52 f. **dum . . . caelum**: 'while the storms and rainy Orion have their fill of fury upon the sea, and his ships are still shattered, and the weather may not be mastered.' In 309 ff. what is here a pretext has now become a mockery.

desaevit: the compound implies the working out of a process to its natural end; so *debellare*, *devincere*, *desaltare* ('to dance a dance out'), *destertere* ('to snore oneself out' to wakefulness).

Orion: the first syllable (short here as in i. 535, x. 763) is long in Greek, and is often kept so in Latin (e.g. vii. 719 'saevus ubi Orion hibernis conditur undis', and iii. 517 'armatumque auro circumspicit Oriona', a grand line). The setting of Orion in November marked the onset of stormy weather (*hiems*); such allusions are not simply learned ornament, but a natural idiom, the stock-in-trade of any farmer or sailor.

53. **quassataeque rates**: sc. *sunt*. *Quassare* is often used of a shipwreck. The implication is 'while his ships are refitting'.

54-89. *Dido hesitates no longer, but arranges a sacrifice in full and correct form. She is on fire with passion, wounded like a deer that some shepherd has hurt to its death. She cannot bear to be without Aeneas, and all the work of building Carthage is at a standstill.*

54. The text of this line varies. *Impenso* is the reading of F (the 'Schedae Vaticanae', early fourth century), and was known to Servius *auctus*; P (the Palatinus, fourth century) has *penso*; a second hand in both has corrected to *incensum*, which is the reading of M (the Mediceus, early fifth century),

R (the Romanus, fifth or early sixth century), and Servius. *Flammavit* is the reading of FPR, *inflammavit* that of M, a second hand in P, and Servius. The word *impensus* is not found elsewhere in Virgil, whereas *incensum* here would be very much in his manner (cf. 197); and although the fact that Virgil does not elsewhere use *flammare* transitively except in the perfect participle need not exclude *flammavit* here, the intensive compound has more force. I should therefore prefer to read, with Mackail, Page, and Goelzer, *his dictis incensum animum inflammavit amore*.

With that text, the caesura in the third foot is blurred by the elision, and there is none in the fourth foot, an unusual and very striking rhythm, giving a metrical picture of the inexorable spread of the fire in Dido's heart. The nearest parallel to such a rhythm is xii. 144 'magnanimi Iovis ingratum ascendere cubile'; others, not so close, are vii. 311 'magna satis, dubitem haud equidem implorare quod usquam est', vii. 623 'ardet inexcita Ausonia atque immobilis ante', xi. 758 'portat ovans. ducis exemplum eventumque secuti'. It is only by collecting such lines that one fully realizes how far Virgil was prepared to go in straining normal rhythms.

55. spemque . . . pudorem: 'she made Dido's wavering mind have hope, and loosed the shackles of her conscience.' For *pudor* see on 27; cf. Medea's cry ἐρρέτω αἰδώς / ἐρρέτω ἀγλαΐη (Apoll. Rhod. iii. 785 f.). Henry's note is characteristically violent.

Note the assonance at the end of the lines, *amore, pudorem*; so 189 f. (*replebat, canebat*), 256 f. (*volabat, secabat*), 331 f. (*tenebat, premebat*), 513 f. (*aenis, veneni*); see Mackail, pp. lxxviii ff. Such 'rhymes' are more common in Virgil than is sometimes realized, and although they are in part due to the exigencies of an inflected language, it is hard not to think that they are sometimes deliberate (cf. Norden on vi. 468); and they certainly reflect a natural taste for 'jingles' that can be discerned in native Latin poetry, as Mackail observes.

For other traces of 'rhyme' cf. 505 (*erecta . . . secta*), 542 (*sentis . . . gentis*), ii. 771 (*quaerenti . . . ruenti*), v. 181 f. (*labentem . . . natantem . . . revomentem*), viii. 620 ff. (*vomentem . . . rigentem . . . ingentem*), xii. 903 f. (*currentem . . . euntem . . . tollentem . . . moventem*); see H. Johnstone, *CR* x, 1896, pp. 9 ff., and my article in *CQ* xxiii, 1929, pp. 51 ff. Such passages hint at the music of rhymed medieval Latin poetry in a way that may perhaps be compared with that in which the rhythms of some of the great Christian hymn-writers echo those of early

Latin (e.g. Ennius *frg. scen.* 196 V. ' o magna templa caelitum/ commixta stellis splendidis', the very same music as in Venantius Fortunatus' hymn 'Vexilla regis prodeunt,/ fulget crucis mysterium'). Cf. F. J. E. Raby, *Christian Latin Poetry* (Oxford, 1927), pp. 20 ff.

56 ff. Virgil draws Dido very carefully. As soon as she hears from Anna the advice that she hopes to hear, her self-struggle ends and her passion has no more restraint. She impulsively carries out her sister's suggestion of making sacrifice, in a ritual which corresponds closely to that followed by Aeneas later in his sacrifice to the chthonic powers (vi. 243 ff.). It is an expiatory ritual, just as Aeneas' rite is (vi. 153 'ea prima piacula sunto'), and if she performs it carefully and correctly, she has every right to expect absolution, just as Aeneas has in vi, l.c. Very close precision was necessary in such a ceremony, as the slightest flaw might invalidate it, and Virgil's description here shows as usual his deep love for Italian religious tradition and his exact knowledge of its detail (cf. Bailey, *Religion in Virgil*, pp. 54 f.); much of our information on such matters comes from him.

56. adeunt: the verb is a t.t. for going to a holy place for worship (*Thes. L. L.* s.v., col. 624. 1 ff.); cf. Lucr. v. 1229 'non divum pacem votis adit ac prece quaesit'; so Pliny (*Epp.* iii. 7. 8) records of Silius Italicus' reverence for Virgil's tomb at Naples 'monimentum eius adire ut templum solebat'. *Pax divum* is a phrase from old ritual, and all Roman ceremonial prayer was directed to maintain 'the peace of the gods' (so Helenus in iii. 369 f. 'exorat pacem divum', with a sacrifice)—see Bailey, op. cit., p. 47, and on Lucr. l.c. Livy states, with reference to a plague (i. 31. 7) 'unam opem aegris corporibus relictam si pax veniaque ab dis impetrata esset credebant'; cf. Heinze, op. cit., p. 128, note 2. *Per aras* means 'from altar to altar'.

57. mactant: an ancient religious term for a ritual offering, perhaps not originally implying the actual slaughter; see L. R. Palmer, *CQ* xxxii, 1938, p. 60.

bidentis: another ritual t.t., used of a sheep two years old; at the end of the first year the two middle of the eight 'milk' teeth drop out, and are replaced by two bigger teeth, the first of the permanent ones, which are so much bigger than the rest that they alone seem to be there. See Henry ad loc.

58. Note the Roman deities. Virgil finds no more difficulty in making Dido perform an Italian ritual, than in making her speak Latin. Ceres and Apollo and Bacchus had special connexions with marriage, although Juno was of greater importance still. *Legifera* is applied to Ceres as θεσμοφόρος is

to Demeter; she first gave men a settled, civilized life (cf. *G.*
i. 7); *Lyaeus* ('the loosener', from λύειν) is a frequent poetic
cult-title for Bacchus. The term *pater* is often given to gods
and heroes, as a mark of respect (somewhat like Chaucer's
use of 'Dan').

Observe the rare rhythm, with a trochaic caesura in both
fourth and fifth foot; so 101, 123, 218, 335, 521, 559, 626, 651.
There are only about 100 examples of this in the whole *Aeneid*,
and of these more than half begin with a word with -*que*
attached (many of these in turn involve a double -*que*);
a large proportion contain a prepositional phrase (as in 101
'traxitque per ossa furorem'). The reason for this rarity is
obvious: such a rhythm produces the effect of a line-ending
in the middle of the fifth foot (cf. Maas, *ALL* xii, p. 527, note),
thus giving the line a 'double-ending' as it were (e.g. 123
'*nocte tegentur*| opaca', 335 '*meminisse pigebit*| Elissae'). Some-
times it is very effective, as in 335 (see note), ii. 380, 465.
See Norden on vi. 140, 789, and Appendix VII (he reduces the
number of such lines very considerably by not including
those where the ending is attached by -*que*), and Platnauer,
op. cit., p. 10.

60. ipsa: the rite is Dido's own peculiar and personal responsibility; it is she, not the priest, who holds the sacred dish
(*pateram*); in vi. 249 it is Aeneas, *ipse*, who actually strikes
down the victims. Virgil stresses her beauty here, as in i. 496
('forma pulcherrima Dido'): she is the Queen, a noble and
commanding figure.

61. candentis: contrast the black victims in vi. 243 ff., offered
to the powers of darkness (cf. *G.* iv. 546).

fundit: i.e. wine from the *patera*; so vi. 244 'frontique in-
vergit vina sacerdos' (here Dido does what the priest does
there).

62. ante ora deum: before the gods' images; yet the gods' eyes
watch Dido, and they know that she is only covering her fault.

pinguis: rich with the fat of victims, as often in Homer; cf.
vii. 764 'pinguis ubi et placabilis ara Dianae'. *Spatiatur*
means the stately walk which formed part of the ritual (see
Mackail).

63. instauratque diem donis: *instaurare* is a religious t.t., used
of 'renewing' an offering or ritual if there had been some flaw
in the original ceremony or else to prevent such a flaw (see
Page on iii. 62, and Henry's long discussion there). Dido
repeats her offerings throughout the day, to ensure that she
will gain the *pax divum*; her dreadful earnestness shows how
desperate she was. Virgil has experimented in language;
instead of writing 'dona die toto instaurat', as he could have,

he makes Dido 'renew the day with offerings', a most vivid phrase: she keeps making a fresh start, and with each fresh start she has fresh hope. Statius imitates him (*Th.* ii. 87 f. 'sociorum sanguine fuso / instaurare diem').

63 f. pecudumque . . . exta: Virgil describes a Greek practice ('extispice'), learnt by the Romans from the Etruscans, but never official at Rome. This is his only mention of it: and Dido was a foreigner (cf. Bailey, op. cit., p. 24, Heinze, op. cit., p. 316). Dido's anxiety is such that she does herself what the priest would normally do. The details are gruesome enough (*reclusis, inhians, spirantia*), but Virgil's restraint can be seen by comparing the horrors of Lucan i. 584-638. For *exta* cf. Warde Fowler, *Aeneas at the Site of Rome*, p. 56.

64. pectoribus inhians: *inhiare* (note the scansion *ĭnh-*) is a very strong word; Virgil has it of an open-mouthed crowd (vii. 814) and of a gloating look (*G.* ii. 463). Dido 'pores eagerly over the opened bodies of the beasts, and seeks the guidance of the throbbing entrails'. The plural form *pectoribus* is very rare in poetry (it occurs twice in Virgil, four times in Statius, once in Lucan, and not at all in Valerius Flaccus), even in the dative, where the singular was impossible metrically without involving a violent elision (see on 684); see Maas, *ALL* xii, pp. 541 f.

Note the prosody *pectoribŭs*, although the next word begins with a vowel (so *adloquitŭr*, 222). When this rare licence occurs in Virgil, the syllable so treated is always in 'arsis', i.e. it bears the metrical ictus, and is generally before the main caesura in the line, where a pause is either marked or felt. A number of examples reflect an original prosody preserved by Virgil as an echo from early Latin: such are imperfect tense-endings in *-bāt*, which occur in Ennius (so v. 853, x. 383, xii. 772), forms such as *pavōr* and *labōr* (ii. 369, *G.* iii. 118; cf. note on 4), a prosody used by Ennius and Plautus, and terminations in *-ēt* and *-īt* (*vidēt*, i. 308; *peterēt*, i. 651; *subiīt*, viii. 363; *enituīt*, *G.* ii. 211), also Ennian and Plautine. But a larger group cannot be explained in this way, since in these lines Virgil has lengthened a vowel that was originally short, as here and in 222, or as in *G.* ii. 5 *gravidŭs autumno*, *G.* iii. 189 *invalidŭs etiamque tremens*, *A.* ix. 610 *terga fatigamŭs hasta*. Sometimes a Greek line-ending is combined with the licence (in either group), e.g. *E.* vi. 53 *fultŭs hyacintho*, *G.* iv. 137 *tondebāt hyacinthi*, *A.* xi. 69 *languentīs hyacinthi*, vii. 398 *canīt hymenaeos*, x. 720 *profugŭs hymenaeos*.

Virgil appears to have used such lengthenings for the sake of variety, either because he wished to recall Ennius and

other early poets, or to echo a Greek rhythm from Homer or
Alexandrian epic, or simply for a special artistic effect
(sometimes there is more than one such motive). In this line,
pectoribŭs inhians seems plainly intended to suggest metrically Dido's lingering look at the *exta*, just as in ix. 610 *fatigamŭs hasta* depicts the energy of the sturdy Rutulians. In
his handling of metre Virgil listened to the voice of imagination as well as to that of rule. For a detailed investigation
of the problem see F. Vollmer, *Sitzungsberichte d. kön. bay.
Akad. d. Wissenschaften*, phil.-hist. Kl., 1917, pp. 19 ff.,
where among other points the important suggestion is made
that when such a lengthening occurs at the end of a clause (as
in *tum sic Mercurium adloquitur*, 222) the prosody may reflect the influence of the *syllaba anceps* which was allowable
at the end of a rhetorical *kolon*, and that the phenomenon
is akin to and parallel with certain types of hiatus in the same
position. See also Norden, *Aeneis VI*, Anh. X, where stress
is laid on the influence of later Greek epic; and R. G. Kent,
Mélanges Marouzeau (Paris, 1948), pp. 303 ff., who also looks
upon the licence as a counterpart to hiatus, but would
explain it by· a theory based primarily on pronunciation.
Whatever the technical explanation of the matter, Virgil's
pleasure in using the device is obvious, and his skill as plain.

65. vatum . . . mentes: Virgil means that nothing could really
help Dido, for her offerings were no more than lip-service to
the gods, and her soothsayers (*vates*) were powerless to diag-
nose and heal her mental disorder (*furentem*). We are not
told what the omens were; presumably the *vates* were satisfied, or perhaps they deliberately produced the favourable
signs that Dido so plainly desired; but at least she had formally expiated her fault (cf. note on 56), and that was the
main thing. Cf. Apuleius, *Met.* x. 2 'heu medicorum ignarae
mentes! . . . quam facilis licet non artifici medico, cuivis
tamen docto Veneriae cupidinis comprehensio, cum videas
aliquem sine corporis calore flagrantem'.

furentem: Dido's passion is now shown in its full strength
(cf. Warde Fowler, *Roman Essays and Interpretations*, Oxford,
1920, p. 186); she is maddened and reckless, and Cupid has
done the work that he was sent to do (i. 659); cf. Apuleius l.c.
'ubi completis igne vesano totis praecordiis immodice baccha-
tus Amor exaestuabat, saevienti deo iam succubuit'. But the
line does not apply only to Dido: it is a general truth as well.

66 f. est . . . vulnus: 'all the time a flame devours her molten
heart to its core, and beneath her breast the living wound
keeps its secret.' *Est* is from *edere*; *mollis* must be taken with
medullas (note the interweaving of object and subject). For

medulla in such a context, see Catull. 45. 15 f. 'ut mihi maior acriorque/ ignis mollibus ardet in medullis', and cf. Plaut. *Most.* 243 'videas eam medullitus me amare'. Virgil does not use the singular form; Catullus has it once (35. 15), where the metre makes a plural epithet impossible.

67. **vivit**: graphic and unexpected; how different from the wound which spoke her death (689).

68. **uritur ... vagatur**: a symmetrical verb-pattern as a 'frame' to the line, very characteristic of Virgil (see Norden, *Aeneis VI*, Anh. III).

infelix: 'ill-starred'; cf. i. 712 'infelix, pesti devota futurae'; *felix* implies happiness primarily in the sense of 'luck'.

69 ff. Dido is compared to a wounded deer, taken off its guard, a poor tender creature, innocent of harm, injured by one who did not even know of the wound he had inflicted. Virgil's pity is clear, even though he has just shown Dido as not candid. Some personal experience must lie behind both this passage and vii. 483 ff., the picture of the tame fawn which, wounded, 'nota intra tecta refugit,/ successitque gemens stabulis, questuque cruentus/ atque imploranti similis tectum omne replebat' (cf. xii. 749 ff.). Note Cowper, *The Task* iii. 108 ff. 'I was a stricken deer, that left the herd/ Long since. With many an arrow deep infix'd/ My panting side was charged', and Shelley, *Adonais*, 'Of that crew/ He came the last, neglected and apart,/ A herd-abandoned deer, struck by the hunter's dart'; and remember Marvell's poem 'The Nymph complaining for the Death of her Fawn'. Such a genealogy of thought is of the very stuff of poetry.

69. **qualis ... sagitta**: 'like a deer after an arrow-shot'; *coniecta* implies simply the act of shooting; the creature has not been aimed at.

70. **incautam:** and so was Dido; and she too was wounded 'from afar'.

Cresia: a 'literary' epithet, such as Virgil likes to use to give colour to what would otherwise be a black-and-white drawing; a good example is xi. 773 'spicula torquebat Lycio Gortynia cornu'; 'Cretan' in itself has no special significance here, except that the Cretans were famous archers. Cf. Kroll, *Studien zum Verständnis der römischen Literatur*, Stuttgart, 1924, pp. 278 f.

71. **agens**: cf. i. 190 f. (of Aeneas hunting stags) 'tum vulgus et omnem/ miscet agens telis nemora inter frondea turbam', *G.* iii. 411 f. 'apros/ latratu turbabis agens'. The participle is almost adverbial (cf. Conway on i. 191); *agens telis* = 'ruthlessly hurling his shafts' (one of which, though he never knew it, pierced the deer).

COMMENTARY

72. nescius: Virgil's picture, by implication, of Aeneas and Dido could hardly be more poignant. Note the run-on (see on 23): the vivid contrast between this emphatic *nescius* and *illa* ('*he* does not know, but she . . .') adds to the unconscious cruelty. (For the change from *quam* to *illa* see note on 445.)

73. Dictaeos: Cretan (from Mt. Dicte in Crete); Virgil keeps the geographical colouring.

haeret . . . harundo: note the elaborate alliteration *h, l, l, h*, and also the inner repetition of *e, r, t*. The 'arrow of death' sticks fast in Dido too.

lateri: the dative is used as if after *inhaerere*, to avoid the metrically impracticable *latere* (so ii. 553 *lateri . . . abdidit*, x. 270 *ardet apex capiti*); contrast x. 361 'haeret pede pes': see Norden on vi. 350. Conversely, in x. 845 the ablative is used with *inhaerere* to avoid an impracticable dative (*corpore inhaeret*).

74. nunc: correlative with *nunc* in 77. By day and night she forces herself upon Aeneas; so much of her tragedy is her own doing.

75. Sidoniasque . . . opes: 'and flaunts Phoenicia's power.' Virgil uses Tyre and Sidon indifferently in speaking of Dido's Phoenician origin; so Statius has *Tyrias opes* (*Th.* x. 3) and *Sidonios duces* (ibid. 126), both referring to the Thebans (Cadmus was a Phoenician). The prosody of *Sidonius* varies: in Greek, the -o- can be short (as here), or long, and Virgil makes it long himself in what is almost a formula, *Sidōnia Dido* (i. 446, 613, ix. 266, xi. 74); the elegists show the same variation (Platnauer, op. cit., p. 54), and so does Statius. The reason for the variation is metrical convenience: a nominative *Sidŏniă* is impossible without elision, and an accusative *Sidōniās* is impossible without synizesis (Conway on i. 678 unwisely states that *Sidoniam* is 'probably trisyllabic').

paratam: hardly 'built', for it was not; it is a city 'all ready' for the cityless Aeneas, a temptation to him to end his wandering.

76. incipit . . . resistit: 'she begins to speak her heart, but stops when the word is half-begun'; a sensitive piece of psychology (and more concisely put, and in a more fitting context, than Apoll. Rhod. iii. 683 ff. μῦθος δ' ἄλλοτε μέν οἱ ἐπ' ἀκροτάτης ἀνέτελλεν / γλώσσης, ἄλλοτ' ἔνερθε κατὰ στῆθος πεπότητο, etc.). This adversative use of -*que* is more common when a negative has preceded (e.g. vii. 50 f. 'prolesque virilis/ nulla fuit, prima*que* oriens erepta iuventa est'); see Wagner, *Quaest. Virg.* xxxv.

77. eadem: with *convivia* (parallel to *iterum* in 78); she asks for the feast all over again, so that she may hear the tale of Troy anew.

78. demens : note how quickly her wild love is openly shown; her fierce, uncontrolled Eastern passions are in marked contrast with Aeneas' self-imposed restraint.

79. pendetque . . . ore: Page well remarks on the vividness of this phrase.

80 ff. post . . . videtque: 'later, when he and she have parted, and the dimmed moon darkens her lamp in turn, and the setting stars bid sleep, she is alone, in a home that is empty, in misery, flinging herself upon the couch that he has left. He is not there, and she is parted from him, but him she hears, him she sees.' Virgil brings out with dramatic force the contrast between Dido's excited animation when she is with Aeneas and her lonely agony when he has left her. Fanshawe translates:

> When every one was parted to his rest,
> And the dim moon trod on the heels of day,
> And setting stars show'd it high time to rest,
> She in the empty house languisht away,
> And on the couch, which he had pressed, lay.

Note the varied vowels, the repeated *s* sounds, the gentle assonance of 'sua*dent*que ca*dent*ia', the sadness of 'do*mo* *m*aeret'. The rhythm of 81 itself suggests sleep (cf. 486), with no strong caesura, and the regular diminishing of the three final words (cf. v. 856 'cunctantique natantia lumina solvit', *G.* iv. 496 'conditque natantia lumina somnus'); the line echoes ii. 8–9 ('et iam nox umida caelo/ praecipitat, suadentque cadentia sidera somnos'), but there, all impatient to hear Aeneas' tale, Dido did not want sleep, here she cannot get it.

80. vicissim: it is comparatively seldom that Virgil ends a line with an adverb (there are 18 examples in this book), or with colourless words like *ille* (13, 421), *quicquam* (317), *istam* (318); see Norden, *Aeneis VI*, Anh. III, B. 2.

82. maeret: a startling word, for which Virgil has not prepared the reader, the more vivid by its position between *domo* and *vacua. Relictis* is parallel to *vacua*: Aeneas is nowhere, though he was present so lately.

83. incubat: the run-on, with the following pause (cf. 23) gives the word a fearful force; the couch is like a treasure to her (cf. *G.* ii. 507, of a miser, 'incubat auro', *A.* vi. 610), and she broods over it in misery.

  illum . . . videtque: such a line shows the magic of an inflected language; Dido locks Aeneas in her thoughts, and this is shown in the word-order. A fresh sleepless night has strengthened her passion; it is not simply the face and words of Aeneas now that are imprinted in her heart, but he is

himself present to her as she thinks of him. 'Stands he, or
sits he? Or does he walk, or is he on his horse? O happy
horse, to bear the weight of Antony!' This is one of those
Virgilian lines of which F. W. H. Myers remarks (*Essays
Classical*, London, 1911, p. 118) that 'they come to us charged
with more than an individual passion and with a meaning
wider than their own'.

  auditque videtque: the second *-que* only is a true connective
(joining *videt* to *audit*); the first is redundant, and needs no
translation; cf. 94 *tuque puerque tuus*, 146 *Cretesque Dryopesque*, 438 *fertque refertque*, 581 *rapiuntque ruuntque*, 589 *terque
quaterque*, 682 *populumque patresque*. These passages show
that the usage tended to be employed with words related in
sense or type, sometimes almost as formulae (e.g. 438, 589,
and the frequent *itque reditque*, *noctesque diesque*); cf. further
nomenque decusque (ii. 89), *caelique marisque* (v. 802), *miseret-
que pudetque* (ix. 787), *tectumque laremque* (*G.* iii. 344); see
H. Christensen, *ALL* xv, pp. 164 ff.

  This use of double *-que* is a mannerism of high epic style,
very common in Virgil, Lucan, and Statius; it is never found
in classical prose. It goes back to Ennius, who took it over
from Homer's use of τε . . . τε (e.g. *Il.* i. 167 σοὶ τὸ γέρας
πολὺ μεῖζον, ἐγὼ δ' ὀλίγον τε φίλον τε); its metrical convenience is
obvious, especially at the end of a line (cf. Norden on vi. 336).
It should not be regarded as a native Latin idiom, in spite of
its occurrence in Plautus: see Fraenkel, *Plautinisches im
Plautus* (Berlin, 1922), pp. 209 f., where it is shown that
Plautus has it only in his more elevated passages and under
certain clear limitations, which again point to its Ennian
origin. (*-Que* itself belongs to very early Latin, e.g. the laws
of the XII Tables and the archaic prose of Cato; but Plautus
and Terence already use it less than *et* or *atque*, and it •had
disappeared from common speech by the time of the early
Empire, as can be seen from Petronius and the Pompeian inscriptions; see L.-H., p. 656, Löfstedt, *Per. Aeth.* p. 87.)

84. Ascanium: Aeneas' little son, often called Iulus (cf. note on
140): he is so like his father that Dido is enraptured (*capta*) by
the likeness, and she imagines that she holds him in her lap
(as she did in i. 718, when Cupid had in fact been substituted
for him by Venus), just as she sees Aeneas with her, actually
present. *Aut* must mean 'at another moment', as in 62: first
she imagines Aeneas there, then Ascanius. I cannot believe
the theory of Page and others that Dido 'tries to cheat her
love by petting the boy as a substitute for Aeneas'. The
picture in 83–85 is a unity: as Dido sorrows alone in the
empty palace, Aeneas is there, the child is there, the whole

vivid scene is present again, and by re-living it she tries to pretend that she is not racked with misery (*si fallere possit amorem*). *Maeret* (82) has shown her grieving for Aeneas' actual absence; now we see her playing at his presence, with Ascanius there as well.

85. **infandum**: a very strong word; her love is something agonizing, a thing which 'ought not to be told', and so practically 'wicked'; Virgil has it of Sinon's 'day of death' (ii. 132), of the portents at Caesar's death (*G.* i. 479), of Clytaemnestra the adulteress (xi. 267), of a war begun against all the omens (vii. 583), of death and slaughter and punishment.

86 ff. Virgil now shows the cumulative effect of Dido's sleepless passion; note the spondees, to represent the slowing down of work on the city.

87. **exercet**: here of plying tools (*arma*); see Conway on i. 499.

88. **tuta**: with *bello* (for *in bellum*), 'to give safety against war'.

88 f. **minaeque murorum**: probably *minae* has its literal sense of something projecting, like *pinnae*, 'battlements', just as *minax* is sometimes used (viii. 668 f. 'te, Catilina, minaci/pendentem scopulo'). Others take it figuratively, like *rotarum lapsus* (ii. 235), but this gives far less vividness.

89. **ingentes** : *ingens* is a very dear word to Virgil, as it was to Ennius before him. See Mackail in *CR* xxvi, 1912, pp. 251 ff., and Conway, ibid., pp. 254 ff. (also on i. 114). Mackail compares the development of its use to that of *vast* and *extreme* in English. Henry has a portentous but light-hearted note on v. 118 'ingentemque Gyas ingenti mole Chimaeram' ('*Ingens* is our author's maid of all work—cook, slut, and butler at once. . . . Seville's famous barber was never busier: it is Ingens here, Ingens there, everywhere Ingens', and so on for six pages). But he is not altogether fair (cf. Conway on i. 453, a good note), and in any case why should not a poet have a special weakness for a favourite word? (Tacitus, no doubt under Virgil's influence, shows a like fondness for it; cf. Gudeman on Tac. *Dial.* 6. 5, Kroll, *Studien zum Verständnis der röm. Literatur*, p. 272.)

machina: perhaps a crane (see Irvine's note), as often in Vitruvius' technical descriptions of building operations; Virgil has it elsewhere (ii. 46, 151, 237) only of the 'contraption' of the Wooden Horse. Henry argues that it means the whole 'device' or 'fabric' of the walls, so that *machina* is a variation of *minae murorum* and both particularize *opera* (his examples are all post-Virgilian, but Valerius Flaccus' expression *machina muri*, vi. 383, is an interesting parallel). If 'crane' is accepted, *pendent* need not be used 'only loosely' with *machina* (so Page); the picture is of a crane high up,

towering to the sky, its burden left in mid-air because no one
is now there to work it. Note the alliteration of *p*, *m*, *n*, and
the harsh clattering effect of *aequataque machina caelo*, sug-
gesting the din and hammering of the work now stopped.

90–128. *An interlude : Juno and Venus plot concerning Aeneas.
Juno, annoyed at Venus' success in making Dido fall in love
with Aeneas, suggests a truce to quarrelling : she will assent to
their marriage, and Carthage shall be Dido's dowry. Venus
pretends to be doubtful of the success of what she knows to be a
trick to make Carthage all-powerful, but she demurely accepts
Juno's assurances and her scheme to bring about the marriage.*

Virgil draws the goddesses with subtle humour (for their
part in the epic see Warde Fowler, *The Death of Turnus*,
pp. 82 ff., and *Virgil's Gathering of the Clans*, pp. 39 ff.). Juno
is at her grandest, and Venus' respectful awe of her is sheer
naughtiness, for she knows her power over Jupiter and has his
promise that Aeneas shall reach Italy (i. 257 ff.). But behind
this feminine sparring, feminine hardness can be discerned:
neither goddess has any pity for the woman Dido. The scene
slightly relieves the tension, placed as it is between two
deeply emotional passages (so too, though more dramatically,
the Charon-scene in vi. 387 ff.; cf. the porter-scene in *Macbeth*). Contrast the opening of Apoll. Rhod. iii.

90. persensit: 'felt quite sure'; Juno has waited for her moment.
peste: the word, like *teneri* and *furori*, shows how inescap-
ably Dido is committed to her fate. Note the alliterative
pattern *t, p, p, t, c, . . . c, f. . . . f.*
91. cara: cf. Page on x. 611, xii. 144. Juno is still *cara Iovis
coniunx*, although she is doing her best to ruin Jupiter's
plans.
    nec . . . furori: 'that her pride was no hindrance to her
passion' (*famam = famae curam*).
92. adgreditur . . . dictis: an archaic phrase (see Norden on vi.
387). Note the juxtaposition *Venerem*)(*Saturnia*, a syntacti-
cal picture of their conference.
93 ff. egregiam . . . duorum est: 'a fine distinction this, to be
sure, and a noble triumph for you and your son to win—a
great and glorious pair of powers. One woman crushed by the
guile of two gods!'
93. egregiam: ironical; cf. vi. 523 'egregia interea coniunx' (of
Helen), vii. 556 'egregium Veneris genus' (said by Juno of
Aeneas).
94. tuque puerque: see note on 83. *Puer* is often used for the
metrically intractable *filius*; but it may be contemptuous

here (cf. Apul. *Met.* v. 28, where Venus calls Cupid *illud incrementum*, 'that limb').

numen: so the older MSS. and Donatus; later MSS. read *nomen*, which many editors adopt. *Numen* is generally taken in apposition with *tuque puerque* (cf. Ovid, *Met.* iv. 451 f. 'illa sorores/ nocte vocat genitas, grave et inplacabile numen'); the brackets of the Oxford text would be better changed to commas, as in Mackail. But *erit* could be supplied, and the clause attached to the next line ('your divinity will be great and renowned in story, for . . .'). *Nomen* would be parallel with *laudem* and *spolia*; it has been approved in spite of its less good MSS. authority, because *memorabile nomen* is a collocation found a number of times elsewhere (see *Thes. L. L.* s.v. *memorabilis*, col. 663. 30), e.g. Ovid, *Met.* x. 607 f. 'habebis/ Hippomene victo magnum et memorabile nomen', and Virgil himself has it in ii. 583 f. 'etsi nullum memorabile nomen/ feminea in poena est'. But it is more obvious here and has less colour; the 'imitations' do not necessarily confirm it (and, for that matter, cf. Ovid, *Met.* iv. 416 f. 'Bacchi memorabile Thebis/ numen'); and as for the evidence of ii. 583 f., it points rather to *numen* in this line, for when Virgil echoes himself it is in his mann. r to make some slight change of tone or word.

95. Note the art of the line: *una* contrasted with *duorum*, *dolo* paired with *victa* and completing its sense, *divum* contrasted with *femina*. *Si* is explanatory, not hypothetical, as often in *si quidem*.

96. nec . . . fallit: '*I* am not so unable to see.' Generally, *adeo* emphasizes the single word which it follows (like γε), e.g. ii. 567 'iamque adeo super unus eram' ('*now* I was the only one left'), iii. 203 'tris adeo incertos caeca caligine soles' ('for three whole days'), *E*. iv. 11 'teque adeo decus hoc aevi, te consule, inibit' ('and it will be in *your* consulship'); see *Thes. L. L.* s.v. col. 614. 43 ff. Here it formally stresses *me* ('others may be blind, but I am not'), but its effect is felt in the tone of the whole sentence ('*I* know *perfectly* well'). Many Latin particles represent a look or stress or gesture, rather than any exact English equivalent.

moenia nostra: this juxtaposition of noun and adjective in agreement at the end of a line is not common; cf. 213, 'conubia nostra', ix. 379 'divortia nota', x. 445 'iussa superba', xii. 482 'agmina magna', 877 'iussa superba'; and in the reverse order, 151 'invia lustra', ix. 283 'omnia dona', 493 'omnia tela', 708 'immania membra', x. 141 'pinguia culta', 639 'inania verba'.

97. suspectas habuisse: the phrase *suspectum habere* is normal

for 'to suspect' (*suspicere* in its finite forms is not found in
this sense except once in Sallust). The use of *habere* with a
perfect participle is common in all periods; for an examination of its development see P. Thielmann, *ALL* ii, pp. 372 ff.,
509 ff., and cf. L.-H., p. 561. In late Latin it becomes the
normal method of expressing the perfect tense, thus paving
the way for romance forms (*datum habes = tu as donné*).

altae: a favourite epithet in Virgil, even more frequent
than *ingens*; it is often almost mechanically used as a kind of
standing epithet, without much real colour (unlike *ingens*,
which generally does add colour), and it is one of the very
rare adjectives of that sort to be found quite frequently at the
end of a line, where normally an adjective is placed only if it
bears some special emphasis. It is almost as if Virgil felt it to
be part of the noun that it qualifies. Cf. 265, vii. 108, ix. 697,
xii. 181, etc.

98. sed . . . tanto: 'but what limit shall we set? Where are we
drifting in all this rivalry?' Juno magnanimously pretends to
want to 'forgive and forget'. The construction is difficult;
quo may mean 'to what end'; *certamine tanto* is used in a
conversational ellipse, which has perplexed scholars from Servius onwards. It is possible to supply a verb of motion, such
as *tendimus*, taking *quo* in its ordinary sense of 'whither',
and *certamine tanto* as a modal ablative; others would rather
understand *opus est* (with *c. t.*, taking *quo* as 'to what purpose'); Conington takes the construction as exactly parallel
to that of Hor. *Epp.* i. 5. 12 'quo mihi fortunam, si non con-
ceditur uti?' (where some MSS. have *fortuna*), i.e. as an
ellipse with no clear verb understood (cf. Wilkins, ad loc.).
Against this last view is the fact that the accusative is
always found elsewhere in this particular ellipse; see Palmer
on Ovid, *Her.* 2. 53 and Wilkins, l.c.; hence Heinsius proposed
certamina tanta ('what is the point of all these quarrels?')
which Heyne reads. The latter is an easy way out, but the
corruption would then be hard to explain, while the occurrence of *certamina tanta* two lines after *moenia nostra* (see
note on 96) would be suspicious. Mackail translates 'whither
away in so hot a contest?', observing that 'the wording,
though compressed, presents no difficulty', and I should prefer to go no further than that: it is an intelligible ellipse,
whatever the exact construction.

99 f. quin . . . exercemus?: 'why not rather dwell in the ways of
peace for ever, by making a marriage-contract between them?'
99. quin: this use, with an indicative (cf. *E.* ii. 71) or an imperative (cf. 547), is from conversational speech and marks
impatience or annoyance; cf. Plaut. *Curc.* 84 'quin tu taces?',

Men. 416 'quin tu tace modo?', *Most.* 815 'quin tu is intro
atque otiose perspecta?', Cic. *ad fam.* vii. 8. 2 'quin tu urges
istam occasionem?' (Cicero has it twice only with the imperative in the speeches, *Rosc. Com.* 25, *Mil.* 79). Virgil introduced
it into poetic style, especially in the formula *quin age* (*E.* iii. 52,
G. iv. 329, *A.* v. 635); so Ovid, *Met.* vii. 70, ix. 383 (imperative), Lucan ii. 319, viii. 441 (indicative), ix. 282 (imperative),
Statius, *Th.* xi. 685, xii. 160, *S.* ii. 1. 208 (indicative), *Th.* i.
260, v. 140, *Ach.* i. 949, *S.* iii. 1. 154 (imperative). Livy
also uses it in lively style (i. 57. 7 'quin . . . conscendimus
equos?').

   pactosque hymenaeos: this is explanatory of *pacem* (*-que* is
often used to append an explanation or an extension of
thought); the wedding is to be the basis of the *pax*. For the
phrase, cf. x. 649 'thalamos ne desere pactos'; here the
name of the marriage-god is transferred to the marriage
itself (the plural is used by analogy with *nuptiae*). Note the
quadrisyllabic ending, which Virgil allows only with a Greek
word (as here, 146, 316) or for some special effect (as 215, 667);
it is often accompanied by some form of metrical irregularity,
as in 667 (cf. note on 64).

100. **exercemus**: a Virgilian experiment in language. *Exercere*
is often used of practising an attitude of mind, generally with
ira, odium, inimicitiae, etc., but sometimes with the opposite
type of word (*amicitia* Sen. *Epp.* 9. 8, Tac. *H.* i. 14. 1, *amores*
Catull. 68. 69), and with both together in Sall. *Cat.* 51. 16
'neque illum in tanta re gratiam aut inimicitias exercere'.
Virgil seems to have extended this use to cover *pacem*, and
then to have extended *pacem* in its turn by the definition
pactos hymenaeos, keeping the same verb by a curious piece
of straining which would not have been present if he had
chosen to write *pactis hymenaeis*. Juno says, in effect, 'let us
make it up by making a match'. (*Thes. L. L.* includes the passage in a very improbable category, s.v. *exercere*, col. 1377. 37.)

   tota . . . mente: cf. *simulata mente* 105; this type of phrase
is the ancestor of the Romance forms of adverbs (*vivement,
vivamente*); see C. H. Grandgent, *An Introduction to Vulgar
Latin*, p. 26.

101. **ardet . . . furorem**: 'Dido is ablaze with love, and has
drawn her passion through and through her frame'; her
madness (*furor*) is like a disease, sweeping her body.

102. **communem . . . auspiciis**: 'so then, let it be in common
that we rule this people, with equality of power'; *communem*
is the important word, expanded by *paribus auspiciis* (cf. vii.
256). *Auspicium* ('command', cf. 341) is a metaphor from
military language: the commander-in-chief alone had

authority to take the *auspicia*, in virtue of his *imperium*, and so the *auspicia* could themselves be regarded as a symbol of *imperium*.

103. **liceat . . . marito**: 'let her be allowed to marry her Phrygian and be his slave'; a venomous line, for *Phrygius* is often a term of contempt used by the enemies of Troy (cf. note on 216), and *servire* implies the abjectness of Dido's love. For *maritus* cf. 35, 536.

104. **dotalisque . . . dextrae**: 'and let her, for her dowry, assign her Tyrians to your control'; Dido's subjects (*Tyrii*, cf. 75) are to be thrown into the bargain. Juno pretends in all this to be making a concession to Venus, who, she says, will have the real power over her son's and his wife's subjects.

105. **olli**: an archaic form (so too *ollis*, *olli* nom. pl.), used by Virgil 'in narratione gravi et sedata' (Wagner, *Quaest. Virg.* xxi, p. 483), especially with reference to the gods. It is normally placed in an emphatic position at the beginning of a line, as Homer uses the demonstrative article in such phrases as τὸν δ᾽ ἐπιμειδήσας (cf. ix. 740 'olli subridens'; see Gloeckner, *ALL* xiv, pp. 185 ff.). Virgil inherited it from Lucretius and Ennius, but it must have long disappeared from spoken Latin, since neither Plautus nor Terence uses it; it occurs (with the non-Virgilian forms *ollos*, *olla* neut. pl.) in a number of old laws quoted by Cicero (*de leg.* ii. 19 ff.). *Olim* is connected with the same root. Quintilian (viii. 3. 24) remarks on Virgil's supreme judgement in his use of such archaisms, '*olli* enim et *quianam* et *moerus* et *pone* et *porricerent* aspergunt illam, quae etiam in picturis est gratissima, vetustatis inimitabilem arti auctoritatem'. We might roughly compare Coleridge's use of 'eftsoons' or 'clomb' in *The Ancient Mariner*.

106. **Italiae**: the first syllable in this word and in *Italus* is properly short; Catullus (i. 5 *unus Italorum*) seems first to have lengthened it, and Virgil regularly uses *Ītalia* (otherwise the word would have been impossible in hexameters), occasionally *Ītalus* when that prosody is needed also (iii. 185 *Ītălă regna*, vii. 643 *Ītălă . . . terra*, ix. 698 *Ītălă cornus*; contrast vi. 757 *Ītălā de gente*). See Norden on vi. 61.

107 f. **quis . . . abnuat**: Richard Stanyhurst translates 'What niddipol hare brayne/ Would scorne this covenaunt?' His translation of *Aeneid* i–iv appeared in 1582, at Leyden; two copies only of the original book exist, but a reprint was made by Arber in the *English Scholar's Library of Old and Modern Works* (Constable, 1895). It is in quantitative English hexameters, such as Robert Bridges experimented with in his *Ibant Obscuri* (Oxford, 1916), and is a repository of linguistic

conceits; his metre was described by T. Nash in 1592 as 'a foule lumbering boystrous wallowing measure', and in 1617 Barnabe Rich wrote of him 'he tooke upon him to translate Virgill, and stript him out of a Velvet gowne, into a Fooles coate, out of a Latin Heroicall verse, into an English rifferaffe'. It is a bewildering experience to pass to his translation from that of Henry Howard, Earl of Surrey, written some forty years earlier. Cf. G. Saintsbury, *History of English Prosody*, i. p. 319, ii, pp. 175 ff.

109. si modo: for *utinam*; cf. vi. 187 f. 'si nunc se nobis ille aureus arbore ramus/ ostendat'.

110. fatis ... feror: 'the fates make me full of doubt and misgivings'; another experiment in language which it is difficult to force into the formal conventions of grammar. *Feror* is often used of movement, either physical or mental, over which one has little control; cf. 376, x. 630 f. 'aut ego veri/ vana feror', G. iv. 497 'feror ingenti circumdata nocte'. Here, *incerta* is added, to stress the pretended doubts in Venus' mind: she 'drifts about in uncertainty'. *Fatis* seems to depend on the combined concept *incerta-feror*, and must be causal (Henry's 'doubtful of the fates' is surely impossible); it is the existence of Fate and its possibilities that makes Venus feign such doubts—Jupiter, she says, may not allow the scheme. In fact, of course, she had no doubt whatever of Aeneas' destiny.

si: 'whether'; this use occurs already in Plautus, to introduce an indirect question after *video*, etc., and is common in prose after verbs of attempting or expecting; see Löfstedt, *Per. Aeth.* p. 327, L.-H. p. 697. The whole clause *si . . . iungi* is formally dependent on *incerta feror*, but it is also an expansion of *fatis* (for the identification of 'fate' with the will of Jupiter see Bailey, *Religion in Virgil*, pp. 228 ff.): the fates fill her with doubt as to what they may do, they cause retrospective and prospective misgivings.

111. Troia: dependent on *profectis* ('the men who sailed from Troy'). Note that the dative of possession stresses the object possessed (whereas the genitive marks the possessor); Venus doubts whether Jupiter will 'let the Tyrians and Trojans have a single city'.

112. In the end, it was a very different fusion that took place, that of Trojans and Italians; see xii. 835 ff.

113. tu ... precando: 'now *you* are his wife, *you* cannot break the law by working on his mind with prayers.' Venus naughtily pretends to be awed by Juno's importance; *fas* ('God's law') is amusing in the context (Conway remarks, on i. 77, that the word always implies a law whose commands

are mainly negative). Venus knows well that she can twist
Jupiter round her fingers when she wishes. Note the emphatic *tu . . . tibi.*

114. excepit: 'took her up' in reply; *sic* ('like this') anticipates
the actual words (cf. 8, 107), like *hoc, illud, haec.*

115 f. mecum . . . docebo: 'That will be *my* task. Now, as to how
the matter in hand can be accomplished—pay attention—I
will tell you in a few words.' Juno puts on her grandest airs
(*regia*).

115. mecum: 'mine'; see Mackail on i. 675, and cf. Livy iv.
32. 5 'memores secum triumphos . . . esse'.

116. confieri: a rare form (but *confici* is metrically impossible);
so Lucr. ii. 1069, v. 891; Servius Sulpicius ap. Cic. *ad fam.* iv.
5. 1, Tac. *Ann.* xv. 59. Terence has *defieri* (*Hec.* 768), Plautus
ecfieri (*Pers.* 761) and *interfieri* (*Trin.* 532). See Kühner,
Lat. Gr. i, p. 821. The *-i-* in *fio* was originally long in all
forms, but in the classical period became shortened in *fieri,
fierem.*

   paucis . . . docebo: a formula; cf. viii. 49 f. 'nunc qua ratione
quod instat/ expedias victor, paucis (adverte) docebo', xi.
314 f. 'nunc adeo quae sit dubiae sententia menti,/ ex-
pediam et paucis (animos adhibete) docebo'.

117. miserrima: a gibe, not pity; 'his love-sick Dido'.

118 f. ubi . . . orbem: 'when to-morrow's Sun has shown forth
his early rising, and with his rays unveiled the world'; there
is a heightening of style after the matter-of-fact manner of
the previous passage; *ortus efferre* is more picturesque than
oriri, and *Titan* more splendid than *Sol* (the Sun was the
child of the Titan Hyperion, and so the poets give him this
name, just as the moon is sometimes called *Titania* or *Titanis*;
cf. *1 Henry IV,* ii. 4. 135 'Didst thou never see Titan kiss a
dish of butter?').

118. crastinus: adjective for adverb, often convenient metrically (cf. *nocturnus,* 303, 490, v. 868, *G.* iv. 521; see Kroll,
op. cit., p. 258).

   ortus: a frequent 'poetic plural' (more common than the
singular), by analogy with ἀνατολαί (see Maas, *ALL* xii, pp. 487,
494); cf. vi. 255, *G.* iv. 544, etc., and note Ovid, *Met.* v. 445
'solis ab occasu solis quaerebat ad ortus'.

119. retexerit: cf. v. 64 f. 'si nona diem mortalibus almum/
Aurora extulerit radiisque retexerit orbem', ix. 461 'iam sole
infuso, iam rebus luce retectis'; see note on 6 f.

120. his ego: the juxtaposition effectively suggests Juno's
power. The short final syllable of *ego* is invariable in classical
poetry (cf. note on 50, and see *Thes. L. L.* s.v. col. 252. 7 ff.).
Virgil likes to set it against a demonstrative, as here, or a re-

lative (536), or *non* (425), *aut*, *en*, etc.; note iii. 45, xi. 392,
xii. 882, where there is a strong pause after elided *ego* (a less
marked pause in xi. 441)—how were such passages read?

nigrantem . . . nimbum: 'black hail-mixed rain', a typical
Virgilian compound expression; note the heavy spondees, and
the massed consonants, rhythm and words alike conveying
the picture of darkness and thunder (*nimbus* implies thunder-
rain); note also the curious assonance in *grandine*, *indagine*,
perhaps also suggestive of noise.

121. **dum . . . cingunt**: 'while the beaters are scurrying about
and ringing the coverts with a cordon'; *alae* is used here of
the horsemen who are driving up the game, and *indago* is a
t.t. for a ring of beaters, equipped with nets (cf. 131).

122. **tonitru . . . ciebo**: 'I will make the whole sky a chaos of
thunder'; the elisions in the line give a metrical picture of the
violent storm.

123 ff. **diffugient . . . devenient**: 'their companions will scatter
for shelter, and will be enwrapped in impenetrable darkness;
but Dido and the hero of Troy shall reach a cave together.'
For the rhythm of 123 see on 58; note the absence of a contrasting particle in 124, where English needs one (a common
Latin way of expressing an antithesis).

124. **et**: postponed (see on 33).

eandem: cf. 165, 678. This is an idiomatic use of *idem*, to
give the meaning of being 'together'; cf. Ovid, *Met.* iv. 328
'thalamumque ineamus eundem', Cic. *Cael.* 36 'fuisti non-
nunquam in isdem hortis' ('you were together with him in
the Park'), and somewhat similarly *A*. ii. 716 'hanc ex diverso
sedem veniemus in unam'. For the pattern *speluncam . . .
eandem* see note on 7.

125. **devenient**: the pause is effective; Juno waits a moment to
let Venus appreciate her plot to the full.

adero: Juno will be there in her capacity as goddess of
marriage (cf. 166); for the success of the marriage she depends
on Venus (*tua si mihi certa voluntas*).

126. **conubio**: the t.t. for a formal marriage; cf. 167 f. 'fulsere
ignes et conscius aether/ conubiis'.

The word has an odd poetic history, and its prosody presents a problem. The nominative *conubium* occurs nowhere
in classical poetry, the accusative twice only (Catull. 62. 57,
Stat. *Th.* i. 69); the only occurrence of the word in elegy is in
Ovid, *Her.* 2. 81, 11. 99; it is used to any extent only by Virgil,
Ovid (in hexameters), and Statius; and by far the most common form is the nominative or accusative plural *conubia*. In
prose, it is most often used as a t.t. of *ius publicum*, and even
here the nominative singular is very rare, except in the

formula *conubium est cum*; for 'marriage' in a general sense
it is almost entirely poetic.

Is the prosody *conŭbium* or *conūbium*? In the nominative
and accusative plural, *conŭbia* is regular and unavoidable
(e.g. 316), except in Lucr. iii. 776 'denique conubia ad
Veneris partusque ferarum' and in seven examples in Statius:
in these, the *-u-* may be long by synizesis (*-i-* being treated as
consonantal), or it may be short. In all other forms (as here)
there is always similar ambiguity of prosody; but scansion by
synizesis can nowhere be said to be *necessary*, because there
is no example anywhere of such forms where the *-u-* bears
the ictus and therefore cannot be short. Servius, however,
expressly states, on i. 73 (of which this line is a repetition, if it
is not an interpolation—see below), that the *-u-* is naturally
long and that Virgil has here shortened it. In late Latin the
word occurs in two lyric passages where there can be no
ambiguity (Prudentius, *Cath.* 3. 75, Sidonius 14. 1), and there
the *-u-* is short.

The poets' practice in the matter of synizesis differs. Virgil
often admits it; Ovid avoids it (see Norden on vi. 33);
Statius has very few examples, and to assume it in the six-
teen lines where he has forms of *conubium* with ambiguous
prosody seems very unsafe. Müller, therefore, (*de re metrica*[2],
p. 303) argues for *conūbium*, and this is supported by Munro
on Lucr. iii. 776. Maas (*ALL* xiii, pp. 433 ff.), arguing *inter
alia* from the relative frequency of forms of *conubium* and
coniugium (which he takes as completely synonymous), deduces that the pre-Augustan and Augustan prosody was
conūbium, and that synizesis is necessary in Lucr. l.c. and the
other passages where the *-u-* does not bear the ictus; but, in
view of the practice of Statius and other post-Augustans in
the matter of synizesis, he admits the prosody *conūbium* as
coexistent with *conŭbia* in these poets. More recently the
view of Müller and Munro has been revived in an important
paper by Wackernagel (*Festschrift für Paul Kretschmer*,
Vienna–Leipzig 1926, pp. 289–306). He examines the problem from a philological as well as from a metrical angle, and
also discusses the use and meaning of *conubium* (which he
takes to have been distinct from *coniugium* in its proper use);
he concludes that *conūbium* is the normal and original prosody, and that it was metrical convenience alone which
dictated *conŭbia* where the *-u-* bears the ictus. This would
bring *conūbium* into line with *innŭba, pronŭba, subnŭba* (cf.
Conway on i. 73): note Ovid, *Met.* vi. 428 'conubio Procnes
iunxit; non pronuba Iuno'. For the lengthening in *conūbia* he
suggests the analogy of *Lemŭres* and *Lemŭria*, or Lucretius'

variations between *lĭquidus* and *līquidus*, *prŏpago* and *prō-pago*.

Wackernagel's arguments seem to me to point clearly to-wards the prosody *conŭbium*, with *conŭbia* as a licence (in spite of Servius' statement). Thus here the scansion will be *conŭbiō iungam*, and there is no unpleasant assonance such as syni-zesis would involve (-*ŭbjo* followed by *iung*-), though it must be admitted that euphony is not a very safe guide in such matters (e.g. the rhythm of vii. 333—'fama loco, neu conu-biis ambire Latinum'—might seem unwarrantably harsh if *conubiis* is made a trisyllable, were it not for the exactly similar rhythm of ii. 607 'iussa time, neu praeceptis parere recusa'). But undoubtedly the word has something queer about it: why the avoidance of the forms in -*um*, and why did Virgil never think of beginning a line with *conŭbia* fol-lowed by an elision, as Statius does? And why are the oblique forms so much rarer than *conubia*?

propriamque dicabo: 'and I will consecrate her as his true wife.' *Dicare* is a religious t.t., used of 'setting apart' some-one or something (cf. *dedicare*).

The line is repeated from i. 73, where Juno promises a bride to Aeolus. It is in all the MSS. here, and Servius knew it. But it does not fit the context easily: 'her to him' has to be supplied with *iungam*, and the sense of *propriam* similarly completed, since Juno is not here speaking to the person who is to receive the bride (contrast i. 73). Mackail and others reject the line as irrelevant, but I am inclined to agree with those who would retain it in spite of its difficulties; for with-out it the speech would end on too light a structure, and Juno's part be shorn of its solemnity.

127. hic ... erit: 'this shall be their wedding'; cf. Catull. 66. 11 'novo auctus hymenaeo'. (If 126 is omitted, *hic* must mean 'here'.)

128. atque: one of the rare instances of unelided *atque* in the *Aeneid*; of the thirty-five lines where it is so found, eight only occur in Books I–VI; see B. Axelson, *Unpoetische Wörter* (Lund, 1945), pp. 83 f., and Platnauer, op. cit., pp. 78 ff., *CQ* xlii, 1948, pp. 91 ff., for some interesting conclusions.

dolis ... repertis: probably ablative absolute; Venus laughs 'as she realises Juno's cunning trick'. It suits her to keep Aeneas safely at Carthage, and the stratagem appeals to her: again, there is no pity for Dido. Henry has one of his pleasantly discursive notes here.

Cytherea: for the prosody cf. note on 6. Venus was wor-shipped in the Aegean island of Cythēra, but the form *Cythērēa* is intractable in hexameters, and so Virgil took over

the Greek alternative *Cythĕrēa* (Κυθέρεια) ; see Bednara, *ALL*
xiv, p. 330.

129–59. *In the bright morning the hunt assembles; Dido's horse is
waiting, brilliantly caparisoned, and presently she comes, with
a golden quiver, gold in her hair, a golden buckle in her splendid
dress. Aeneas joins her, as glorious as Apollo ; and the hunt
begins, with young Ascanius enjoying himself as much as anyone.*

Note the happiness of the passage, beauty and colour and
excitement everywhere, with no hint of the misery to come
(cf. viii. 585 ff., and Henry *ad loc.*, Warde Fowler, *Aeneas at
the Site of Rome*, p. 98). Virgil can describe light marvel-
lously : e.g. his picture of a falling star in ii. 693 ff., or of the
moonlit sea in vii. 9, or of the funeral procession of Pallas in
xi. 143 f.; and cf. ii. 569, vii. 73 ff., 526 f., viii. 391 f., 585 ff.
Chaucer has caught the mood in *The Legend of Good Women*,
1188 ff.:

> The dawening up-rist out of the sea ;
> This amorous quene chargeth her meynee
> The nettes dresse, and speres brode and kene ;
> An hunting wol this lusty fresshe quene ;
> So priketh her this newe joly wo.
> To hors is al her lusty folk y-go ;
> Un-to the court the houndes been y-broght,
> And up-on coursers, swift as any thoght,
> Her yonge knightes hoven al aboute,
> And of her wommen eek an huge route.
> Up-on a thikke palfrey, paper-whyt,
> With sadel rede, enbrouded with delyt,
> Of gold the barres up-enbossed hye,
> Sit Dido, al in gold and perre wrye ;
> And she is fair, as is the brighte morwe,
> That heleth seke folk of nightes sorwe.

129. Repeated in xi. 1, a Homeric picture.
130. it . . . iuventus : ' out from the gates, when the sun's light
has sprung up, there streams the pride of Carthage.'
   iubăre : an Ennian word, only here in Virgil, but used a
number of times by Ovid, Statius, and Valerius Flaccus. It
is used of the light of the sun, as here, of the morning star
(cf. Ovid, *F.* ii. 149 f.), of the rainbow (Stat. *Th.* x. 136), etc.
131. There is no verb to this line, and no great need to supply
one : the meet begins at dawn (130)—nets, spears, galloping
horsemen, hounds and all. An ancient hunt was not very
sporting to our minds ; nets of various kinds were so arranged

that the game could be driven into them and then killed. Virgil here distinguishes two sorts of net, those with wide meshes (*retia rara*), used to surround a cover, and 'trap-nets' (*plagae*) which would be set in the known track of the game, made of very fine material (cf. Pliny, *NH* xix. 11); cf. Seneca, *Phaed.* 44 ff. 'alius raras cervice gravi/ portare plagas, alius teretes/ properet laqueos'. See Mair's notes on Oppian, *Cyneg.* i. 147 ff. (Loeb edition) for a good account, and J. Aymard, *Essai sur les chasses romaines* (Paris, 1951), for an exhaustive study of the whole subject, with some interesting illustrative plates.

lato . . . ferro: 'broad-bladed hunting-spears'; the descriptive ablative acts for a compound epithet.

132. **Massylique . . . vis**: 'the African horsemen gallop up, and keen-scented powerful hounds.' The Massyli were a people in N. Africa. The hounds would probably be named (see the list of dogs' names in Ovid, *Met.* iii. 206 ff., and J. M. C. Toynbee, *Beasts and their Names in the Roman Empire*, in *Papers of the British School at Rome*, xvi, 1948, pp. 24 ff., a fascinating study).

odora canum vis: lit. 'the keen-scented strength of hounds'; so Lucretius has *promissa canum vis* (iv. 681), *fida canum vis* (vi. 1222), a development from *fortis equi vis* (iii. 8) and *carbonumque gravis vis* (vi. 802) where *vis* has its literal meaning. It is a form of phrase that belongs to old Latin, and probably goes back to Homer (e.g. *Il.* xxiii. 720 ἴς Ὀδυσῆος). 'Copied from Lucretius', says Page, absurdly; in such a point, Virgil takes over what he regards as a legitimate poetic heritage, adding a new beauty which gave fresh honour to the earlier poet: a reflection passes from the one to the other.

The line ends with a monosyllable, and the effect of such an ending should be clearly understood. A glance at any page of Virgil shows two normal patterns in the last two feet, either that of *delecta iuventus*, or that of *venabula ferro*: i.e. the last word is a disyllable or a trisyllable, and the last two feet are shared between two words only. Thus the metrical beat or 'ictus', in a normal ending, falls on the same syllable as that which bears the accent of the spoken word; for that accent falls on the penultimate syllable of all disyllabic words, and of all longer words if that syllable is long, but on the antepenultimate of trisyllabic or longer words if the penultimate is short; and this rule gives *delécta iuvéntus*, *venábula férro*, with word-accent and ictus coinciding. When the normal end-pattern is disturbed, the rhythm is disturbed too, so that there is no longer this coincidence: the ictus falls thus, *odóra canúm vis*, but the accent thus, *odóra cánum vís*,

and so with an abnormal end-pattern an abnormal rhythm is
obtained. The line has a bustling, agitated close instead of a
calm, smooth one, and the metre itself shows the excitement
of the scene, with the hounds poking about vigorously and
appearing in unexpected places. Any such monosyllabic ending is worth careful study (cf. Page on x. 2): e.g. viii. 43
'inventa sub ilicibus sus' (the surprising sow), v. 481 'procum-
bit humi bos' (the ox crashes down), xii. 552 'summa nituntur
opum vi' (a mortal fight), G. i. 181 'saepe exiguus mus' (the
mouse pops up), Ovid, *Met.* xiv. 515 'et levibus cannis
nutantia semicaper Pan' (Pan playing tricks). Some are
traditional, e.g. i. 65 'divum pater atque hominum rex'; see
Norden, *Aeneis VI*, p. 439, and cf. Bridges, *Ibant Obscuri*,
pp. 8 f.

This interplay of ictus and accent is an integral feature of
the hexameter as Virgil writes it (see L. P. Wilkinson, *CQ*
xxxiv, 1940, pp. 30 ff.); it is bound to occur, since the ictus can
never fall on a short syllable and the accent can; but Virgil
manipulates it with supreme skill (for the whole subject
see W. F. J. Knight, *Accentual Symmetry in Vergil*, Blackwell
1939). Just as coincidence is the norm in the last two feet of
the line, so clash regularly appears somewhere at least in the
first four. An analogous kind of interplay can be felt in much
English poetry: take Wyatt's line 'The longe love that in my
thought I harber' (cf. G. Saintsbury, *History of English Prosody*, i, p. 306), or Donne's 'Blasted with sighs, and surrounded with tears', or Dryden's 'Not a sigh, nor a tear,
my pain discloses'—in all, the metrical beat can be heard
to clash at certain points with the normal word-accent.

133. reginam: the word is put first for emphasis; its position
could be interchanged with that of *Poenorum* or *cunctantem*,
but an inappropriate word would then be stressed. Cf. *at regina* (1), and note there; she is named as queen here on the
special day that was to bring her 'wedding', in 296 (when she
hears of Aeneas' imminent departure), in 504 (the building
of the pyre), in 586 (when she sees that the fleet has left).

thalamo cunctantem: her hesitation is not due to a desire
to be impressive, nor (as the old commentators thought) because she was taking so long to dress; she hesitates as a bride
might, even though she did not know what was to be the out-
come of the day (so Manlius' bride delays through *ingenuus
pudor*, Catull. 61. 79); Virgil's choice of the word *thalamus* is
significant (he could have written *tecto*).

limina: the plural is much more frequent than the accusative singular, perhaps influenced by such plurals as *aedes*,
fores.

135. **stat . . . mandit**: 'there stands her steed, and proudly champs the foaming bit'; *sonipes* suggests the ring of the hoofs as the horse paws the ground—it is a word that goes back to Accius and Lucilius, and Virgil first used it in epic, followed by all his successors (see Rittweger, *ALL* vii, p. 326); for the whole picture cf. vii. 277 ff. *Ferox* means 'mettlesome', 'high-spirited', not 'fierce'. Note the alliteration, and the assonance of 'spu*ma*ntia *ma*ndit', to suggest the noise of the horse's jaws. Nailed horseshoes were not used at this period in Italy, although there is evidence of their use in Roman times in both Gaul and Britain. The references to 'shoes' in Catull. 17. 26, Sueton. *Vesp.* 23, *Nero* 30, Pliny, *NH* xxxiii. 140, Vegetius, *Mulomed.* i. 26. 3, ii. 82. 2, are to shoes of broom or to leather socks, sometimes with a metal plate attached either for ornament or as a protection to injured feet. I owe this information to Miss S. White, who remarks that *sonipes* 'probably refers to the hollow noise made by the air-space between the sole of the foot and the ground, which is the sign of a sound unshod foot; this would be more obvious to people who were not accustomed to the sharper, clearer ring of the iron-shod foot'.

137. **Sidoniam . . . limbo**: 'wearing, flung about her, a Phoenician cloak with embroidered hem'; *picto limbo* acts as a compound epithet.

   chlamydem: direct object of *circumdata*, which is used like a Greek 'middle' participle denoting an action 'done to oneself' (cf. Nettleship on *G.* iv. 337); the construction is especially common (in poetry) with verbs of dressing, wearing, etc. (cf. 493, 518, 644, 659), and not with a participle only (cf. 493, ii. 510, vii. 640). It occurs also in the poetically-coloured prose of Livy (xxvii. 37. 12) and Tacitus (*Ann.* ii. 17, *Hist.* ii. 20); see Landgraf, *ALL* x, pp. 218 ff.

138 f. **cui . . . vestem**: 'she has a quiver of gold, her hair is knotted into a gold clasp, golden is the brooch that underfastens her purple dress.' The whole picture is one of gleaming brilliance and beauty (*purpureus* is a bright shade, cf. i. 590 f., xi. 819); and Dido's hair was golden (590; so Chaucer, 'her brighte gilte here'). The *vestis* may be a robe beneath the *chlamys*, or the *chlamys* itself. Cf. xi. 776 'fulvo in nodum collegerat auro', v. 313 'tereti subnectit fibula gemma'.

139. **vestem**: the plural form is more common in Virgil; but cf. v. 619, 685 (also at the end of a line), xii. 825 (*vestes* P); see Maas, *ALL* xii, p. 519.

140. **nec non et**: a use introduced into poetry by Virgil, generally at the beginning of the line (but cf. vii. 521, ix. 310, *G.* ii. 452). It was originally a usage of familiar speech, as is shown

by its occurrences in Varro's *de re rustica* (see Löfstedt, *Per. Aeth.* pp. 95 ff.; cf. L.-H., p. 686).

Phrygii comites: 'the Trojan company', in their turn; *Phrygius* is not derogatory here (cf. 103). Iulus is *laetus*, 'excited'; Virgil draws him with affectionate care (cf. 156 ff.), and 'he grows all through the *Aeneid*' (Warde Fowler, *The Death of Turnus*, p. 90, note 1, in a fascinating discussion which is itself a loving biography of the boy; see also some wise remarks by Heinze, op. cit., pp. 157 f.).

141. incedunt: the word suggests a stately progress; the pause after it marks the moment of their waiting for Aeneas to take up his position.

pulcherrimus: as Dido was *pulcherrima* (60); Aeneas is worthy of her, just as Manlius was worthy of his young bride's beauty (Catull. 61. 189 ff.). Another of Virgil's heroes, Turnus, was also *ante alios pulcherrimus* (vii. 55).

142. infert se socium : 'steps forward to join her'; the two splendid figures join their companies into one. In the elaborate simile that follows, with the high-sounding names adding splendour, Aeneas is compared to Apollo, just as in i. 496 Dido, on her first appearance, is likened to Apollo's sister Diana leading the dance *per iuga Cynthi* (cf. 147): both Dido and Aeneas are like the most nobly beautiful of all the gods.

143. qualis ubi: a compendious form of comparison; *qualis* looks forward to *haud segnior* in 149 (which takes the place of *talis*); cf. xii. 4 ff. 'qualis . . . haud secus', and see Conway on i. 430–1.

hibernam: 'Lycia his winter home'; Virgil imagines Apollo as living in winter at his famous shrine of Patara in Lycia, on the river Xanthus, and paying a visit to his island birthplace Delos when navigation became practicable, to hold high festival there.

fluenta: the plural is invariable in the classical period; see *Thes. L. L.* s.v.

145. instauratque choros: 'starts up the dance anew' on his return, a renewed solemnity of ritual (cf. 63).

146. A fine-sounding line; people travelled from everywhere, and *fremunt* ('make a din') well suggests the excitement of these visitors to the festival, some of them rather rustic. The Dryopes were said to live near Mount Parnassus, the Agathyrsi perhaps came from Thrace; *picti* probably means 'tattooed' (cf. *G.* ii. 115), though Servius refers it to the colour of their hair, which Pliny calls *caeruleus* (*NH* iv. 88). Virgil likes to make geography romantic, as Milton does.

Cretesquē Dryopesque: for the doubled *-que*, see on 83.

Virgil has made the first -*que* long, by a metrically convenient but abnormal treatment of the syllable, based on Greek practice. The consonant-group *dr*, with which the following word begins, consists of a mute (*p, b, f, d, t, c, g*) and a liquid (*l, r*), and such a group could either be pronounced as a unit or be treated as two independent consonants (contrast a group like *gm, nt*, which could never be pronounced as a unit). The first of these two methods is the norm if such a group occurs in mid-word, and the normal syllabic division of such a word as *tenebrae* is *tenĕ-brae*, with -*nĕ*- an open syllable (cf. *ă-prum*, 159); but here the poets sometimes used the second method, pronouncing *tenēb-rae*, i.e. separating the mute from the liquid and attaching it to the previous syllable, which thus becomes closed and the vowel is necessarily long (cf. *āg-ros*, 163). But if such a group begins a word, the first method of pronunciation is alone possible, unless a very unusual licence is taken, such as Virgil has taken here: for in this line he has treated a word-division as if it were a syllable-division and availed himself of the second method just mentioned, detaching the mute from the liquid in *Dryopes* and attaching it to the vowel at the end of the preceding *word*, thus giving the pronunciation *Cretesquēd-ryopes*. This is obviously abnormal (a rough analogy is to be seen in Butler's *Hudibras*, 'And pulpit, drum ecclesiastick/ Was beat with fist instead of á stick'), and Virgil can only treat the syllable in this way because it bears the ictus; mark that in *Dryopesque*, where -*que* does not bear the ictus, the vowel keeps its normal quantity and does not have the *f* of *fremunt* attached to it. Further, Virgil treats -*que* in this way only when a second -*que* follows, as here (cf. Housman, *CQ* xxi, 1927, p. 12); other examples are vii. 186, xii. 181, *G*. i. 352. Cf. note on 159, and see Christensen, *ALL* xv, pp. 181 ff., Norden, *Aeneis VI*, p. 451, Postgate, *Prosodia Latina*, pp. 32 ff.

Thus this line contains a Greek metrical practice (cf. Homer's method of treating τε), to match the Greek names, and the Greek 'atmosphere' is further shown by the quadri-syllabic ending (see on 99).

147. ipse: Apollo (*ipse* often means 'the master', like αὐτός). Cynthus (cf. i. 498) was a hill in Delos, and Apollo is described as he often appears in art, a sensitive beautiful figure, wearing a bay-wreath and carrying a quiver. Note how the simile-structure has become a statement of fact, as if Apollo were actually present. The whole picture shows with great precision the nobility of Aeneas' appearance (cf. 12).

147 ff. mollique . . . ore: 'and with clinging leafage shapes and confines his flowing hair and entwines it with gold, while his

arrows clang upon his shoulders; no less vigorous than his
was Aeneas' bearing, and just so much grace and radiance is
in his noble face.' Virgil does not, of course, mean that
Apollo was dressing his hair as he walked, but that this is the
way he looked as he walked. *Egregio, decus, enitet* all contribute to the fine picture of Aeneas: *egregius* means 'out of
the ordinary', *decus* implies the grace of physical beauty,
enitere the glow and sheen of health (like *nitor, nitidus*). 'Decent' in English once bore the Latin sense of 'lovely', but it
has now lost the colour of its original.

151. ventum : for *ventum est*, impersonal; see on 416.

invia lustra: 'trackless forest-lairs' (cf. note on *moenia
nostra*, 96). A mosaic from Halicarnassus in Asia Minor shows
Aeneas and Dido hunting a tiger (see Pease); in the Low Ham
mosaic (see on 158) no quarry is shown.

152 f. ecce . . . iugis: 'see, racing down from the hills come the
wild mountain-goats, driven downwards from a rocky pin-
nacle': *deiectae*, i.e. by the beaters (the *alae* of 121).

153. alia de parte: the phrase suggests that Virgil had a painting
in mind; cf. Catull. 64. 251 'at parte ex alia florens volitabat
Iacchus', where Kroll compares Cic. *Arat.* 367, Manil. i. 319
(all descriptive passages).

154. transmittunt cursu: 'go skimming across'; in this transitive use of *transmittere* there generally seems a feeling of
speed (Henry takes it to imply the way in which a moving
thing passes what is static, so that the object passed seems
itself to move); so in vi. 313 'stabant orantes primi transmittere cursum' (where *cursum* is an 'internal' accusative), it is
a quick passage that the ghosts long for, not just the passage
only.

155. Note the rushing dactyls, to show the frightened, crowding
creatures as they 'mass their dusty columns in flight'; in
montisque, the connecting particle is explanatory.

156. at: in marked contrast: young Ascanius has to stay on
lower ground, but he has a grand time, galloping past one
group after another (Heyne comments 'iuvenilem exsulta-
tionem facile sentis'); note *acri* at the end of the line, marking the importance of the epithet—the boy has a 'spirited
horse', not some quiet animal 'used to children'.

157. iamque . . . iam: Virgil first introduced *iam . . . iam* for
modo . . . modo (which he nowhere has, in contrast to Ovid who
uses it constantly, cf., e.g., *Met.* vi. 371 ff.); the usage was
not often imitated, though Statius has a number of examples.
But he prefers *nunc . . . nunc* (cf. 285, 442), and this is common in poetry after him and in silver prose. See Wölfflin,
ALL ii, pp. 242 ff.

158. inertia: cf. ix. 730 'immanem veluti pecora inter inertia tigrim'; the deer seem tame sport to him (but the adjective also suggests the mute terror of the helpless beasts); a 'foaming boar' (cf. i. 324) would be much better. In 1945 a remarkable mosaic pavement, made of local material, was uncovered at Low Ham in Somerset, showing scenes from the story of Dido and Aeneas, including the hunt (see *JRS* xxxvi, 1946, p. 142 and plate xi); Ascanius is shown galloping, his cloak streaming in the wind, with a set face and vigorous action; he and Dido ride white horses, Aeneas a black one. (For the story of Dido in various forms of art see Pease, pp. 70 f.; a series of Italian seventeenth-century tapestries, now in the Cleveland Museum, U.S.A., is described by D. M. Schullian in *Vergilius*, 1940, no. 4, pp. 23 ff., with plates.)

votis: either dative after *dari*, or, perhaps better, ablative with *optat* ('prays longingly'); *votum* is used both of the vow and of the accompanying prayer, and *optare* implies longing for an ideal (cf. x. 279 'quod votis optastis, adest', Hor. *Epp.* i. 14. 43 'optat ephippia bos, piger optat arare caballus').

159. Note *ă-prum*, and contrast *āg-ros*, 163 (cf. note on 146); occasionally both methods of treating a vowel before mute and liquid can be seen in the same line, e.g. ii. 663 'natum ante ora pătris, pātrem qui obtruncat ad aras', Ovid, *F.* iv. 749 'sive săcro pavi, sedive sub arbore sācra' (cf. Platnauer, op. cit., p. 55, Norden on vi. 791, Kroll on Catull. 62. 63).

160–72. *The sky darkens, and there is a storm of hail and thunder. All run for shelter, and Dido and Aeneas reach a cave together. The powers of Nature bear witness to their union, and thus their sorrow began.*

160. A fine onomatopoeic line (cf. 122), recalling Lucr. v. 1193 'et rapidi fremitus et murmura magna minarum'; Virgil makes an abrupt transition from the brilliant light of the previous passage to black darkness and impending misery.

misceri: the sky is all a mass of noise (cf. i. 124, of the sea); for an interesting note on Virgilian storms see Warde Fowler, *The Death of Turnus*, p. 94. Chaucer has 'Among al this to-romblen gan the heven,/ The thunder rored with a grisly steven.' Marlowe (*Dido Queen of Carthage*, Act IV) thus embroiders Virgil: 'I think it was the devil's revelling night,/ There was such hurly-burly in the heavens:/ Doubtless Apollo's axle-tree is cracked,/ Or aged Atlas' shoulder out of joint.' Berlioz's *Royal Hunt and Storm* will be familiar.

161. Note the echo of 120, and the repetitions below from 124–5.

162. Tyrii comites . . . Troiana iuventus: cf. 140, 130.

163. Dardaniusque . . . Veneris: Ascanius. The periphrasis, so strange to our ears (cf. 258), is part of Virgil's allusive manner; it is a method that could easily be overdone, and Juvenal often parodies it (e.g. *Sat.* iii. 118 'ad quam Gorgonei delapsa est pinna caballi'). The sporting columns of many daily newspapers will supply a form of modern counterpart. Cf. Kroll, op. cit., p. 266; E. R. Curtius, *European literature and the Latin Middle Ages*, pp. 275 ff.

163 f. diversa . . . petiere: 'terrified, made for shelter (*tecta*) at scattered points among the fields.' They went by different paths to different places for cover (*diversi* would have been equally possible, cf. *G.* iv. 500, of Eurydice, 'fugit diversa'); note that here Virgil does not simply echo the *diffugient* of 123.

164. petiere: the perfect of sudden action, as in *G.* i. 329 f. 'quo maxima motu/terra tremit; fugere ferae'.

ruunt . . . amnes: the dry river-beds are flooded in a moment. Observe the rhythm of this line; although the strong caesura (normally the main pause in the line) follows *ruunt*, the real rhythmic pause is after *petiere*, at the weak caesura in the third foot, so that the line falls rhythmically into two nearly equal parts (contrast 146, 183, a like metrical pattern, but with the rhythmic pause in its natural place after the strong caesura). See also 316, 417, 582, 604. The rarity of this rhythm is one of the ways in which the Latin hexameter differs fundamentally from the Greek, for a glance at any page of Homer will show that it is a characteristic of the Homeric line. See Hardie, *Res Metrica*, pp. 8 f., 27 f., and Norden, *Aeneis VI*, Anh. VII, B 2 (d).

165. See notes on 124. C. Pitt, in a note to his translation (1753), refers to a remark by Steele in the *Tatler* (no. 6) on Virgil's use of *dux Troianus* here, and adds, ''Tis said, that Mr. Addison communicated this remark to Steele, and by Steele's making use of it in the Tatler, first discovered him to be the author of those papers.'

Chaucer thus describes Virgil's picture:

> And shortly, fro the tempest her to save,
> She fledde her-self into a litel cave,
> And with her wente this Eneas al-so;
> I noot, with hem if ther wente any mo,
> The autour maketh of hit no mencioun.
> And heer began the depe affeccioun
> Betwix hem two; this was the firste morwe
> Of her gladnesse, and ginning of her sorwe.

166 ff. The witnesses to the union of Dido and Aeneas are no

mortals, but the Elements, primeval Earth, Fire, Air; Juno,
goddess of marriage, is there (cf. 125) taking the place of the
pronuba, the matron who was in charge of the wedding-cere-
mony on the bride's side and gave her to her husband
(cf. vii. 319 'et Bellona manet te pronuba', Catull. 61. 179 f.).
Prima tellus (cf. vii. 136 f. 'primamque deorum/ tellurem')
represents the bread of the marriage-rite (see Mackail), the
lightning is the marriage-torch (*taeda*, cf. 18), and the air is
witness (*conscius*); the wedding-chant is sung (*ulularunt*) by
the mountain-nymphs. Heinze (op. cit., p. 361) well remarks
on the heroic grandeur of the lines.

Virgil thus makes the wedding ritually correct, as one would
expect him to. But it remains a supernatural ceremony, and
an uncanny one for all its seeming correctness; nothing here
resembles the unalloyed happiness of the union of Adam and
Eve, when 'All Heaven,/ And happy constellations, on that
hour/ Shed their selectest influence; the Earth/ Gave sign of
gratulation, and each hill' (Milton, *PL* viii. 511 ff.); the feel
of the passage is nearer to those other lines (ibid. ix. 782 ff.)
when, after the Fall, 'Earth felt the wound, and Nature from
her seat, Sighing through all her works, gave signs of woe/
That all was lost'.

167. dant signum: as if for the bridal procession.

168. conubiis: for the prosody, see on 126.

ulularunt: carefully chosen: the word is often associated
with ritual cries (and might be so taken here), but it more
usually means a cry of sorrow or horror (cf. 667), and so could
be a terrifying sound on such a day.

169 f. ille dies . . . fuit: 'that day in the beginning was the
cause of death, that day in the beginning was the cause of
sorrow.' *Primus* is adverbial, as in i. 1 (see Mackail's note),
and in vii. 117 ff. 'ea vox audita laborum/ prima tulit finem
primamque loquentis ab ore/ eripuit pater' (where *prima*,
primam are nearly 'at once', as Mackail notes). It is repeated for special emphasis; there is no need to explain it by
transferring it to *causa* by some alleged process of logic, nor
(with Henry) to take *leti* and *dies* together. Virgil makes it
plain that all the succeeding misery of both Dido and Aeneas
stems from the way in which both regarded the events of this
critical day: neither understood the mind of the other.

169. ille dies: Virgil never writes *illa dies*; but with ordinary
adjectives, although he always has a masculine form with an
oblique case of *dies*, both singular and plural, in the nominative he always has a feminine (often a virtual formula, *longa
dies, nulla dies, postera . . . orta dies*)—obviously because the
feminine offers a metrical convenience with a nominative but

gives no advantage with an oblique case. See E. Fraenkel,
Glotta viii, 1917, pp. 24 ff.. and Norden on vi. 429; Fraenkel
examines the use of *dies* exhaustively, and concludes that in
classical prose the masculine only can sharply fix a single
day, while the feminine is used for 'time allowed, including a
final day' (cf. Nisbet on Cic. *de domo* 45); he examines the
poets' practice also (l.c., pp. 60 ff.), showing how metrical
considerations made them often deviate from ordinary prose
usage (note that Ovid has *illa dies* regularly, Statius both *ille*
and *illa* indiscriminately). See further Hofmann in *Philologus*
xciii (NF xlvii), 1938, pp. 265 ff.

170. neque enim: Conway (on i. 198) takes this as a compound
particle, meaning 'indeed not', in spite of the following *nec*;
this seems strained and unnecessary, even though elsewhere
neque enim generally has this sense (with *enim* bearing its
old asseverative meaning).

  specie famave: i.e. by how things look or by what is said.

171. furtivum: 'secret' (cf. Catull. 7. 8); so *furtum* often means
a secret love-affair.

172. coniugium: wedlock, lawful marriage; yet Aeneas made no
such pretence (338 f. 'nec coniugis umquam/praetendi taedas'),
whereas Dido deliberately stifles her better self, making the
name of wedlock 'a covering for her wrongdoing'; the antithesis between *coniugium* and *culpam* (the normal word for
unfaithfulness in marriage) is strikingly shown by the position of the two words 'framing' the line. For *praetexit* cf.
500 'novis praetexere funera sacris' (the English *pretext* has
lost the colour of the Latin word).

  Note how short this paragraph is in which Virgil describes
so simply and directly the happening that brought tragedy to
both lives; a less great poet might have blunted its dramatic
force by verbiage.

173–97. *Rumour at once runs through Libya, a swift and hideous
monster, mingling truth and lies; she puts it about that Dido
and Aeneas are living together, forgetful of all but themselves;
and in particular she reaches Iarbas with her tale.*

'Enter Rumour, painted full of tongues' (2 Henry IV, *In-
duction*). This description of *Fama* acts as an interlude,
covering the passage of time (cf. Heinze, op. cit., p. 380) and
enabling Virgil to tell Aeneas' fall from grace more objec-
tively. Virgil may have a painting in mind, as some have
thought. His description is highly rhetorical, and some
editors (e.g. Page and Irvine) have much disliked it, yet the
rhetoric is a subtle handmaid of tragedy: *Fama*, with her
omnipresent eyes and babbling tongues, might have taken

her tale anywhere else without necessarily evil results, but
she chooses, almost casually as Virgil shows it, to go to
Iarbas, whom Dido had especially snubbed; and from this
comes an inescapable train of ill. Virgil has written a warning
parable on the theme 'Be sure thy sin will find thee out':
what may appear a private concern of two individuals is in
fact the concern of many whom it indirectly affects.

The passage was pillaged by later imitators (cf. Ovid, *Met.*
ix. 137 ff., Stat. *Th.* iii. 425 ff., Val. Flacc. ii. 116 ff.), and
should be compared with Ovid's picture of the home of
Fama in *Met.* xii. 39-63, a fine description yet lacking the
deeper undertones of Virgil. Chaucer (*Hous of Fame*, iii.
251 ff.) has made a fusion of Virgil and Ovid. Stanyhurst
begins:

Fame, the groyl ungentil, than whom none swifter is extant;
Limber in her whisking, her streingth in journye she treb-
    bleth;
First like a shrimp squatting for feare, then boldlye she
    roameth
On ground prowd jetting: shee soars up nimblye toe sky-
    ward.

175. viget: her moving gives her strength, not weariness; the
second half of the line, appended by *-que*, explains the first.
Virgil has in mind Lucr. vi. 340 ff. (of a falling thunderbolt)
'denique quod longo venit impete, sumere debet/ mobilitatem
etiam atque etiam, quae crescit eundo/ et validas auget viris
et roborat ictum'. It is a good example of his way of drawing
on what had sunk into his memory as he read, adapting it to a
different purpose and with different shades of meaning:
Lucretius' scientific picture has become a moral fantasy.
Note further how the roughness of *mobilitatem*, which Lucretius has to force into the line by an uncomfortable elision,
has been changed by Virgil just enough to make his line
swift and smooth instead of bumpy.

eundo: 'in the going', instrumental. Closely akin to this use
is the modal ablative of the gerund, as in ii. 6 f. 'quis talia
fando/ . . . temperet a lacrimis?'; in both uses the gerund is
not far off in meaning from a present participle ('while going',
etc.), and the relationship is clear from such a passage as Tac.
Ann. xv. 38. 4 'incendium . . . in edita adsurgens et rursus
inferiora populando, antiit remedia velocitate mali': so that
the ancestry of the modern Romance participial forms becomes evident.

176. primo: the adverb, followed as usual by a contrast: *Fama*
is nervous at first, but later grows through confidence (and

how easily a rumour can be scotched if it is taken in time).
Virgil has in mind Homer's picture of Strife (*Il.* iv. 442 f.
ἥτ' ὀλίγη μὲν πρῶτα κορύσσεται, αὐτὰρ ἔπειτα / οὐρανῷ ἐστήριξε κάρη
καὶ ἐπὶ χθονὶ βαίνει), but the detail of 'fear' is his own effective addition. See S. Eitrem, *Symbolae Osloenses* v, 1927,
p. 85, for a theory that certain traditions of magic lie behind
the manifold eyes and tongues of *Fama*.

178. deorum: 'against the gods'; objective, as in ii. 413
'ereptae virginis ira'. Virgil represents *Fama* as a sister of
the Giants whom Earth produced in anger at the gods' treatment of her other children the Titans.

179. extremam: born after the rest. Coeus was properly a
Titan, Enceladus a Giant; Virgil stresses the horrible associations of Rumour.

    ut perhibent: 'as the story goes', a very common usage of
the verb (note *pĕrh-*, like *inhians*, 64).

180. Note the swift rhythm and the hard, clattering consonants.

181. So the Cyclops is 'monstrum horrendum informe ingens,
cui lumen ademptum' (iii. 658); the elisions and the rhythm
make a violent and ungainly picture (cf. Norden on vi. 186).
Virgil likes this position for *ingens*: cf. vi. 552 'porta adversa,
ingens', vii. 170 'tectum augustum, ingens', xii. 897 'saxum
antiquum, ingens'.

183. subrigit: *subrigere* (not a common word) is the·transitive
form of *surgere*. Virgil does not use it elsewhere.

184. medio: 'the midspace' between sky and earth, where she
may see all that is happening. So Ovid (*Met.* xii. 39 f.) puts
the House of Fame *inter terrasque fretumque/ caelestesque
plagas*.

185. stridens: here of whirring wings; Virgil uses the verb of a
whizzing missile, of the noise of hinges or wheels, of the hiss
of hot metal in water. Note the emphatic position of the
participle, strengthened by the pause after it; cf. ix. 418 f.
'it hasta Tago per tempus utrumque/ stridens, traiectoque
haesit tepefacta cerebro'. A glance at any page of Virgil will
show how seldom the first foot of a line is occupied by a
single spondaic word, with no overlap to the second foot
(24 such lines in this book, four of which are in Dido's last
speech, 651, 655, 657, 658); and a pause after the spondee, as
here, is rarer still (contrast 562 with 390), cutting the word
off from the rest of the line. See Norden, *Aeneis VI*, Anh.
VIII, Wagner, *Quaest. Virg.* xiii, p. 432, Conway on i. 26; and
see further on 453 below.

    declinat: note that the coincidence of word-ending with
the end of a foot causes coincidence of ictus and accent here,

as well as in the next two lines (again in 191–3); a long run
of this rhythm in the fourth foot is unusual in the *Aeneid*. Cf.
note on 522, and see Knight, *Accentual Symmetry in Vergil*,
pp. 36 ff., A. Woodward, *The Fourth Foot in Vergil* (*Philological Quarterly*, xv, 1936, pp. 126 ff.).

187. aut: postponed (see on 33). *Territare* seems to belong
otherwise to comedy and prose (cf. xii. 852 'aut bello territat
urbes'); its use in poetry appears to be a Virgilian innovation.

188. pravi: 'crooked', the invariable implication of the word.
The essence of Rumour is its warped mixture of truth and
lies (cf. 190).

189. populos: the various peoples of Africa (not 'people'). See
on 54 for the 'rhyme' in *replebat, canebat* (the imperfects
imply repeated action).

190. gaudens: see note on *stridens*, 185. With this punctuation,
the rhythm is parallel to that line ('she it was then that kept
filling the nations with her manifold tattle, delighting in it');
Page objects that this is harsh, and takes *gaudens* with *canebat*, making *et* postponed—an unlikely view.

  facta atque infecta: cf. ix. 595 'digna atque indigna relatu';
the assonance (both here and in *canebat, replebat*) effectively
suggests the way in which *Fama* keeps hammering away
remorselessly.

191. cretum: a passive participle from the intransitive *cresco*
(mainly a poetic use, with ablative of origin, or with *a*, which
is a variant here).

192. cui . . . Dido: 'whom Dido, in all her beauty, thinks fit to
take as her wedded lord'; cf. vi. 142 'hoc sibi pulchra suum
ferri Proserpina munus', where the Golden Bough is a tribute
to Proserpina's beauty (here, Dido's beauty is in contrast to
her conduct, as *Fama* reports it).

193. hiemem: with *fovere*; they 'keep the winter warm', i.e.
they pass it comfortably. Page thinks this is an 'incredible'
interpretation, and takes *hiemem* as accusative of duration of
time (with *inter se* for *se inter se*, as often in reciprocal expressions, e.g. Cic. *de am.* 82 'neque solum colent inter se ac
diligent, sed etiam verebuntur'), but I find this most un-
imaginative: Virgil means that their love has made them
oblivious to externals, they are 'snug' and happy together,—
and the cold in their lonely hearts has gone too; such a
picture of other people's happiness would be an easy target
for the malignant, as *Fama* knew so well.

  luxu: 'wantonness', a common meaning of *luxus, luxuria*;
quam longa, 'all its livelong time' (sc. *sit*, cf. viii. 86 'ea . . .
quam longa est, nocte').

fovere: the basic sense is that of keeping warm and comfortable ('cherish' is generally an absurd translation); so the bees 'keep house snugly underground' (*G.* iv. 43 'sub terra fovere larem'), and in Cic. *de nat. deor.* ii. 129, birds after hatching out their chicks 'ita tuentur ut et pinnis foveant ne frigore laedantur'; cf. note on 686, and Mackail on x. 838; in ix. 57 'castra fovere' is ironical, as *Fama* (but not Virgil) means *fovere* to be here.

194. regnorum immemores: a lie, as is clear from 260 (unless Aeneas can be blamed as forgetful of a kingdom that does not yet exist). The words, and the whole passage 191–4, show what Virgil means by *facta atque infecta* above: it is true that Aeneas has come to Carthage, and that Dido is living with him; but *luxu* and *turpique cupidine captos* ('enthralled by vile passion') is a malicious twist to truth, and so is *immemores*.

195. foeda: 'loathsome'; here is Virgil's own comment upon the importance to be attached to Rumour (*dea foeda*, cf. *malum* 174). Note that he writes *in ora*, not *in aures*: the *populi* do not only hear the tattle, but it is on their lips and they keep passing it on.

196. cursus detorquet: 'swerves in her course', making a dead set at Iarbas, the one person who could do the most harm.

197. animum: 'feelings'; Conway has an interesting note on i. 149.

aggerat iras: a variation of *incenditque animum dictis*. *Aggerare* means 'to pile up' (like an *agger*); this metaphorical use is one of Virgil's experiments (again in xi. 342), and Statius and Silius Italicus imitate it.

Virgil prefers the plural accusative of *ira* to the singular (seventeen times in the *Aeneid*, as against four examples of the singular, three of which occur with reference to Juno and the other refers to Jupiter). The plural suggests repeated 'fits of anger' (so 532), or 'angry actions' (see Mackail on i. 25; cf. ii. 381 'attollentem iras', of a snake, vii. 15 'iraeque leonum', of angry roaring, Livy ix. 9. 18 'in haec ferrum, in haec iras acuant'); so Tacitus has 'ferendas parentium iracundias . . . dictitans' (*Ann.* xiv. 4. 2). See W. Havers, *Festschrift für Paul Kretschmer*, p. 42, Riemann, *Études sur la langue et la grammaire de Tite-Live*, p. 55, Landgraf, *ALL* xiv, p. 74.

198–218. *Iarbas has served Jupiter loyally, and has built him many shrines—and on hearing this sour tale, he is full of angry reproach: has all his service been in vain? A vagabond woman, whom he has honoured with his charity and help, has scorned*

*his offer of marriage, preferring a fop and a libertine! Is this
Jupiter's idea of reward?*

Iarbas, King of Numidia, is represented as the son of the
Libyan god Hammon, who was identified with Jupiter (cf.
Catull. 7. 5). Virgil shows him as a conscientious servant
of his divine father, in the simple faith that one good turn
deserves another. Fierce barbarian despot as he is, he regards Dido as a chattel, a woman to whose love he has a
natural right; his attitude to Jupiter is childlike and naïve,
and Virgil has drawn a subtle picture of primitive mentality.
Other versions of the story make Iarbas seize Dido's throne
after her death (Ovid, *F.* iii. 551 ff., Sil. It. viii. 50 ff.), and in
the legend as told by Justin (xviii. 4 ff.) it was to avoid
marriage with him that Dido destroyed herself on the pyre.
Marlowe gives him a leading part in his *Dido, Queen of Carthage*: it is he who first welcomes the shipwrecked Trojans, still
parted from Aeneas; he quarrels with Dido, Anna falls in
love with him, and the play ends with both Anna and Iarbas
stabbing themselves after Dido's death.

198. **Hammone . . . nympha**: 'sprung of Hammon, on the ravish-
ing of a Garamantian nymph'; the Garamantes were an
African people (cf. *E.* viii. 44).

199. **immania**: the temples are bigger than the normal size (cf.
vi. 19). The word is another of Virgil's favourites (see Mackail
on i. 616), and often implies cruelty or horror, 'monstrosity,'
of behaviour: one of Virgil's most effective uses of it (with
both senses present) is vi. 576 'quinquaginta atris immanis
hiatibus Hydra'.

201. **excubias . . . aeternas**: 'sentinel of the gods to everlasting',
a picturesque extension of *vigilem*, itself vivid enough
('never sleeping'). *Cruor* is especially used in connexion with
sacrifices.

202. **pingue solum**: cf. 62; *solum* and *limina* may be nominative
(sc. *erant*), or accusative after *sacraverat*; the change of tense
from *posuit* to the pluperfect seems of little significance (but
see Page's note).

variis . . . sertis: 'the entrances all aglow with gay garlands.'
Variis and *florentia* support each other, and make a bright
and coloured picture. *Varius* (cf. ποικίλος) is used of anything
'variegated', especially where the changing colours fuse into
a gay whole: Catullus (61. 87) has it of a flower-garden,
Horace (*C.* ii. 5. 12) of autumn tints, Ovid (*Met.* iv. 619) of a
mottled snake, Petronius (45. 1) of a striped pig. Lucretius
has *florere* of the sea, gay with sailing-ships (v. 1442), Virgil
has it of a glittering line of armed men (vii. 804 'agmen agens

equitum et florentis aere catervas'). *Serta* is found in the plural only (cf. Bednara, *ALL* xiv, p. 548).

203. amens animi: 'utterly distraught in mind' (cf. 300); *animi* is usually taken as a locative, and Virgil often has it with adjectives (*inops*, *infelix*, *furens*, etc.); Löfstedt, however, regards it as a true genitive of reference (*Synt.* i, pp. 172 ff.; cf. L.-H., p. 402), pointing out that one never finds *animi cogitare*, *animi habere*, etc., where a locative would be expected if *animi* were in fact locative. The phrase *amens animi* is itself curious, and seems to be a Virgilian experiment: Lucretius often has *mens animi* (iv. 758, etc., cf. Catull. 65. 4), 'the understanding of the mind', and it looks as if Virgil chose his phrase here as an echo of it ('bereft of mental understanding').

amaro: cf. x. 368 'dictis virtutem accendit amaris', again of the smarting bitterness of a gibe.

204. dicitur: odd, as if Virgil were telling the incident at second-hand. See an interesting discussion in Heinze, op. cit., p. 242; he suggests that Virgil for the moment imagines himself with Aeneas and Dido, hearing a report of what happened; cf. ix. 82 f. 'ipsa deum fertur genetrix Berecyntia magnum/ vocibus his adfata Iovem'.

media . . . divum: 'in the very presence of the majesty of the gods' (cf. 62 'ante ora deum'). *Numen* is a word that belongs to the old Italian religion; see Bailey, *Religion in Virgil*, pp. 60 ff.; sometimes it means the 'will' of the god, sometimes the god himself visualized as a 'power' or 'spirit'. Here *numina divum* resembles *numina Palladis* (iii. 543), *Iunonis numen* (iii. 437), which Bailey explains as a periphrasis for the name 'with possibly an added note of majesty or dignity'. The gods' presence seems to fill the *arae* (cf. note on 269).

205. supinis: 'turned upwards'; the word means literally 'on one's back' (cf. ὕπτιος), and is then used metaphorically of mental 'lolling'; the English 'supine' has lost the colour of its Latin original. As a term in grammar, the supine form of a verb is so called because in it the action of the verb has 'fallen on its back', so to speak: for it is the only part of a verb that can never stand alone without some further support.

206. omnipotens: pointed; the whole burden of Iarbas' bitter complaint is that Jupiter's power seems worse than useless. And as if to refute the gibe, Jupiter hears the prayer and acts promptly upon it (220). The word is itself Ennian, and its use by Plautus (*Poen.* 275) points to the influence of tragedy upon the style of comedy; see Fraenkel, *Plautinisches im Plautus*, pp. 207 ff., and cf. note on -*que* . . . -*que*, 83.

nunc: Iarbas himself had introduced the cult of Jupiter, as
Henry explains.

207. **Lenaeum libat honorem**: 'offers the wine-god's rich libation'. *Lenaeus* (cf. ληνός, a wine-press) is a frequent cult-
title for Bacchus (cf. *Lyaeus*, 58); *libare* = 'to touch with the
lips' and so 'to make libation' (cf. v. 77 'mero libans car-
chesia Baccho'); *honorem* here has the concrete sense of
'offering', 'gift' (cf. iii. 118 'meritos aris mactavit honores',
where the *honores* are explained as cattle), but there is present also the idea of the beauty and richness of the gift.

208 ff. **an . . . miscent?**: 'can it be in vain, my father, that we
shiver as you whirl your thunderbolts? Are they blind,
those flames among the clouds that make our hearts to
quake? Is it empty mutterings that they stir?' *An*, as
often, expresses ironical scepticism.

209. **nequiquam**: Virgil prefers this to *frustra* (cf. Wölfflin, *ALL*
ii, pp. 1 ff.). The stress lies upon it here, and upon *caeci* (i.e.
'aimless') and *inania*.

210. **terrificant**: a Lucretian word, of a pattern that Virgil likes,
used after him by Statius and Silius Italicus. Note the admirable use of alliteration and assonance in these lines. To
be struck by lightning was the traditional punishment of a
perjurer (cf. Juv. iii. 145, xiii. 223): is it all a fraud, Iarbas
asks, is it of no avail to be honest?

211. **femina**: the normal word in poetry for a woman; Cicero
only uses it to contrast with *vir* or when dignity or distinction
is implied, while Tacitus prefers the poetic word. Iarbas uses
it in contempt; he sees nothing of Dido's bravery in exile
(contrast the very different tone of *dux femina facti*, i.
364).

212. **exiguam**: 'puny'; all her efforts could not amount to
much, and yet she has no gratitude for his fine offer of marriage. The position of the word gives it special emphasis
(cf. xi. 62 f. 'solacia luctus/ exigua ingentis').

    pretio: 'in return for payment'; see i. 367 f. 'mercatique
solum, facti de nomine Byrsam/ taurino quantum possent
circumdare tergo' (so Marlowe has 'Where, straying on our
borders up and down,/ She crav'd a hide of ground to build
a town'). Iarbas flung her a strip of land at a bargain price;
note the snarling contempt in '*pretio posuit*': 'a little town,
bought at an easy rate' (Dryden).

    litus arandum: 'a piece of shore to plough'; another sneer
—the land would not be good for pasture, and Iarbas would
not realize its value as the site of a port—and there is further
point in the fact that *litus arare* is proverbial for 'wasting
pains'.

213. loci leges: 'conditions of holding'; Iarbas is her feudal lord.

conubia: see on 126, and on 96 for the collocation *conubia nostra* (here *nostra* at the end of the line adds a touch of self-importance).

214. reppulit: 'has thrust away', a strong word in an emphatic position.

dominum: also emphatic; Dido is Aeneas' slave (cf. *servire*, 103), as Iarbas had fully expected her to be to himself.

215 ff. Iarbas has a fierce barbaric contempt for Aeneas, as a dressed-up womanish creature, just as Turnus calls the Trojans *genus femineum* (ix. 141 f., cf. ix. 614 ff., xii. 99). His attitude is that of the Romans in Virgil's own time for eastern peoples (cf. *G.* i. 57 'mollesque Sabaei'), but there is something more universal here, for Iarbas shows all the age-old distrust, jealousy, and inward fear felt by the rough and primitive for a softer and more sophisticated people, while his scorn for Aeneas' dress shows all that suspicion of 'foreign fashions' that an untravelled, insular person might feel.

215. et: 'indignantis', as in i. 48 'et quisquam numen Iunonis adorat?' (cf. 'And did those feet in ancient time . . . ?').

ille Paris: Stanyhurst has 'This smocktoy Paris'; Iarbas takes Paris as a typical effeminate Phrygian—and one who stole another's wife as well.

semiviro comitatu: such 'easterners' are no better than the eunuch priests of Cybele, the *Magna Mater* of the Gods, whose orgiastic worship was later to spread from Phrygia to Rome. Note the quadrisyllabic ending (cf. 99), a Greek-type ending to suit the 'foreign' picture, upsetting the normal pattern (cf. note on 132).

216 f. Maeonia . . . subnexus: 'his chin and essenced hair wound about with a Lydian turban.' The alliteration and assonance is admirable, as Iarbas mouths his mocking taunts. Virgil uses 'Lydian' as he uses 'Phrygian', to denote the Asiatic origin of the Trojans, as well as for variety (Maeonia was the old name for Lydia, cf. the name *Maeonides* for Homer).

216. mitra: an oriental head-dress, tied with ribbons (ix. 616) · round the head, turban-manner, and under the chin (a feminine fashion, cf. Catull. 64. 63, where Ariadne wears a *mitra*); it can be seen in representations of Paris (see Pease). Iarbas is not used to such a headgear, and does not quite understand how it works, so he is suspicious and contemptuous of it; similarly, the Romans felt that there was something queer and not quite decent about the trousers worn by some foreigners (cf. Cic. *ad fam.* ix. 15. 2 'cum in urbem nostram

est infusa peregrinitas, nunc vero etiam bracatis et Trans-
alpinis nationibus')—so Chloreus wears *barbara tegmina
crurum* (xi. 777), and Valerius Flaccus says of an oriental
soldier (vi. 700 ff.) 'subligat extrema patrium cervice tiaran/
insignis manicis, insignis acinace dextro;/improba barbaricae
procurrunt tegmina plantae'.

madentem: cf. xii. 99 f. (a like context) 'crinis/ vibratos
calido ferro murraque madentis'. Iarbas dislikes the 'ele-
gance' of Aeneas.

217. subnexus: this is read by two inferior MSS. only, for *subnixus* of the primary MSS. and of Servius; it was adopted by
Henry (with vigour), Conington (with hesitation), and Ribbeck. Henry's defence rests on such parallels as x. 138 'molli
subnectens circulus auro', Val. Flacc. ii. 103 'tereti crinem
subnectitur auro', Stat. *S.* v. 3. 115 'specieque comam subnexus utraque', on the ground that *subnixus* is grammatically
impossible and does not present the required sense of 'tying'.

I cannot see any justification for abandoning *subnixus*, and
would prefer to remove *subnexus* from the Oxford Text here,
with the support of Page and Mackail. *Subnixus* (a participial
form, although the verb *subnitor* does not occur) means
'leaning on', 'supported by', with *mentum* as accusative of
'part concerned'; Iarbas can only understand the out-
landish headgear by supposing that Aeneas' chin and hair
are so languid that they need support from the bands of the
mitra (see Sidgwick's note); *crinem* probably refers to a bun
of thick long hair at the back, bulging out from the support-
ing *mitra*. The translation would accordingly be (reading
subnixus) 'propping up his chin and essenced hair with a
Lydian turban'.

rapto potitur: 'enjoys what he has filched'; Iarbas regards
Dido as a piece of stolen property. *Raptum* is used here as a
noun (cf. vii. 749 'vivere rapto', viii. 317 'parcere parto').
Note the third-conjugation form *potitur* here and in iii. 56
(*potiuntur* is the only other finite form used by Virgil).

nos: in sharp contrast, with no connecting particle; cf. ii.
374 f. 'alii rapiunt incensa feruntque/ Pergama: vos celsis
nunc primum a navibus itis?', xii. 662 ff. Iarbas has kept
faith, but Jupiter has looked on while Aeneas breaks all the
rules.

217 f. nos . . . inanem: 'while *we* keep bringing presents to
your shrines—yes, to yours—and cosset your great name, for
nothing.'

218. quippe: Mackail compares i. 59, xii. 421 f. 'subitoque
omnis de corpore fugit/ quippe dolor', and remarks that
Virgil never uses *quippe* except at the beginning of a line,

even if its clause does not begin there. It is an explanatory
particle, used in conversational manner, often introducing an
answer to a question (either formal or imagined); cf. i. 39
'quippe vetor fatis', Cic. *de or.* ii. 218 'leve nomen habet
utraque res. quippe: leve enim est totum hoc, risum movere'
(where *quippe* = 'naturally'). Like *scilicet* and *nimirum*, it
is often ironical, as here; it should probably be taken closely
with *tuis*, although its effect colours the tone of the whole
sentence (cf. Cic. *Mil.* 33 'movet me quippe lumen curiae').
See Mackail and Conway on i. 59; for the rhythm of the end
of the line see on 58. Statius, unlike Virgil, often has *quippe*
in mid-line.

fovemus: cf. note on 193. Iarbas has done all he can to
'coddle' Jupiter's reputation, and it turns out to be a sham.
Note how this grimly sarcastic speech ends dramatically with
the angry adjective *inanem*; and observe the cumulative
f-sounds (unpleasant to Roman ears, cf. Quintil. xii. 10. 29).

219–37. *Jupiter hears and acts; he sends Mercury to Aeneas, to
tell him that he is belying the high promise that his mother held
out for him, and is forgetful of his destined greatness: he is to
sail at once.*

219. arasque tenentem: cf. vi. 124 'talibus orabat dictis arasque
tenebat' (where see Norden), xii. 201 'tango aras, medios
ignis et numina testor'. The altar is grasped in supplication;
cf. the account of the oath taken by the nine-year-old
Hannibal in Corn. Nep. *Hannibal* 2. 4 'simul me ad aram
adduxit . . . eamque ceteris remotis tenentem iurare iussit
nunquam me in amicitia cum Romanis fore'. The plural
aras is used by analogy with *altaria*; see Landgraf, *ALL* xiv.
p. 68, Löfstedt *Synt.* i, p. 43.

220. omnipotens: see on 206. *Torsit* need mean no more than
'turned'; but it might suggest the suddenness of Jupiter's
reaction to reproach.

221. oblitos . . . amantis: 'those lovers who had forgotten their
better repute.' Aeneas and Dido are alike at fault.

222. sic: parallel with *talia* (cf. note on 114). Mercury is sent
just as Hermes was sent in *Od.* v. 28 ff. to free Odysseus from
Calypso.

adloquitur: for the prosody -*ŭr* see on 64; cf. v. 284 'olli
serva datūr, operum haud ignara Minervae', *G.* iii. 76 'altius
ingreditūr et mollia crura reponit'. There is no question here
of an 'originally long' syllable; but there is a very slight
pause before *ac* (cf. Conway on i. 308, 668), and the lengthening (at the 'rise' of the foot, where the ictus falls) may suggest a certain solemnity in Jupiter's utterance.

223. vade age: again in iii. 462, v. 548; cf. *ergo age . . . imponere,* ii. 707, *quare agite . . . succedite,* i. 627 (see Conway's note), *fare age,* vi. 389; it is a lively conversational turn (*age* so used is common in Plautus, see *Thes. L. L.* s.v. *ago*, col. 1403. 66).

labere pennis: 'wing your way smoothly'; *labere* well suggests Mercury's effortless motion, helped by the mild Zephyrs.

224. Note the antithesis of the names: a Trojan commander should not be dallying in Tyrian Carthage.

qui nunc: this is not an example of the monosyllabic effect discussed on 132, for the double monosyllable is metrically equivalent to a spondaic disyllable, and so the line has a normal end-pattern; for some statistics of Virgil's usage see Norden, *Aeneis VI*, Anh. IX. 4 (b).

225. exspectat: Servius interprets 'moratur, deterit tempus' (cf. 235, 271), a curious absolute use ('waiting', without object or aim, as Page remarks), for which there is no exact parallel (the examples quoted by Pease are not really relevant). Housman (*CR* xix, 1905, pp. 260 f.) denies that such a meaning is possible, since it is the essence of *exspectare* to have an object, either expressed or implied, which is 'awaited'; he proposed *Hesperiam* for *exspectat*. But Aeneas *is* 'waiting expectantly' for something—the completion of Carthage, the work on which Mercury finds him busy (260): and the object to *exspectat* can be supplied from *urbes*; it is in Carthage that he is awaiting his city, without any thought for the cities that Fate has already made his. I see little reason for Housman's emendation, nor for Campbell's *exceptat* (*CR* lii, 1938, p. 162); there is perhaps something to be said for the proposal *Tyrias* for *Tyria* in 224 (see *CR* ii, 1888, p. 226), as providing an epithet to balance *fatis datas* (cf. Campbell, l.c., p. 163), but certainly not enough to make it necessary in the text. I prefer to accept the MSS. reading, which is not incompatible with common sense unless the reader is perverse.

respicit: the verb implies careful, concerned attention (colloquially, 'to bother about'). Note that this is the first time that Aeneas is directly made responsible for wrong.

226. celeris: a vivid epithet (cf. 270, 357); the winds provide the speed with which Mercury travels. For this form of the feminine accusative see Conway on i. 187.

227 f. non illum . . . armis: 'it was no such man as this that his noble mother promised us in him (that is why she rescued him twice from Grecian arms).' For the emphatic use of the pronoun cf. xi. 45 f. 'non haec Euandro de te promissa parenti/ discedens dederam'.

228. Graium: Virgil prefers this genitive form; cf. Page on
iii. 53.

ideo: i.e. because of the virtue that Venus expected him to
show; the clause is parenthetic.

bis vindicat: Venus had saved Aeneas once in battle (*Il.* v.
311 ff.), once at the sack of Troy (*A.* ii. 620, 665). Virgil
uses the present tense, because although the act of rescuing is
past, Venus is still 'his rescuer'; cf. ix. 266 'cratera antiquum,
quem dat Sidonia Dido', where Dido remains 'the giver'
of the bowl, though the occasion of the gift was part of a
vanished world, vii. 363 'at non sic Phrygius penetrat Lace-
daemona pastor', where Paris is still 'the invader of Sparta',
though he stole Helen long ago, ii. 663 'natum ante ora
patris, patrem qui obtruncat ad aras', where Pyrrhus is
still 'the butcher', though the time of his butchery is past.

229. gravidam . . . frementem: 'big with many a power of command, a seething land of war'; cf. x. 87 'quid gravidam bellis
urbem et corda aspera temptas?' *Imperiis* refers to the occasions for generalship that would arise when Aeneas reached
Italy: it was a warlike Aeneas that Venus had led Jupiter to
expect, not a languishing lover of a foreign queen. Some
editors interpret *imperiis* as 'empires', i.e. the different
states of Italy over which Aeneas was to rule, but this suits
the context less well, and the plural in such a sense seems
most unlikely.

230. Italiam: see on 106. *Genus . . . Teucri* has an archaic ring
(cf. Norden on vi. 500); Teucer was the ancestor of the Trojan
race, and *alto* can imply either antiquity or nobility.

231. leges: the civilizing force of law in general, brought to a
lawless world; the reference is ultimately to the rule of
Augustus, the greatest of Aeneas' descendants (cf. *G.* iv.
561 f. 'victorque volentis/ per populos dat iura').

232 ff. si nulla . . . arces?: 'if in no way is he fired by the
splendour of so proud a state, if for his personal glory he
toils not at his heavy task, does Ascanius' father grudge his
own son the citadel of Rome?'

233. super ipse sua: cf. xii. 638 'vidi oculos ante ipse meos'.
Ipse sua is a common type of juxtaposition, emphasizing
the owner in relation to what he owns; here *ipse* gains in
force because it intrudes between *super* and *sua*, as in Ovid,
Her. 12. 18 'et caderet cultu cultor ab ipse suo'.

molitur: the *l*-sound is repeated in *nulla . . . gloria . . . laude
laborem*. The verb implies 'tackling' a difficult task (cf. vi. 477
'inde datum molitur iter'), just as *moles* contains the idea of
weightiness and difficulty (cf. Conway on i. 33).

234. Ascanione: for the metrically impossible *filione* (for *-ne* see

on 32); it is incredible, says Jupiter, that a father should forget his duty to his son, even if he forgets his duty to himself;
Aeneas is beset by *pietas* in all its forms.

235. struit: the word suggests some deep design (cf. 271).
There is no elision between *spe* and *inimica*. Virgil has a
good many experiments with hiatus, particularly where
Greek names are used (e.g. i. 617 'Dardanio Anchisae')
or where a special Greek effect is sought (e.g. 667 'femineo
ululatu ').

Elsewhere, hiatus occurs most commonly before a marked
pause, as if the speaker or narrator pauses for reflection, unconscious of what is to follow: e.g. iii. 606 'si pereo, hominum
manibus periisse iuvabit', ix. 291 'hanc sine me spem ferre
tui, audentior ibo', xi. 480 'causa mali tanti, oculos deiecta
decoros', xii. 31 'promissam eripui genero, arma impia
sumpsi'; another type shows hiatus before an adverb of place,
or before a demonstrative pronoun, where a fresh start is
made in speech or narrative, e.g. i. 16 'posthabita coluisse
Samo: hic illius arma', v. 735 'concilia Elysiumque colo.
huc casta Sibylla', x. 141 'Maeonia generose domo, ubi
pinguia culta'; another type occurs in enumerations, before *et*
(*E*. iii. 63, *G*. i. 341, *A*. iii. 74, vii. 226) or *aut* (*E*. viii. 44, *A*. x.
136). In all these lines the ictus falls upon a long vowel which
is kept unelided. A smaller group consists of lines where a
long vowel, which does not bear the ictus, is shortened in
hiatus according to the Homeric practice—such are *G*. iv.
461 'implerunt montis; flerunt Rhodopeiae arces', *A*. iii.
211 'insulae Ionio in magno', v. 261 'victor apud rapidum
Simoenta sub Ilio alto' (note the Greek names with the
Greek prosody). In *E*. ii. 53, *A*. i. 405, hiatus occurs after
a short vowel which does not bear the ictus.

This line, though the pause after *spe* is not as clearly
marked as in the lines mentioned above, does nevertheless
show a slight pause at the hiatus, as if Jupiter were musing
over the possible reasons for Aeneas' behaviour, or trying to
decide exactly how to refer to the Carthaginians: Wagner
saw this (*Quaest. Virg.* xi, p. 421), and interprets 'aut qua
spe moratur, et quidem inimica in gente'. Such a hiatus at
a pause is clearly akin to Plautus' practice at a change of
speaker or where a fresh start is made in the narrative (the
same thing can be seen in Juvenal, cf. Friedländer, p. 60):
Lindsay (*Early Latin Verse*, Oxford 1922) regards its
occurrence in Virgil as 'native Roman' (the Plautine examples quoted there are remarkably close to the Virgilian
ones). See Hardie, *Res Metrica*, pp. 45 ff.; Shipley, *TAPA* lv,
1924, p. 141, Platnauer, op. cit., p. 57; and cf. note on 64.

moratur: the parallelism with 224–5 seems to support the retention of *exspectat* in 225; I cannot understand why Housman remarks (*CR*, l.c.) that 'even *cunctatur* would be inconsistent with *non respicit'* in 225, when we have here *moratur* followed by *nec . . . respicit*. *Tyria Karthagine* there corresponds to *inimica in gente* here, *fatis datas urbes* there to *prolem . . . arva* here.

236. Ausoniam: i.e. 'Italian'; the Ausonians were the early inhabitants of central and southern Italy. *Lavinia arva* (a reference to the future city of Lavinium) is a limitation of *prolem Ausoniam*, appended, as often, by *et* (cf. Conway on i. 2). This is the only occurrence of the adjective *Lāvinius* in Virgil, except as a variant form in i. 2 for *Lavina*; the name *Lāvinia* has the same prosody except in vii. 359, where it is *Lăvinia*; the name of the town is always *Lăvinium*. Mackail compares the solitary example of *Sȳchaeus* (i. 343) and of *Dīana* (i. 499) as showing a like variation.

237. naviget! . . . esto: 'he is to sail! This is the sum of it, let this be our message.' Jupiter ends with a peremptory order; *nostri* shows his royal power. *Haec summa est* = 'this is what it amounts to'.

238–78. *Mercury obeys : he puts on his winged sandals and takes up his messenger's staff, and goes air-borne to Carthage, stopping only on the peak of Atlas. He finds Aeneas busy with the building of Carthage, wearing a sword and cloak that Dido had given him. He delivers Jupiter's message, and vanishes from sight.*

Virgil has made his own adaptation of Homer (*Od.* v. 43 ff.), in lines which are very close to the Greek and yet are pure Virgil in sound and 'feel'; it would have been absurd for him to make any change of detail in such a traditional description, which shows Mercury putting on his official dress as Divine Messenger.

238. pārere părabat: a type of rhetorical assonance (increased by *patris*) involving something like a word-play, which seems to have pleased Roman ears: cf. *E.* iii. 109 f. *amores . . . amaros*, *G.* ii. 328 *āvia . . . ăvibus*, *A.* i. 646 *cari stat cura parentis*, ii. 606 f. *părentis . . . părere*, vi. 204 *auri . . . aura* (see Norden), x. 191 f. *cănit . . . cānentem*, x. 417 f. *cănens . . . cānentia*. In prose cf. Vell. Pat. ii. 39. 3 'pārendi confessionem extorserat părens', Nepos *Cim.* i. 2 'non magis amore quam more ductus'; see Norden, *Die Antike Kunstprosa* i, p. 208. Cf. E. R. Curtius, *European Literature and the Latin Middle Ages*, pp. 278 ff.

239. talaria: a t.t. for Mercury's winged sandals; cf. Keats, *Endymion* iv. 330 ff.

> when lo!
> Foot-feather'd Mercury appeared sublime
> Beyond the tall tree-tops; and in less time
> Than shoots the slanted hail-storm, down he dropp'd
> Towards the ground; but rested not, nor stopp'd
> One moment from his home: only the sward
> He with his wand light touch'd, and heavenward
> Swifter than sight was gone;

and compare Milton's description of Raphael (*PL* v. 266 ff.):

> Down thither prone in flight
> He speeds, and through the vast ethereal sky
> Sails between worlds and worlds, with steady wing
> Now on the polar winds; then with quick fan
> Winnows the buxom air. . . .
> Six wings he wore, to shade
> His lineaments divine: the pair that clad
> Each shoulder broad came mantling o'er his breast
> With regal ornament; the middle pair
> Girt like a starry zone his waist, and round
> Skirted his loins and thighs with downy gold
> And colours dipt in heaven; the third his feet
> Shadow'd from either heel with feathered mail,
> Sky-tinctured grain. Like Maia's son he stood,
> And shook his plumes, that heavenly fragrance filled
> The circuit wide.

240. Note the steady rhythm which carries the reader on to the fourth-foot caesura; *sublimem alis*, 'air-borne on wings' is Virgil's own detail, but *rapido . . . flamine* is a close translation of Homer's ἅμα πνοιῇς ἀνέμοιο.

aequora: note that Virgil never uses the dative or ablative plural form *aequoribus*, although it would suit the metre; but *aequorum* is avoided because it is metrically intractable.

241. rapido: 'whirling', in an active sense; see Mackail on i. 59.

242. virgam: the *caduceus* or herald's staff, which Mercury carried as a mark of his office. What follows is an explanatory aside, such as a modern prose-writer would put in a footnote.

242 ff. hac . . . resignat: 'with this staff he beckons the spirits, the pale spirits, up from Orcus, and with it he sends others again down to dismal Tartarus, with it he gives sleep or withholds it, and unseals men's eyes in death.' Virgil describes the use of the *virga* by Mercury in his capacity as ψυχοπομπός.

242. evocat: the word is particularly used of the 'summoning' of spirits; it may not mean more than ghostly visitations in general, but more probably Virgil is influenced here by Orphic–Pythagorean beliefs in reincarnation: Norden (on vi. 749) thinks that his immediate model was the Orphic Hymn to Hermes, 57. 6 ff. αἰνομόροις ψυχαῖς πομπὸς κατὰ γαῖαν ὑπάρχων, / ἃς κατάγεις, ὁπότ' ἂν μοίρης χρόνος εἰσαφίκηται, / εὐιέρῳ ῥάβδῳ θέλγων ὑπνοδώτιδι πάντα, / καὶ πάλιν ὑπνώοντας ἐγείρεις.

Orco: the lower regions in general; Tartarus (*Tartara* is an irregular plural form, used for metrical convenience) was the special place of punishment. Note the *t*, *s*, and *l* sounds in these lines.

244. lumina morte resignat: a beautiful and mysterious phrase. *Morte* is a loosely used accompanying ablative (cf. Mackail, pp. 513 ff.); *resignat* was explained by Turnebus, the sixteenth-century French scholar, as referring to the custom of opening the eyes of the dead upon the pyre, so that they might see their way to their new home (cf. Pliny, *NH* xi. 150), a meaning now generally accepted (cf. Stat. *Th*. iii. 129 *lumina signant*, of closing the eyes of fallen soldiers). This is doubtless the literal sense; but who can tell what further meaning the words had for the poet who wrote of the blessed dead 'largior hic campos aether et lumine vestit/ purpureo, solemque suum, sua sidera norunt' (vi. 640 f.)? R. J. M. Lindsay (*CP* xlvii, 1952, p. 165) takes *morte* as 'at the moment of death' and *resignat* as 'opens up', interpreting the words as meaning Mercury's power to restore to life a man who is on the border line between life and death.

Editors have been annoyed because Virgil seems to refer, first to Mercury's power over the dead (242–3), then to his power over the living (*dat somnos adimitque*), then, in this phrase, again to his power over the dead. Hence Henry chose to take *morte* as 'sleep', making the phrase a variation of the first part of the line, a singular view. Too much has been made of this alleged awkwardness: death is too nearly the twin-brother of sleep to make it matter to Virgil whether he gives an orderly catalogue of Mercury's functions or not. But if analysis is necessary, may we not say that in these lines Virgil first describes Mercury's power over the waking dead, then his power over the waking and sleeping living, then his power over the sleeping dead?

245. illa: Virgil now resumes his account of Mercury's journey. Mackail regards *illa* as awkward after *hac* in 242, 'as though they were things opposed to each other'; this is captious, for *hac . . . resignat* is clearly an aside, describing the general functions of the *virga*, while *illâ fretus* ('with its power') takes up *virgam* and gives the particular use which Mercury makes

of it at this moment. However, Mackail and others are probably right in regarding the passage as a whole as lacking in
revision.

agit ventos: Mercury rides the winds and 'drives' them as
he rides; Henry pictures him as exhorting the winds, crying
'age, age, age!'

246. nubila: the strong pause after the run-on word gives it an
exaggerated emphasis (contrast the force of the pause after
conspicit, 261, and cf. note on 22); it looks as if this is the
end of a rough draft, only temporarily fitted to the rest of the
line. Another indication of possible lack of finish is the re-
currence of *et* in three consecutive lines in the second half of
the line, and the group of five lines (243–7) ending with a verb.

247. duri: this suggests both the physical aspect of the grim
mountain, and the inflexible hardness of Atlas as he 'makes
his head the stay of heaven'; see R. W. Cruttwell in *CR* lix,
1945, p. 11, for a theory that *Durus* may have been a Roman
soldier's nickname for Mt. Atlas.

248 ff. This description of Atlas (perhaps based on a painting)
has power, but is out of place here, and the narrative would
run better if it went straight on from 247 to 252. Mackail
suggests that the four lines are an early draft, 'meant to be
struck out and replaced by the single line 247'. The repetition of *Atlantis* gives a curious prominence to the name,
which does not seem to need such a stressing; and the
similar rhythm of 248, 249, and 251 is noticeably monotonous
(249 and 251 are identical, and in each the third-foot caesura
is blurred by the monosyllable *et*, so that the effective caesura
is in the fourth foot, as in 248); yet this cannot be pressed as a
weakness, in view of such a couplet as i. 115 f. 'in puppim
ferit: excutitur pronusque magister/ volvitur in caput; ast
illam ter fluctus ibidem' or ii. 29 f. 'hic Dolopum manus,
hic saevus tendebat Achilles;/ classibus hic locus, hic acie
certare solebant'.

250. From using *vertex* and *caput*, which suit the mountain as
well as the human figure, Virgil passes to purely human
features in *umeros, mento, barba*, while the mountain has
become a *senex*; Page regards the effect as 'childish', a harsh
criticism if one remembers, for example, some of the rock-
formations on the Cornish coast, or those near Dawlish. It
is a fantastic picture, to which no exception need be taken in
itself, but in its context here it all sounds a little strange.

252. Cyllenius: Mercury was born on Mt. Cyllene in Arcadia
(cf. viii. 139); the allusive name is useful, as it provides an
alternative metrical pattern. The god 'came to a halt by
effort of balanced wings', perfectly poised as he glided to rest; the

present participle *nitens* suggests that his flying and alight-
ing are virtually simultaneous, a vivid and observant picture.

253. constitit: the pause here is effective. Mercury flies evenly
to Mt. Atlas, then dives down to sea-level near Carthage, like
a sea-bird coasting round before landing. Page strangely
thinks that he assumed a bird's form.

253 f. hinc . . . misit: 'from here he dived down seaward,
plunging with all his body's force'; note the interlacing of
adjective, pronoun, and noun in *toto praeceps*)(*se corpore*.

254. The repeated *circum* clearly shows the bird's wheeling
flight as it gets nearer and nearer shore, flying 'low and close
to the sea'.

256–8. Some editors, including Ribbeck, have condemned these
lines as spurious ('sunt autem versus tam ieiuni et salebrosi
ut vix de fraude facta dubitare liceat' is Heyne's comment);
they are not needed for the sense, and their absence would
not spoil the picture. Possibly 253–5 and 256–8 may represent two originally alternative versions in Virgil's mind. The
interesting rhythm suggests that the lines are Virgilian: in
256 there is no mental pause in mid-line, as *inter* is so closely
connected in sense both with *terras* and with *caelum*, so that
the line depicts metrically a steady unending flight (note also
the assonance of *aliter terras inter*); this effect is carried on in
the next line, where there is no pause till after *Libyae* (cf. i.
301 'remigio alarum ac Libyae citus astitit oris', in the description of Mercury's first visit to Carthage). The 'rhyme' in
volabat, secabat has been criticized, but it is quite characteristic
(cf. note on 55). Mackail speaks of the 'clumsy phrasing and
the needlessness' of the lines, Page finds them 'dull and
frigid', Irvine calls them 'bad in technique'; but they have
sound MS. authority, and I cannot really see that they are
unworthy of Virgil, even though he had plainly not made up
his mind about the final form of the whole passage 245–58.

258. materno . . . avo: this might well be termed 'frigid'; yet
the reference to Atlas as Mercury's 'maternal grandfather' is
really no odder than *Dardanius nepos Veneris* (163). What is
more relevant to criticism is the impression given that Atlas
was somehow responsible for Mercury's flight. But *Cyllenia
proles* following *Cyllenius* in 252, which Mackail criticizes, is
exactly in Virgil's manner—see ii. 371–82 (*Androgeos . . .
haud secus Androgeos*), xi. 806–14 (*Arruns . . . haud secus . . .
Arruns*), xii. 1–9 (*Turnus . . . haud secus . . . Turno*).

259. māgalia: cf. i. 421 'miratur molem Aeneas, magalia quondam' (of the new buildings of Carthage, contrasted with the
'shacks' that they had been). There is a kindred word in *G.*
iii. 340 ('raris habitata măpalia tectis'), and both are used

specifically of African hutments, described by Sallust (*Iug.*
18. 8) as 'oblong, with curved sides, like ships' hulls'. Conway (on i. 421) conjectures that *magalia* are round enclosures,
with many separate huts inside, *mapalia* single huts. I
imagine that Little Em'ly in *David Copperfield* would have
recognized them easily enough.

260. Note the effective placing of *Aenean*: Aeneas is the first
person that he sees, 'building battlements and making new
dwellings'—so that *regnorum immemores* (194) is a patent lie.
There is no inconsistency with 86–89 as Pease thinks: there,
Dido, racked by her love, loses all interest in the work of
building; here, the work is being continued by Aeneas in
happy partnership, now that she has won him—a subtle
point. Yet it is an Aeneas with a jewelled sword and purple
cloak, a Tyrian Aeneas, dressed out in magnificence by Dido,
not a grave and sober man of destiny. I cannot understand
why Mackail regards 261–4 as 'a rather infelicitous parenthesis': the lines are a glimpse, seldom seen, of Virgil's hero
as a happy man.

fundantem . . . novantem: note the internal 'rhyme'; the
elision before *arces* prevents the line from being a true
'leonine' (such as 288, *E.* viii. 80, *A.* iii. 36, v. 853, x. 756, xii.
561).

261. conspicit: 'catches sight of' (not 'sees'); the pause is
admirable.

atque: the word suggests the immediate, sudden point that
strikes him first (cf. the Plautine *atque eccum video*, etc.); see
Page on i. 227.

262. ensis: the sword itself is put for the scabbard, which was
'starred with tawny jasper' (Mackail compares xi. 11 *ensem
. . . eburnum*, a sword in an ivory sheath).

ardebat: a good word; the purple cloak 'glows'. The whole
picture is dazzling—and oriental.

murice: properly the shell-fish from which purple dye was
obtained. Tyrian was the richest and finest of all purple
shades. Pliny makes fascinating reading on the whole subject (*NH* ix. 124 ff.); he states (135) that the Tyrian hue
resembled that of clotted blood, *nigricans aspectu idemque
suspectu refulgens*. The conjunction here of Tyrian purple
with jasper is surely not casual: in the *Memoirs of Lady
Fanshawe* (written in 1676), the wife of Virgil's translator
describes a visit to the Alhambra at Granada, 'whose buildings are, after the fashion of the Moors, adorned with vast
quantities of jasper-stone. . . . Here I was showed in the
midst of a very large piece of rich embroidery made by the
Moors of Grenada, in the middle as long as half a yard of the

true Tyrian dye, which is so glorious a colour that it cannot
be expressed: it hath the glory of scarlet, the beauty of
purple, and is so bright, that when the eye is removed upon
any other object it seems as white as snow.' Had Virgil met
some Moorish merchant in Rome?

263 f. dives . . . auro: 'gifts which Dido in her wealth had made,
dividing off the web with a subtle strand of gold'; *tenui*
shows the fineness of the interweaving of the cloak, and *et*
introduces a clause explanatory of *fecerat*. Long after, when
an anguished Aeneas saw his friend Evander's son Pallas
dead in his cause, he set upon him robes of gold and purple
'quas illi laeta laborum/ ipsa suis quondam manibus Sidonia
Dido/ fecerat et tenui telas discreverat auro' (xi. 73 ff.).
Sparrow suggests (op. cit., p. 67) that the same garment is
meant in both passages; even if it is not, the repetition is
poignant enough, with its fleeting glimpse of Dido, *laeta
laborum*, happy and proud of her Aeneas.

265. continuo: a favourite word of Virgil's, and frequent in
earlier poetry, but rare in post-Virgilian verse (e.g. it occurs
once only in Lucan, and three times only in Statius).

   invadit: Mercury wasted no time (*continuo*), but 'went for'
Aeneas the moment he caught sight of him; cf. Tac. *Ann.* vi.
4 'Agrippa consules anni prioris invasit, cur mutua accusa-
tione intenta nunc silerent'.

   tu: emphatic ('you, *Aeneas*!'); cf. Stat. *Th.* x. 206 ff. 'tune,
inquit, inertis/ Inachidas . . ./ . . . tantam patiere amittere
noctem,/ degener?'

   Karthaginis altae: see note on 97. It should be an Italian
city that Aeneas is building.

266. uxorius: this is Mercury's own sneer; note the juxtaposition with *pulchram*: Aeneas is so much tied to Dido's apron-
strings that he is building *her* fine city for her (*uxorius* is
almost 'so fond of your wife as all that').

268. ipse: this, with the repetition in 270, shows the gravity of
the message; various shades of meaning converge in it, (*a*) the
decision is Jupiter's own, (*b*) it is Jupiter in person who sends
the message, (*c*) his power is supreme and unquestionable
(for *ipse* 'the master' see on 147). Note the effective juxtaposition in *tibi me*.

269. numine: cf. xii. 180 'cuncta tuo qui bella, pater, sub
numine torques' (of Mars). *Numen* here is connected with
the idea of Jupiter's 'nod' (cf. note on 204), by which he
controls all things. Sometimes this 'power' is a mysterious
abstract feeling of 'divinity', as in Ovid, *F.* iii. 295 f. 'lucus
Aventino suberat niger ilicis umbra/ quo posses viso dicere
"numen inest"'.

270 ff. Note the skilful echoes of Jupiter's own words (in a different order of lines), and the changes made to adapt them to a direct address.

271. Cf. xii. 796 'quid struis? aut qua spe gelidis in nubibus haeres?' (Jupiter to Juno); note that Virgil does not repeat the bold hiatus of 235—he knew when to let well alone.

teris otia: 'idly waste your time'; cf. Stat. *S.* iii. 5. 61 'otia tam pulchrae terit infecunda iuventae': an unjust sneer, for whatever Aeneas has done wrong, he is clearly not *otiosus*. The *s*-sounds are noteworthy (cf. 305); of course, *teris* and *terris* would not have been pronounced alike. The plural *otia* is necessitated by the metre, and is foreign to classical prose (see Maas, *ALL* xii, p. 545); Horace and Catullus have the singular in lyrics (Löfstedt, *Synt.* i, p. 46).

273. The line is omitted in the primary MSS.; the changes from 233 are very perfunctory, and it is clearly suspect.

274 f. The adaptation of 234 and 236 is notable. Mercury ends as Jupiter had done (but *regnum Italiae Romanaque tellus* is even more solemn than Jupiter's own words), with an instruction to Aeneas to 'remember Italy'; but he does not reproduce the command *naviget*, for he knows that the terror of his appearance will be enough.

274. spes . . . Iuli: either 'the hopes that Iulus has' of being Aeneas' heir, or 'the hopes that Iulus inspires' as heir; the former is preferable, both in view of *Ascanione pater* (234) and of *cui . . . debetur* here: the foundation of a dynasty is implied (cf. *prolem Ausoniam*, 236). Cf. vi. 364 'per genitorem oro, per spes surgentis Iuli', and Norden's note.

276. debetur: note how Mercury's speech ends abruptly with a single run-on word, exactly as in 570, and then he vanishes; cf. viii. 583, where Evander ends a speech similarly, and then faints (contrast 387 below, where Dido's speech ends with a line, before she faints). For a somewhat different effect with the same metrical device cf. x. 495, 744, 776, xii. 45.

tali . . . ore: more than 'with such words'; *os* implies not only the spoken words upon the lips, but the way they were said and the whole expression or 'mien' of the speaker.

277. medio sermone: 'while he was still speaking' (but he had finished his message; contrast 76 'incipit effari mediaque in voce resistit'). The completeness of Mercury's disappearance is shown by the piling-up of *procul, ex oculis, in auram* (*tenuem*, 'insubstantial', though a conventional epithet, adds to the effect of mysterious evanescence). The elision after *tenuem* is subtle: the syllable vanishes, just as the god does; Virgil might have written 'in tenues oculis evanuit auras' (the precise words of Ovid, *F.* ii. 509), but he chose a more

graphic pattern; see further on 692. Line 278 is repeated in
ix. 658 (Apollo's appearance to Iulus); Wagner observes that
these are the only two passages where Virgil has the singular
aura after a preposition (*Quaest. Virg.* ix, p. 409).
278. Virgil likes this type of line, with an elision (generally
a strong one) at the end of the second foot, and the caesura in
the third foot either absent or weakened by a preceding
monosyllable belonging closely in sense (as here) to the word
that follows the caesura: the pattern occurs in 8, 99, 122, 130,
142, 150, 151, 201, 214, 222, 229, 248, 257, 275, 291, 396, 397,
405, 410, 431, 465, 470, 513, 546, 554.

279–95. *Aeneas is horrified at the apparition: he is in haste to
obey, but he is grievously torn in mind : how shall he even begin
to break the news to Dido? In the end he orders some of his
men to make the fleet ready in secret, and he will find a way of
approach that will least hurt her. And his orders are obeyed with
alacrity.*

These lines bring us suddenly and dramatically to the
tragic contrast of the divergent characters of Aeneas and
Dido. So far in the book Aeneas has been almost wholly subordinated to Dido, and his presence has been felt rather than
seen: the last direct mention of him was in 165, and even
there it is Dido's attitude, not his, to their union that is
stressed; since then we have heard of him through *Fama*,
and we have seen him in the mind of Iarbas and through the
eyes of Mercury acting as Jupiter's messenger. Now for the
first time he is before us in person, not as an appendage to
Dido, and his character is at once made clear. In contrast to
the impulsive, headstrong, passionate Dido, who has gone to
all lengths to quell the still small voice of conscience, Aeneas
at once recognizes its dictates, and he does not question
obedience. But his cruel dilemma is also clear. He loves
Dido (291), Carthage is sweet to him (281), and although he
knows from the first that he must and will go, his chief concern is to soften the blow that is to fall on Dido. The conflict
of duty and desire is plain; and the speed of events adds to
the suffering they bring: all in a moment, the happiness of
both is shattered, for ever.

279. at vero: a very strong expression of contrast. Aeneas is
brought up with a jolt, and is 'distraught and tongue-tied at
the vision': *obmutuit* suggests that he tried to speak, but that
his voice was blocked. The next line is a variation of the
same picture.
280. arrectaeque . . . haesit: 'his hair stood bristling with dread,
and his voice stuck fast in his throat.' The line is repeated in

xii. 868, when Turnus is terrified by the Fury; cf. ii. 774
(Aeneas' vision of Creusa), iii. 48 (his vision of Polydorus);
the repetition is characteristic of epic, but Virgil's use of it
differs in effect from Homer's method (cf. 7, note, and see
Sparrow, op. cit., pp. 80 ff.). The Latin *horror* is primarily a
literal 'bristling', just as Milton's Dragon in the *Nativity
Ode* 'swindges the scaly Horrour of his foulded tail'; so too
Milton writes 'a horrid front/ Of dreadful length and dazzling
arms' (*PL* i. 563 f.), and Keats in *Lamia*, 'A deadly silence
step by step increased,/ Until it seem'd a horrid presence
there,/ And not a man but felt the terror in his hair'.

281. Here is the dilemma: he is afire to go, and to go quickly
(*fuga*), but the land that he must leave is sweet; in *dulcis*, we
have a fleeting glimpse of Aeneas' real feelings. *Abire* (the
infinitive after *ardet* is poetic, cf. Page on ii. 64) would have
been enough; *fuga* shows that Aeneas had to 'run away' from
the desires of the flesh.

283 f. agat . . . audeat . . . sumat: indirect deliberatives; Aeneas
said to himself 'quid agam?', etc.

     quo nunc . . . adfatu: 'what words should he now have the
courage to use, to get round the queen in all her passion?';
nunc, i.e. now that things have gone so far—once it might
not have been so bitter for both of them.

283. ambire: literally, 'to canvass', a good word here, but Page
is wrong in thinking that it 'hints at cunning and treachery';
the sense of pleading or persuading is uppermost, as in Hor.
C. i. 35. 5 'te pauper ambit sollicita prece/ ruris colonus'.
(The only other passage where Virgil uses *ambire* metaphorically is in vii. 333, where the sense of deception is clear, but
the word is in the mouth of Aeneas' enemy Juno.) Aeneas
knows that he must prove false to Dido, but it is an involun-
tary betrayal, and his heart rebels against it; *furentem* shows
that he sees only too well how hard the task will be.

284. exordia: properly of the laying down of a web, and so
again appropriate; here too I cannot see how Page finds a
sense of falsehood in it. Virgil simply means 'how is he to
set about a beginning?' The plural form is due to metrical
necessity only, not to any idea that Aeneas had to try out
a number of 'beginnings' (cf. Maas, *ALL* xii, p. 485). Such
pleonasms as *prima exordia* are very characteristic of Latin
style; they have their origin in a wish for emphasis or for
clarity (see Löfstedt, *Synt.* ii, ch. 9): cf. Plaut. *Pseud.* 399
'neque exordiri primum unde occipias habes', Livy iii. 54. 9
ubi prima initia incohastis libertatis vestrae'.

285–6. These lines are repeated in viii. 20–21, and are ignored
by Servius here; and 286 is added only by a later hand in F

and P (see Mackail); hence some editors regard them as an
interpolation (cf. Sparrow, op. cit., p. 143). Heinsius, con-
sidering *atque* suspect, conjectured *utque*, omitting the stop
after *versat*. I cannot see that *atque* is awkward, or that the
lines are otiose: Aeneas' dilemma is so sudden and so cruel,
that they show well his desperate search for a solution, and in
fact 287 would surely be too abrupt without them; *atque* is
quite natural, joining the idea of 'he wonders how best to
act' (283-4) with that of 'he puzzles it out in his mind'—it is
simply the form of 283-4 that makes *atque* seem at first sight
out of place. For *nunc . . . nunc* see on 157.

288. The particularizing by name is characteristic of Virgil; cf.
i. 611 f., ix. 171, etc.; this line is repeated in xii. 561 (see
on 260 for the internal or 'leonine' rhyme).

289. classem . . . taciti: 'they are to fit out the fleet and never
say a word' (cf. viii. 79 f. 'geminasque legit de classe bire-
mis/ remigioque aptat'). The subjunctives *aptent, cogant,
parent, dissimulent*, are oblique jussive.

sociosque . . . cogant: 'and they must call their mates to
join them at the shore.'

290. arma: 'tackle', 'gear' (cf. 86): they are to pack up, ready
to go. But it might mean 'arms', in case the Carthaginians
caused trouble.

quae . . . dissimulent: 'they are to make up an excuse to
explain the change of plan'; *rebus novandis* suggests a revolu-
tion (and to Aeneas, this was just what it seemed to be).

291 f. quando . . . amores: 'since Dido, his best, knew nothing
and never dreamed of the breaking of so strong a love.' The
words represent Aeneas' thought, as Irvine remarks, and this
explains the epithet. *Optima* is heart-breaking in its context;
it is not 'benignant' or 'gracious' (Mackail), nor 'that excel-
lent woman' (Pease, who further believes that the epithet is
'slightly disparaging'), still less 'a wistful bit of retrospection
to the days when she was still bearing herself with decorum'
(Hahn, see Pease ad loc.). It means what it says, that Dido
was all the world to him; it is one of the tiny revelations of
Aeneas' true feelings, like *dulcis terras*, 281.

292. speret: used of 'anticipating' what is in fact actually happening, with a present infinitive.

293. aditus: 'ways of approach', explained by *quae . . . tempora,
quis . . . modus* (sc. *sint*); Aeneas wants to soften the blow, to
break it gently to Dido that he must leave her.

Virgil prefers the plural accusative form of *aditus*, sometimes where (unlike this line and 423) the singular would have
been expected and would be used in prose, i.e. as a 'poetic
plural'. Examples of this latter use are v. 441 f. 'nunc hos

nunc illos aditus omnemque pererrat/ arte locum', and xi.
766 f. 'hos aditus iamque hos aditus omnemque pererrat/
undique circuitum': in both, the singular would have given
the sense required; in the first the plural is needed for metrical
reasons (and even if the singular had been possible metrically,
nunc hunc nunc . . . would have been intolerable); in the
second, however, the singular would have been perfectly
possible if Virgil had cared to write *totum* for *omnem*. This
preference for the plural is further shown in ii. 494 'fit via vi,
rumpunt aditus primosque trucidant', where the plural is not
necessitated by the metre (and in fact *aditus* is a variation on
via), and in ix. 683 'inrumpunt aditus Rutuli ut videre
patentis', where the singular could also have stood and
where *aditus = portam* (675). Possibly the plural use was
suggested in part by Greek usage in ἔσοδοι; the same preference is shown by Ovid, Lucan, Statius, and Valerius
Flaccus. Of the four Virgilian examples of the singular
aditum, two are identical (vi. 424, 635, 'occupat Aeneas
aditum', with a consonant following), where the plural might
have stood on the analogy of ii. 494 and ix. 683, but here
there is no word like *porta* in the near context, and this may
account for the singular. The other two are ix. 58 'lustrat
equo muros aditumque per avia quaerit' and ix. 507 'quaerunt
pars aditum et scalis ascendere muros', where Virgil's usage
elsewhere might have led us to expect *aditus*: it would have
been possible in both (for in 507 Virgil could have written
aditus scalisque, which he no doubt avoided because of the
resultant clash of sibilants), but he has chosen the more precise singular in these similar contexts.

294. quis . . . modus: 'what is a good way for his purpose';
dexter implies both 'skilful' and 'favourable', with the second
sense uppermost. The pause after *modus* (stronger than the
usual pause at such a 'bucolic diaeresis', cf. Hardie, *Res
Metrica*, p. 17) is effective; it is almost as if Aeneas' hopes
were shown as fading into the distance, as he turned over the
problem that he could never solve.

295. facessunt: 'they hurry to do his orders'; *facessere* is used
of eager, quick action. Note how uneasy Aeneas' men have
plainly been in Carthage, and compare their simple alacrity
with his worried indecision: *they* have no problems like his to
complicate their little world. Marlowe understood them
when he makes Achates say (Act iv):

> This is no life for men-at-arms to live,
> Where dalliance doth consume a soldier's strength,
> And wanton motions of alluring eyes
> Effiminate our minds, inur'd to war.

296–330. *But Dido cannot be deceived : she hears a rumour of what is afoot, and is at once whipped to ungovernable frenzy. She flings herself upon Aeneas with a wild speech: 'So this was your scheme, to leave me by stealth, regardless of love or of bonded word? To leave me alone, and unprotected, against those whom you have caused to hate me? With nothing to hope for, not even a child to bear your name and bring you back to me?'*

296. at regina: cf. note on line 1. The words mark a heightening of the drama, and a new chapter as it were in the relations between Dido and Aeneas. *Dolos* here need not preclude my interpretation of *ambire* in 283: Aeneas' plan was a *dolus* in Dido's eyes.

297. praesensit: explained and amplified in *motusque . . . futuros.* Dido 'realized beforehand' what was afoot, for *Fama* took care to tell her. But another meaning is latent: her conscience (never wholly stilled, cf. 172) made her uneasy and half-fearful always that something would go wrong, and she 'had a presentiment' of ill; for being in love she was abnormally sensitive to anything that might threaten her happiness (*quis . . . amantem?*). Virgil is careful not to make it plain whether her knowledge came from *Fama* alone.

  excepit: she 'caught the sound' of the movements to come; *excipere* is especially used of hearing something at a distance (cf. ix. 54 'clamorem excipiunt socii fremituque sequuntur').

  prima: perhaps 'at once' (cf. note on 169); but it may literally mean that Dido was the first person to have any idea of Aeneas' plans, before all others, before even Anna.

298. omnia tuta timens: 'inclined to fear where all was safe.' Virgil thus makes it clear that Dido in her inmost heart was never free from self-blame (see Irvine's note). For this use of the present participle to express tendency see Reid on Cic. *de sen.* 26 'ut senectus . . . sit operosa et semper agens aliquid et moliens'.

298 f. eadem . . . parari: 'that self-same unconscionable Rumour brought her the tale, passion-ridden as she was, that the fleet was being fitted out and a voyage in preparation.' *Impia* shows Rumour as lacking all respect for ordinary human relationships, *tam ficti pravique tenax quam nuntia veri* (188); *furenti* may be proleptic, anticipating *saevit* and *bacchatur* below, but this is not necessary (cf. 283).

300 ff. saevit . . . Cithaeron: 'utterly distraught she raves, and storms aflame all about the city: just like some Thyiad, maddened at the stirring of the holy symbols, when at the sound of Bacchus' name the mystic revels in their cycle prick her on, and midnight Cithaeron loudly calls.'

Dido does not wait for any explanation of what she hears, but at once loses all self-control; in this primitive, passionate aspect of her heart she is so utterly different from Aeneas, and the sufferings of both are the more bitter because of it. Virgil piles up verbs and adjectives to show her state, and adds a simile that would convey far more to his readers than it can to us. She behaves like a Maenad (*Thyias*, from θύειν, to rush violently, used of the wind or the sea, is one of the Greek names for a follower of Bacchus), she is like a person 'possessed': Virgil has deliberately chosen words that would suggest the atmosphere of Euripides' *Bacchae* (cf. 469 f.).

300. **inops animi**: for the genitive see on 203; but it may be the ordinary genitive of 'thing lacking' which is found with *inops* (e.g. *consilii, rationis*). She has lost all the help that reason might have given her.

301. **bacchatur**: used of any wild frenzy (cf. 666, vi. 78), but it has special point here in view of the simile to come.

sacris: either the 'rites' in the abstract, or, more probably, the actual 'symbols' or emblems of the god, brandished in ecstasy; cf. Val. Flacc. iii. 231 f. 'at barbara buxus/ si vocet et motis ululantia Dindyma sacris', *id*. iii. 540 (of Bacchus) 'duceret ac rursus thiasos et sacra moventem'.

302. **audito ... Baccho**: i.e. when she hears the cry *Euoe Bacche* (cf. vii. 389, Catull. 64. 255).

trieterica: literally 'held every third year', that is, 'in alternate years' by our reckoning; the ancient system of reckoning was inclusive, so that in a given group of years ABCD the festival would be held in the years A and C, the latter being the 'third year' inclusive of A. It is a Greek ritual word, used here (like *Thyias* and *orgia*) to add to the precision of Virgil's picture and consequently to the full appropriateness of the simile. Pease has an exhaustive collection of passages where the term is used.

303. **orgia**: equivalent to *sacra* in both the senses noted above, but always with an essentially mystic content, as being known only to the initiate. The festival was held on Mt. Cithaeron in Boeotia (the scene of Euripides' *Bacchae*); Virgil personifies the mountain (cf. Eur. *Bacch*. 726 f. πᾶν δὲ συνεβάκχευ' ὄρος / καὶ θῆρες, οὐδὲν δ' ἦν ἀκίνητον δρόμῳ); for *nocturnus* see note on 118, and cf. *G*. iv. 521 (the death of Orpheus) 'inter sacra deum nocturnique orgia Bacchi'. Notice the many hard *c* and *t* sounds in the whole passage 300–3; the whole effect is one of noise.

304. **ultro**: 'without waiting for him'; Dido takes the initiative (cf. Page's good note on ii. 145), giving Aeneas no time to speak first; and so he never found *mollissima tempora fandi*

and had no chance to defend himself on ground of his own
choosing.

305–30. Dido begins her speech in hissing rage; but her mood
quickly changes, and she presently passes from imperious
anger to almost abject dependence; and the pathos of her
appeal is heightened when we find this proud, splendid
creature, who had spurned Iarbas and many another, re-
duced to terror at the thought of facing her enemies without
Aeneas' protection. Finally, her desire for a child overcomes
all other emotions, and the speech which began so fiercely
ends in what is almost a soliloquy, barely whispered.

Like the others in the book, this speech is composed in the
high tragic-rhetorical tradition of Euripides' *Medea* (e.g.
465 ff.), which was followed by Apollonius Rhodius before
Virgil (e.g. iv. 355 ff.); but the strength of Dido's personality
towers above all the rhetoric. When Ariadne upbraids
Theseus for his desertion (Catull. 64. 132 ff., a speech which
Virgil would remember), she seems ineffectual and almost
tiresome, a silly little thing for all her betrayal; and we need
only look at Ovid's treatment of the deserted Dido (*Her.* 7,
a bland rehash of all Dido's speeches in this book; see Appendix, pp. 203 ff.) to see not only Virgil's supreme art, but his
sympathy and his sensitive understanding of a woman's mind,
and, above all, the nobility of his creation in Dido. See
Heinze's perceptive discussion, op. cit., pp. 133 ff.

Henry observes here: 'while Virgil . . . greatly improves
upon and surpasses his original, those who have re-copied
from Virgil fall short, not only of the improved model with
which he has furnished them, but even of the original itself;
compare Tasso's tedious, spiritless, and unnatural dialogue
of Armida and Rinaldo, in the 16th canto of *Gerusalemme
Liberata*'. What French sixteenth-century rhetoric could
make of Virgil may be seen from the *Didon se sacrifiant* of
Étienne Jodelle, performed in 1558, and based largely on this
book: a typical passage runs (cf. 314 ff.)

> Par ces larmes je dy que, te monstrant à l'oeil
> Combien l'amour est grand, quand si grand est le dueil,
> Et par ta dextre aussi, puis que moy, miserable,
> Ne me suis laissé rien qui ne soit secourable;
> Par les feux, par les traits dont ton frère si bien
> A vaincu ma raison qu'il ne m'en reste rien;
> Par nostre mariage et par nos hymenées
> Qu'avoyent bien commencé mes rudes destinées;
> Par les dieux que, devot, tu portes avec toy,
> Compagnons de ta peine, et tesmoins de ta foy;
> Par l'honneur du tiers ciel que gouverne ta mère,

Par l'honneur que tu dois aux cendres de ton père,
Si jamais rien de bon j'ay de toy merité,
Si jamais rien de moi à plaisir t'a esté,
Je te pry, prens pitié d'une pauvre famille
Que tu perdras, au lieu d'achever une ville . . .

and so on, for another seventy lines.

305 f. For the repeated sibilants in this and the next line, cf. 603 ff., and Eur. *Med.* 476 f. ἔσωσά σ' ὡς ἴσασιν ῾Ελλήνων ὅσοι / ταὐτὸν συνεισέβησαν Ἀργῷον σκάφος (see D. L. Page ad loc.). Dionysius of Halicarnassus, writing some ten years after Virgil's death, observes (*de comp. verb.* 14, cf. Rhys Roberts's note, p. 146) that the sound of *s* is 'ugly and disagreeable and more suited to a beast than to a rational being'; yet it can only be judged in its context, and it is worth while to contrast 562 below 'nec Zephyros audis spirare secundos', or the sadness of ii. 793 ff. 'ter frustra comprensa manus effugit imago,/ par levibus ventis volucrique simillima somno./ sic demum socios consumpta nocte reviso', or Christ's tender words to the woman with an issue of blood (*Ev. Luc.* 8. 48), Θύγατερ, ἡ πίστις σου σέσωκέ σε· πορεύου εἰς εἰρήνην.

dissimulare . . . terra: 'and so, sir traitor, you even sought dissimulation of so impious a sin? You thought to steal in silence from my land?' *Perfide* and *crudelis* (311), as Irvine remarks, are the only reproachful epithets in the speech. *Etiam* must be taken with *dissimulare*: Aeneas could not only do the deed but could hope to conceal it.

306. nefas: something contrary to God's law (cf. note on 113), a piece of cruel irony in this context.

307. noster: probably with reference to their mutual love, as in *conubia nostra* below (316); it is this that she remembers most as yet, and it is not until her second speech (365 ff.) that it has turned to bitter hate: but then again, in her speech to Anna she is softened once more (429), and in all her agony of spirit before her death she alternates likewise, while even on the pyre she thinks tenderly of her former bliss. These changing moods of Dido are eloquent of Virgil's art.

data dextera: in what she wished to believe was a valid marriage-ceremony (cf. Mackail's note); cf. Eur. *Med.* 21 f. ἀνακαλεῖ δὲ δεξιᾶς / πίστιν μεγίστην.

308. moritura: so again in 415, 519, 604, 'a single bell-stroke' (Mackail). Dido, in all her impulsiveness, at once envisages her death—not suicide as yet, for it is not till later, when all her hope has gone, that the idea of self-destruction comes upon her and then grows inexorably in her mind. *Crudeli funere* means simply the bitterness of death in sorrow, and does not imply the manner of it.

309. hiberno . . . sidere: 'in winter's season.' Anna's words in
52–53 have now become a mockery to her: Aeneas is in haste
to get away at all costs, even when no sensible man would
sail. And yet, Dido seems to find concern for his safety
too.

moliris: 'labour at' (cf. 233); the word suggests the hard
work of getting the fleet to sea, as well as the 'devising' of
the voyage, together with the hint of its being a 'trap' for
her; contrast iii. 5 f., where *classem moliri* is used of the
literal building of a fleet. Note the heavy effect of the two
spondaic words *hiberno moliris* in mid-line, and contrast the
quick dactyls of the next line.

310. mediis . . . Aquilonibus: 'when the North winds are at
their worst.' The *Aquilo* was notoriously the wind of rain and
storm; cf. *Acts* 27. 14–15, 'But not long after there arose
against it a tempestuous wind, called Euroclydon. And
when the ship was caught, and could not bear up into the
wind, we let her drive' (where *Euroclydon = Euraquilo* of
the Vulgate, the N.E. wind.)

311. crudelis: the run-over position, and the strong pause that
follows, gives great emphasis to the adjective (cf. note on
impulit, 23). But Aeneas' 'cruelty' is already undergoing a
change in implication; he is not only cruel to her in leaving
her, but cruel to her in risking his life at such a season.

311 ff. quid . . . aequor: 'tell me, suppose it were for no foreign
shore, for no unknown home that you were making now, suppose storied Troy still stood—would *Troy* be still your goal
in a voyage on swollen seas?' Dido means that even if he
had a home left to go to, he would not sail at such a season,
unless for some urgent and compelling cause: why then sail
for an unknown shore?

314. mene fugis?: the truth breaks upon her at last; *she* is the
compelling cause of his flight: 'is it *I* from whom you flee?'
Cf. ix. 199 f. 'mene igitur socium summis adiungere rebus,/
Nise, fugis?', where *mene* contains a like incredulity. In her
simplicity (and Dido is never other than essentially simple)
she can only see the issue as a personal matter between herself and him, and no other considerations occur to her (see
Henry).

There is an echo of these words in vi. 466 'quem fugis? extremum fato quod te adloquor hoc est'; but there it is Aeneas
who speaks, Dido who recoils from him, as they meet in the
lugentes campi. Similarly, Dido's self-address *infelix Dido*
(596) becomes Aeneas' address to her in vi. 456, and her
words to Anna 'hunc ego si potui tantum sperare dolorem'
(419) are echoed in his words to Dido in vi. 463 f. 'nec credere

quivi/ hunc tantum tibi me discessu ferre dolorem'. Cf. note on 331.

per ego has lacrimas: for this (normal) word-order, in which the unstressed pronoun is placed after the stressed *per*, see Kühner-Stegmann, *Lateinische Grammatik*, ii, pp.592 ff., L.-H. p. 611. Such an order is frequent in adjurations, both in Greek and Latin; cf. Eur. *Med.* 324 μὴ πρός σε γονάτων τῆς τε νεογάμου κόρης, Ter. *Andr.* 289 'per ego te hanc nunc dextram oro', Ovid, *F.* ii. 841 'per tibi ego hunc iuro fortem castumque cruorem'. Note further xii. 56 f. 'Turne, per has ego te lacrimas, per si quis Amatae/ tangit honos animum' (see Mackail, p. 517, for the relation of the Amata-episode to Book IV).

dextramque tuam te: cf. 307. Note the effect of the mono-syllabic ending (see on 132); the line is eloquent of Dido's misery, with its violent clashes of word-accent and metrical ictus continued even to the last foot by Virgil's use of this abnormal end-pattern. Observe also how the line is framed, as it were, between *me* and *te*.

Henry quotes *Julius Caesar* ii. i. 270 ff. (Portia to Brutus),

> and upon my knees,
> I charm you by my once commended beauty,
> By all your vows of love, and that great vow
> Which did incorporate and make us one,
> That you unfold to me, your self, your half,
> Why you are heavy.

315. Her tears and his pledge are all that she now has left, by her own action (*ipsa*): she has abandoned all for him.

316. *Conubia* and *hymenaei* both imply legal marriage; see notes on 126 and 99 for these words. The unusual rhythm of this line is Greek in type. There is no strong caesura in the third or fourth foot; the line is divided in the Greek fashion into two rhythmically nearly equal parts at *nostra* (cf. note on 164, but there a strong caesura is technically present after *ruunt*, while here there is none at all). The quadrisyllabic ending upsets the normal pattern (the ictus gives *inceptós hyme-náeos*, the word-stress gives *incéptos hymenáeos*) as in 215, and *hymenaeos* is itself a Greek word. Further, the second foot has what is for Virgil a most abnormal pattern, though it is very common in Lucretius: the end of the foot coincides with the end of a word (*conubia*), and a glance at any page of Virgil will show how very rare this is; cf. 372, 385, *G.* iii. 344 'armentarius Afer agit, tectumque laremque'. Such Lucretian line-beginnings as *exaequataque sunt* (v. 1296), *effervescere cernebant* (v. 1335), *strata cubilia sunt* (v. 1417) are unthinkable in

Virgil. Lastly, the line is an admirable example of Virgil's way of echoing an earlier poet (Catull. 64. 141 'sed conubia laeta, sed optatos hymenaeos') but in a graver tone: even more striking in this way is the famous line (vi. 460) 'invitus, regina, tuo de litore cessi', of which the original (Catull. 66. 39 'invita, o regina, tuo de vertice cessi') might be taken by the unwitting as a parody.

317 f. fuit ... meum: 'or if ever I held any sweetness for you.' For the postponed *aut* see on 33. Editors compare Soph. *Ai*. 520 f. ἀνδρί τοι χρεὼν / μνήμην προσεῖναι, τερπνὸν εἴ τί που πάθοι; cf. also xii. 882 f. 'aut quicquam mihi dulce meorum/ te sine, frater, erit?'. Mackail points out that line 317 is one of the rare instances in the *Aeneid* where there are as many as ten words in the line (on iii. 155; so also vii. 466, ix. 409, x. 242, 903, xii. 48, 917); contrast 542, with four words only (the least number found).

Marlowe incorporates these lines in his play (Act v, 'And woful Dido, by these blubber'd cheeks,/ By this right hand and by our spousal rites, / Desires Aeneas to remain with her,/ *Si bene quid de te merui*', etc., to which Aeneas replies in Virgil's words of 360–1).

318. labentis: her *domus* (i.e. herself and her household) is already falling, now that Aeneas no longer upholds it.

319. oro ... mentem: 'I implore you, if prayer still has any place, put off that purpose that you hold.' The position of *oro*, occupying the first foot with no run-on to the second, and with a pause to follow, gives it more emphasis than it would have in mid-line (cf. note on 185).

320. Dido now appeals to Aeneas' sense of her own danger. It is plain that she had previously been unafraid of the enemies that surrounded Carthage (cf. 39 ff.), but now she cannot face them without him: and her position is now worse, because of the fierce jealousies aroused in Iarbas and probably others as well.

te propter: cf. *quam propter*, xii. 177; not a common inversion (cf. Bailey on Lucr. i. 90). Here the order is due not only to Virgil's wish to stress *te*, but to the fact that *propter te* would make the first foot occupied by a single spondaic word (cf. *oro* above) and one that by its nature was unsuited to the weight and prominence so given it.

Nomadum: the Numidians (cf. 535); *Numidarum* (cf. 41) is metrically rather lumbering (cf. Martial ix. 75. 8, where *Nomas* = Numidia, Stat. *S.* i. 5. 36). *Tyranni* is no more than 'rulers' (cf. vii. 266, 342, x. 448). Dido does not name Iarbas, but he is meant.

321. infensi Tyrii: just as Aeneas' companions had resented his

delay in Carthage, so the Carthaginians resented Dido's pre-
occupation with him; cf. Eur. *Med.* 506 ff. ἔχει γὰρ οὕτω· τοῖς
μὲν οἴκοθεν φίλοις | ἐχθρὰ καθέστηχ᾽, οὓς δέ μ᾽ οὐκ ἐχρῆν κακῶς | δρᾶν,
σοὶ χάριν φέρουσα πολεμίους ἔχω.

te ... eundem: 'again, because of you'; *idem* often corresponds to 'also', 'likewise'; so in 298, Rumour is 'once
again' responsible for a crisis.

322. exstinctus pudor: 'the flame of conscience has been
quenched'; *pudor* here is her sense of loyalty to Sychaeus (cf.
27, 55): but Dido has forgotten that it was she herself who
stifled it.

qua ... prior: 'that pride of other days, by which alone I
was taking my path to the stars'; her only assured way to
immortality lay in her proud repute as a faithful wife, and
this has now perished because of Aeneas. Henry's note is
more than usually exciting.

sidera adibam: Norden (*Aeneis VI*, p. 455) notes that an
elision of -*a* at this point in the line is very much rarer than
that of -*e* (cf. 645).

323 f. These lines, says Servius, Virgil read to Augustus *ingenti
adfectu.* Mackail takes *cui* as meaning 'for what' rather than
'to whom', comparing ii. 677. By *moribundam* Dido means
that life is not worth living any more (see on *moritura*, 308).

323. hospes: a sad word here; Aeneas is now no more than what
he was when they first met (i. 753, cf. *quis novus hic ...
hospes*, 10), a visitor, as it were, a 'friend' in the most formal
sense: English has no proper equivalent for the ancient relation between host and guest (a relation which Aeneas has
forgotten), which was 'a stronger bond than any other but
that of the relation of father and son' (Warde Fowler,
Aeneas at the Site of Rome, p. 91, comparing Aul. Gell. v. 13).
Heinze (op. cit., p. 134, note 1) compares Callimachus fr. 556
(Pfeiffer), νυμφίε Δημοφόων, ἄδικε ξένε. Yet Dido's use of the
word *hospes* here shows that she cannot yet believe the worst
of Aeneas; it is not till later (424) that he becomes a *hostis*, a
'foreign foe'.

325. quid moror?: 'why linger here?': the thought continues
in her mind that life is useless now; either her brother
Pygmalion would come to kill her, as he had killed Sychaeus,
or she would be forcibly carried off by Iarbas, now that
Aeneas' protection has gone. *An* introduces a sardonic
question (cf. 208); the position of *frater* drives home the
irony (note the interwoven arrangement in *mea Pygmalion*)(
moenia frater).

327 ff. saltem ... viderer: 'at least, if I could have held in my
arms a child by you before you leave me, if only I had playing

in my home a baby Aeneas, to bring you back to me—in spite of all—by the way he looked, *then* I should not feel quite trapped, quite forlorn.'

327. saltem: emphatic, both by position and rhythm (cf. note on 185). Virgil uses the word six times altogether, and always with a note of pathos; cf. *G*. i. 500 f. 'hunc saltem everso iuvenem succurrere saeclo/ ne prohibete', *A*. vi. 370 f. 'da dextram misero et tecum me tolle per undas,/ sedibus ut saltem placidis in morte quiescam', vi. 884 f. 'purpureos spargam flores animamque nepotis/ his saltem accumulem donis'.

suscepta: there is no need to take this in any way but in the literal sense (cf. 391 'suscipiunt famulae'); but it could be given the technical meaning that the verb sometimes has, of 'taking up' a child at birth and 'acknowledging' it and one's duty as a parent towards it, so that the sense would then be virtually 'if I had had a child'; the first interpretation is preferable in this context—the picture is clearer and sadder so.

328. parvulus: diminutives belong to intimate, familiar language, and so are very rare in epic style; their natural home in poetry is the personal lyric (e.g. Catullus) and satire. This is the only occurrence of a diminutive adjective in the whole *Aeneid*, and it is one which Ovid does not use in the whole of the *Metamorphoses*. Thus *parvulus* here is a very remarkable word, and Virgil's use of it shows Dido not as an epic heroine but as a real and tender woman. See A. S. F. Gow, *CQ* xxvi, 1932, pp. 150–7, for a detailed study of the use of diminutives by the Augustan poets; their marked decline in frequency after Lucretius and Catullus shows a clear change in poetic fashion; and diminutive adjectives, as contrasted with substantives, tended to become rare even in those authors whose style and manner admitted the diminutive type. See also Axelson, *Unpoetische Wörter*, pp. 38 ff.

There is only one comparable picture in classical Latin to this, and it is in Catullus, who, like Virgil, also came from 'Italia Transpadana': 'Torquatus volo parvulus/ matris e gremio suae/ porrigens teneras manus/ dulce rideat ad patrem/ semihiante labello' (Catull. 61. 209 ff.). The two passages point forward to another Italy, the Italy of the great renaissance painters. Juvenal has a bitter parody of Virgil in his picture of the advantages of childlessnes (5. 137 ff.). Stanyhurst thought fit to make Dido speak of 'a cockney dandiprat hopthumb prittye lad Aeneas'.

329. Aeneas: this is one of the few occasions where Dido uses Aeneas' name (see on 479). Irvine compares Apul. v. 13, where Psyche says to Cupid 'sic in hoc saltem parvulo cognoscam faciem tuam'.

tamen: 'beautiful and untranslatable' is Page's perceptive comment: the reader must complete the ellipse from his
own understanding. The only thing that matters for Dido,
after all, is that she should see Aeneas in a child of his and
hers, no matter what he had done or where he was; we must
not forget *illum absens absentem auditque videtque* (83). For
a similar *tamen* cf. x. 507 ff. 'o dolor atque decus magnum
rediture parenti,/ haec te prima dies bello dedit, haec eadem
aufert,/ cum tamen ingentis Rutulorum linquis acervos!',
E. x. 31 'tristis at ille "tamen cantabitis, Arcades" inquit'.

Ovid, in some vulgar lines (*Her*. 7. 133 ff.), makes Dido
already with child; Chaucer follows him, but with simple
dignity ('I am with childe, and yive my child his lyf').
Dryden judged Ovid well; see his *Dedication of the Aeneis*
(vol. xiv of the 1808 edition, p. 177).

330. capta ac deserta: as if at the sack of a city.

So the great speech ends: the fierce, proud Dido who began
it is now defenceless and broken.

331–61. *Aeneas, remembering Jupiter's warning, fights down his
love, and at last speaks : 'I owe you all you say, and I shall
never forget you, as long as I live. I never meant to leave you
and tell you nothing. But I never claimed to be your lawful
husband. If I were free to choose, the rebuilding of Troy would
be my first care ; as it is, the gods bid me go to Italy. My father's
ghost has warned me, the thought of the wrong I do my son is
ever with me ; and but now I have had clear orders from Jupiter's
own messenger. I will not be tempted. I go to Italy, against all
my heart.'*

This is Aeneas' only speech, and in making it he is at the
bar of judgement before posterity. Page comments 'not all
Virgil's art can make the figure of Aeneas here appear other
than despicable', and he speaks of 'the cold and formal
rhetoric of an attorney'. This is to ignore all the undertones
of the speech, and it is a view that has misled generations of
schoolboys. It is unfair, and it is untrue. Irvine shows a
deeper insight, remarking that 'at the very crisis of a great
book, and writing at the highest imaginative level, Virgil
knew what he was about'.

The speech is Virgil's way of showing the conflict between
Dido's uncontrolled emotion and Aeneas' pale cast of thought.
She has appealed to feeling, he answers by reason and logic.
Her speech gives fact, as she sees it; his gives fact, as he sees
it. He does not disguise the stark and brutal truth, that she
has deceived herself, he has not deceived her. The tone is
cold and formal, and at the end we see why it is so: had he

not controlled himself (and the tenseness of his struggle is
clear from 360–1) he would have broken down and yielded.
His speech, though we may not like it, was the Roman
answer to the conflict between two compelling forms of love,
an answer such as a Roman Brutus once gave, when he
executed his two sons for treason against Rome. It is no fault
of Virgil's that the harsh conflict between duty and desire is
what it is; and given that conflict, Virgil knew that this was
how he must show it. Aeneas has wronged Dido, and he
knows it; he has wronged God, and he knows it; atonement
either way means pain for ever: and it is our pity that we
should give him, not our scorn.

331. Iovis monitis: Virgil shows at the outset that Aeneas was
no free agent.

    immota: cf. 369, *num lumina flexit?* When Dido on a later
day met Aeneas in the Underworld, it was she who turned a
stony face to his pleadings (cf. note on 314): 'nec magis in-
cepto vultum sermone movetur/ quam si dura silex aut stet
Marpesia cautes' (vi. 470 f.)

    tenebat: continuous action? or conative? The answer de-
pends in part upon our view of Aeneas. For the assonance in
tenebat, premebat, see on 55; it is surely deliberate.

332. obnixus: the word shows his mental struggle; 'he wrestled
against' his love (*curam,* see on 1), thrusting it deep beneath
his heart; cf. i. 209 'spem vultu simulat, premit altum corde
dolorem'.

333. tandem: observe how much more effective this order is
than if Virgil had written *pauca refert tandem*: the spondaic
disyllabic word, occupying the first foot with no overlap to
the second, is isolated and emphasized (cf. notes on 185, 319,
320).

    pauca: Aeneas could have said more, if he had been willing
to give way to his emotions. I cannot see how Page deduces
from this that Virgil 'is conscious that as a reply it is inade-
quate'.

333 ff. ego te . . . artus: 'I tell you, all the countless services
that you can ever list in words, O queen, these you have done
for me, and I shall never say you nay; nor shall I ever be
unwilling to keep Elissa in my mind, as long as I bear my
own self in memory, as long as the breath is lord of this my
body.'

333. ego te: English cannot bring out the force of this juxtaposition; the two persons concerned face each other syntactically,
as it were, and the importance for both of what is being said
receives clear emphasis. *Ego* is often used at the beginning of
a reply to a criticism, marking the personal reaction of the

speaker to what has been said (see Nägelsbach, *Lateinische
Stilistik*, p. 745).

quae plurima fando: some editors have taken this to be a
gibe, but that is absurd; Aeneas simply means that Dido's
acts of kindness to him are more than he can ever acknow-
ledge. For *fando* see on 175.

335. nec ... pigebit: cf. vii. 233 'nec Troiam Ausonios gremio
excepisse pigebit'. To a modern ear the phrase sounds odd and
very lukewarm; but it resembles such mannerisms as *minime
contemnendus*, which implies considerable praise. Yet through
out these opening lines, Aeneas seems to be slowly and carefully picking his words, trying not to say what he might wish
unsaid, and this impression is helped by the unusual rhythm
of *meminisse pigebit Elissae* (see on 58), by which the line itself
has a certain reluctance as the words fall slowly into position
to bring it to its close. A very different Aeneas is speaking
now from the Aeneas who once said to Dido (i. 607 ff.) 'in
freta dum fluvii current, dum montibus umbrae/ lustrabunt
convexa, polus dum sidera pascet,/ semper honos nomenque
tuum laudesque manebunt,/ quae me cumque vocant terrae'.

Elissae: Dido's Carthaginian name, which she herself uses
in 610; Virgil avoids inflected forms of the name *Dido* (see
Mackail). Marlowe (like Dryden in his translation) had his own
ideas about it (Act IV, 'Hear, hear, O hear Iarbas' plaining
prayers,/ Whose hideous echoes make the welkin howl,/ And
all the woods Eliza to resound').

336. The words come more quickly now. Note the unusual
pattern of *hos regit artus* (cf. note on 420): since the last two
feet are divided between more than the normal two words,
the ictus does not coincide with the word-accent in the fifth
foot (*hos régit*); cf. L. P. Wilkinson, *CQ* xxxiv, 1940, p. 35.

337. pro re ... loquar: 'let me speak a few words to meet the
case' (*loquar* may, of course, be future): a cool, impersonal,
legalistic remark, showing that Aeneas has once more
mastered his feelings after the warmth of the previous line.
The stress is on *pro re*: all Dido's love for him, all his for her,
must not prevent him from facing the cruel facts.

337 f. neque ... fugam: Aeneas' answer to Dido's opening
charge (305 f.). We must remember that he had hoped to
find *mollissima fandi tempora*; he never meant to leave her,
as she thinks he did, as some sneaking thief might go.

338. ne finge: a common colloquial construction, taken over
into poetry because it is so convenient metrically; it is not
found in classical prose.

338 f. nec ... veni: 'it was no bridegroom's torch that I ever
held before me, it was no bond of this kind to which I came.'

Praetendi is both literal and metaphorical (cf. *praetexit*, 172)
he never 'held out' the torch of marriage (see on 18), no:
'cloaked his purpose' by pretence of it. Note the slow
measured spondees in the first four feet of 339.

Here is the central point of Aeneas' position. He has neve:
once regarded himself as Dido's husband, and he has neve:
said anything to her to make her think that he does: a bruta
truth, which nothing can disguise, but one that he mus'
make clear. Dido's attitude has never been in doubt (cf. 172)
this is the first time that Aeneas' view has been given, and it:
abruptness makes it all the more terrible to hear. The gul
between the two is now plain to see: in Dido, desire could
always deceive duty, in Aeneas, desire could never win the
last battle.

340 ff. me si . . . victis: these lines were quoted by Pitt in hi:
speech on the Preliminaries of Peace, 3 November 1801
'there were periods during the continuance of the war, i:
which I had hopes of our being able to put together the
scattered fragments of that great and venerable edifice; t(
have restored the exiled nobility of France; to have restore(
a government, certainly not free from defects, but built upo:
sober and regular foundations, in the stead of that mad systen
of innovation which threatened, and had nearly accomp
lished, the destruction of Europe. *Me si fata meis . . . .*'

Aeneas answers in words that show by their solemn move
ment, as F. W. H. Myers points out (*Essays Clàssical*, p. 122]
'a long-unuttered pain' . . . 'neither in Carthage, nor yet i:
Italy, can his heart expect a home'. Myers translates:

> Me had the fates allowed my woes to still,—
> Take my sad life, and shape it at my will,—
> First had I sought my buried home and joy,
> Loves unforgotten, and the last of Troy;—
> Ay, Priam's palace had re-risen then,
> A ghost of Ilium for heart-broken men.

Cf. ii. 641 f. 'me si caelicolae voluissent ducere vitam,/ ha:
mihi servassent sedes'.

341. auspiciis: 'authority' (cf. 103), as if he were a commande:
with the right of taking auspices himself. But Aeneas is no'
'the captain of his soul'.

sponte . . . curas: 'arrange to my own liking all tha'
grieves me'; *curas* here means all the sadness that has eve:
clouded his life (contrast *curam* above, 332).

342 f. urbem . . . colerem: 'it would be Troy's city that]
should be tending before all others, Troy and the preciou:
relics of my dear people': note again the slow spondees, an(

the isolation of *urbem* (like *tandem* in 333); *reliquias* may mean 'ruins', or it may mean the ashes of the dead; the tense of *colerem* (contrast *posuissem* below) implies 'this is what I should be doing at this very moment', and the word itself suggests 'dwelling in' as well as 'tending': the passage is a good example of the many facets of Virgilian expression.

343. manerent: some commentators object that this gives an impossible sense, and Peerlkamp and Ribbeck delete the words *Priami . . . manerent*, leaving the line unfinished; Sparrow agrees (op. cit., pp. 143 ff.), holding that the phrase can only mean that the palace in which Priam had lived could itself be standing—he suggests that the words may have been supplied, to complete an unfinished line, from ii. 56 'Troiaque nunc staret, Priamique arx alta maneres'. I think that too much has been made of the alleged difficulty. If Aeneas could have rebuilt Troy, *a* royal palace would 'still be standing', and even if Priam lived there no longer, it would still be 'Priam's palace' in men's minds.

344. recidiva: rebuilt after destruction (cf. vii. 322, x. 58, again with the noun *Pergama*); the literal sense is 'falling back' into position, and so Pliny (*NH* xxx. 104) uses it of a recurrent fever.

manu: 'in person', often coupled with *ipse* to express personal physical exertion (cf. iii. 372 'ipse manu multo suspensum numine ducit').

Pergama: the citadel of Troy, τὰ Πέργαμα.

victis: a revealing word: Aeneas can never forget the pitiful lines of refugees at Troy (ii. 766), when 'urbs antiqua ruit multos dominata per annos' (ii. 363), and all his promised destiny can make no atonement for the bitter past. Bowra's phrase of Book II, 'the poetry of defeat from the point of view of the defeated' (*From Virgil to Milton*, London, 1945, p. 41) is penetrating: and Dido herself had heard the tale.

345. Italiam: for the prosody see on 106. Note the impatient repetition in the next line: not his dear Troy but Italy is his destiny, and he is not allowed to forget it.

Gryneus: for the prosody see on 6. Apollo had a temple at Gryneum in Asia Minor.

346. Lyciae . . . sortes: 'the oracle of Lycia' (for Apollo's connexion with Lycia cf. 143). The *sortes* or 'lots' would be the pronouncements of the oracle, written on tablets. We are not told when these utterances had been given, nor when Aeneas had had the visions of Anchises referred to below (a point which shows how reticent Virgil has been about Aeneas).

capessere: cf. v. 703 'Italasne capesseret oras'; the verb means 'to lay hold of', and so 'to make for' a place, or to 'undertake' a piece of work. Note the unusual assonance in *iussere capessere* (cf. Norden, *Aeneis VI*, Anh. IV, p. 407).

347. hic amor, haec patria est: 'this is my love, this is my homeland now'; but this is not his real feeling, as 361 shows—it is only what his 'nagging gods' have made him feel. Virgil likes this word-pattern: cf. vii. 122 'hic domus, haec patria est' (which suggests that *hic* in this line might be the adverb), vi. 129 'hoc opus, hic labor est', xi. 739 'hic amor, hoc studium', xii. 572 'hoc caput, o cives, haec belli summa nefandi'.

348. Phoenissam: 'Phoenician as you are'; the adjective is in an emphatic position. If it is right for Dido, a Phoenician, to leave her home for distant lands, why should the Trojans be grudged a settlement in Italy?

349. tandem: 'tell me'; often so in lively interrogations, the counterpart of a gesture or look or tone. Note the juxtaposition *Ausonia*)(*Teucros*.

350. invidia: 'grudge', 'prejudice' (often a better rendering than 'hatred').

et nos ... regna: 'we too sin not in seeking a foreign realm.' The plural accusative *regna* is far more frequent in Virgil than the singular; here the singular would not be possible for the epithet. Dido might have answered that Aeneas had no need to go beyond Carthage for his 'foreign realm'. But in itself his argument is logical (and indeed, the whole speech is the battle of logic against emotion), though it is meagre, academic, and even petulant. Yet it should be remembered that behind it all Aeneas is racked by the longing to stay at Carthage; he is catching at words to save himself from giving way.

351 ff. me ... imago: 'to me, each time the night sets her pall of watery shadow upon the earth, each time the fiery stars leap up, there in a dream my father's troubled ghost comes in warning, comes to appal.'

Chaucer, in a different context, has:

'Certes', quod he, 'this night my fadres gost
Hath in my sleep so sore me tormented,
And eek Mercurie his message hath presented,
That nedes to the conquest of Itaile
My destinee is sone for to saile;
For which, me thinketh, brosten is myn herte!'

Aeneas now shows another mood; he leaves his arid logic, and rises to his true height. He loves Dido, but he is shocked at himself, and that shock now finds expression in his deep

awe at the supernatural warnings sent him; he has outraged
pietas towards his father, his son, and the gods alike: how
else then can he act but to flee temptation?

351. **me patris**: another effective juxtaposition. Mackail suggests that the true meaning of such ghostly visitations (see
note on 346) only took shape with Mercury's appearance.
There seems a reference to them in vi. 694 ff., where Anchises
and Aeneas meet in the *laeti loci* of the Underworld: '"quam
metui ne quid Libyae tibi regna nocerent!"/ ille autem: "tua
me, genitor, tua tristis imago/ saepius occurrens haec limina
tendere adegit"'.

353. **in somnis**: 'in a dream', the normal expression in prose
and verse; Virgil has *in somnis* seven times, Lucretius four-
teen times, and neither uses *in somno*: see Löfstedt, *Synt.* i,
pp. 55 ff. for a detailed discussion (so in Greek, ἐν ὕπνοις is
regular, but ἐν ὕπνῳ rare). The varied vowel-sounds of these
three lines are notable; observe further the repeated *u*-
sound, and the subtly interwoven alliteration of *s* and *t*; the
effect is mysterious and uncanny. The double *quotiens* (like
Italiam above) shows how inescapable it all is.

354. **Ascanius**: i.e. the thought of him (sc. *admonet*); cf. i. 662
'urit atrox Iuno', xii. 895 'di me terrent et Iuppiter hostis',
examples which suggest that here it is not simply 'the
thought of Ascanius' but 'the thought of Ascanius and his
rights as a son (*puer*)' that Aeneas means. It is clear that he
has been turning over the problem himself before Mercury
spoke of it (274).

   capitisque . . . cari: 'and the wrong I do to so beloved a
head' (explanatory of *puer Ascanius*). English would use
'soul' rather than 'head'; *caput* is used in such expressions
for the most vital part of a person (cf. 613 'infandum caput',
and the *lepidum caput, festivum caput* of comedy, e.g. Ter.
Ad. 261, Plaut. *Mil.* 725; see *Thes. L. L.* s.v., col. 404. 63 ff.).
So Horace, addressing Virgil on the loss of his friend Varus,
writes (*C.* i. 24. 1–2) 'quis desiderio sit pudor aut modus/ tam
cari capitis?', and Antigone addresses Ismene (Soph. *Ant.* 1)
ὦ κοινὸν αὐτάδελφον Ἰσμήνης κάρα.

355. **Hesperiae**: 'the Western Land', i.e. Italy; Horace has it of
Spain (*C.* i. 36. 4), and Lucan uses *Hesperius* for 'Spanish'
(e.g. i. 555). Note the two strong elisions in the line, suggestive of Aeneas' emotions.

   et . . . arvis: 'the lands, I mean, that are his by destiny'; *et*
appends an explanation of *regno Hesperiae*. *Fatalis* is not the
English 'fatal', but 'fateful', 'fated'.

356. **interpres**: 'messenger', literally an 'agent' or 'go-between'
(ἑρμηνεύς); cf. 608 below, and x. 175 'tertius ille hominum

divumque interpres Asilas', where see Page. Note the adaptation of 268 ff.

357. utrumque caput: a common accusative in adjurations. Servius gives three explanations of *utrumque*, 'meum et tuum', 'Iovis et Mercurii', 'meum et Ascanii'. The first seems most natural; it is only reasonable to take the parenthesis as referring to the speaker and the person spoken to. Mackail objects that this is 'feeble', and suggests that Virgil means Anchises and Ascanius, a curious view since Aeneas is now not speaking of either. Aeneas means that his dreams were terrifying enough, but the culminating apparition of Mercury is almost unbelievable—yet it has happened, and he says, 'I swear it, by your head and my head.'

358 f. ipse ... hausi: 'yes, with my own eyes, in bright light, I saw the god as he came within these walls, with my own ears I drank in his words.' It is no fantasy, and there is only one answer to it. *Lumine* here may of course mean 'daylight'; but it may mean the divine effulgence accompanying the god; cf. iii. 151 (Aeneas' vision of the Penates) 'in somnis multo manifesti lumine', and see Warde Fowler, *The Death of Turnus*, pp. 84 f.

360 f. desine ... sequor: 'have done with burning both our hearts with your sad appeals: to Italy, but not of my free will, I go.'

At last Aeneas' tortured emotions get the better of him. As a servant of duty he must be cold, as a man he is on fire; his mind pulls him one way, his body another, and he cannot bear it; Dido is making things worse for both of them (for *meque ... teque* see note on 83). And so, at the last, he tells her the truth: he does not want to go, he knows he is betraying her, he would even betray the gods, and either way he will sin. In their own way, these lines are as despairing an appeal for pity as any words of Dido's. Marlowe well pictures the physical temptation that beset Aeneas:

> Yet Dido casts her eyes, like anchors, out,
> To stay my fleet from loosing forth the bay . . .
> . . . I fain would go, yet beauty calls me back;
> To leave her so, and not once say farewell,
> Were to transgress against all laws of love.
> But, if I use such ceremonious thanks
> As parting friends accustom on the shore,
> Her silver arms will coil me round about,
> And tears of pearl cry 'Stay, Aeneas, stay!'
> Each word she says will then contain a crown,
> And every speech be ended with a kiss:
> I may not dure this female drudgery:
> To sea, Aeneas! Find out Italy!

361. 'This unfinished line nobody, I suppose, would wish to see completed' (Irvine); see on 44. For *sequor*, 'to make for', cf. 381, v. 629 (again with *Italiam*).

These are Aeneas' last words to Dido: could she not understand his agony? And yet, did he understand her? When he meets her in the *lugentes campi*, he says 'nec credere quivi/ hunc tantum tibi me discessu ferre dolorem' (vi. 463 f.). The utter dissimilarity of their characters is an integral part of the tragedy.

362–92. *Dido turns in fury on him : he is hard and cruel and knows no pity ; heaven has forgotten justice ; she gave him help in his need, and this is her reward. 'Take your course to Italy, and I pray that you may be wrecked in mid-sea; and my ghost shall haunt you always.' She flings herself from him, and her maidservants take her, in a faint, tenderly to her chamber.*

362. iamdudum: cf. 1, where it is love, not anger that has been coming upon her 'all this time'. From Aeneas' very first words, Dido knew that she had failed in her appeal to his love and pity; and 'all the time of his speaking she has been looking on him askance'. For like words used in a very different context cf. viii. 152 f. 'dixerat Aeneas. ille os oculosque loquentis/ iamdudum et totum lustrabat lumine corpus'.

aversa: so, at their last meeting (vi. 469) 'illa solo fixos oculos aversa tenebat'; cf. Arnold, *The Scholar Gypsy*, 'Averse, as Dido did with gesture stern/ From her false friend's reproach in Hades turn,/ Wave us away, and keep thy solitude'.

363 f. huc illuc . . . profatur: 'this way, that way she darts her eyes, she stares him up and down with speechless look, and then she flares up and speaks her mind so.' Virgil's picture is clear and dramatic: her eyes 'keep the secret' (*tacitis*) of her anger till he has finished, and then, untouched by an appeal that she has not understood, *accensa profatur*.

363. volvens oculos: whereas Aeneas *immota tenebat lumina*. 'Rolling' has associations in English which often make it unsuitable in a translation; cf. vii. 251 'intentos volvens oculos', of Latinus, xii. 939 'Aeneas volvens oculos', x. 446 f. 'miratus stupet in Turno corpusque per ingens/ lumina volvit': the predominating sense is 'restlessness'.

365 ff. This is the speech which Charles James Fox said was 'on the whole, perhaps the finest thing in all poetry'. He compared it with Medea's speech in Apollonius Rhodius (iv. 355 ff.), but the resemblance is really superficial only. In Apollonius the speech has no such dramatic setting as this, and there is no such contrast as there is here between Dido's stormy violence and the dreadful chill of Aeneas. Virgil is

closer to Euripides (*Med.* 465 ff.), but there are similar
fundamental differences, stemming from the quite different
characters of the Euripidean tragedy. Jason is shabby and
shallow, Medea is a murderess and a witch (see D. L. Page's
analysis in his edition, pp. xiv ff.). But Dido is a human
woman, still in love for all her anger, and never far from tears,
confronting a human man who is caught in an impossible
dilemma. Her speech is no second-hand adaptation of a
Greek model; it is Virgil's own creation. Her changing
moods are shown as vividly as before: she bursts out angrily,
in mid-thought and mid-phrase, with no preliminaries; but
after three lines she speaks as if Aeneas were not with her,
she is alone with her thoughts as she goes over what he has
said, then suddenly (380) she turns on him again; but the
effort is too much, and her heart is too full, and she faints as
she leaves him.

Dryden begins:

> False as thou art, and more than false, forsworn,
> Not sprung from noble blood, nor goddess born,
> But hewn from hardened entrails of a rock;
> And rough Hyrcanian tigers gave thee suck.
> Why shou'd I fawn, what have I worse to fear?
> Did he once look, or lent a list'ning ear;
> Sigh'd when I sob'd, or shed one kindly tear?;

contrast the fifteenth-century Scots translator, Gavin Douglas,
Bishop of Dunkeld:

> Nouthir was ane goddes thy moder as is said
> Nor yit King Dardanus cheif stok of thy kyn,
> Thow treules wicht, bot of ane cauld hard quhyn
> The clekkit that horribil mont Cawcasus hat.
> Thow schowkit neuir womannis breist, wele I wat,
> Bot of sum cruell tygere of Araby
> The pawpis the fosterit, in the wod hircany.

365. nec . . . auctor: 'no, you had no goddess for mother, no
Dardanus began your line'; the second *nec* is postponed, as in
33. Note the hard initial consonants of this and the next
line, and the vowel-sounds of 367.

auctor: this always implies 'responsibility' in varying
forms (see Nettleship, *Contributions to Latin Lexicography*,
s.v.); cf. vii. 49 'tu sanguinis ultimus auctor', Cic. *Leg. Agr.*
ii. 100 'nulli me vobis auctores generis mei commendarunt'.

366 f. duris . . . tigres: the literary ancestor of this rhetorical
conceit is Patroclus' speech to Achilles, *Il.* xvi. 33 ff., νηλέες,
οὐκ ἄρα σοί γε πατὴρ ἦν ἱππότα Πηλεύς, / οὐδὲ Θέτις μήτηρ· γλαυκὴ δέ
σε τίκτε θάλασσα, / πέτραι τ' ἠλίβατοι, etc.

The discussion of the passage in Macrobius, *Sat.* v. 11. 14, should be consulted as a typical example of the pedantic interests of fourth-century scholarship. The 'literary allusions' add colour to a bare statement; Virgil uses names of places in the mysterious North to express coldness and cruelty, just as in *G.* iv. 517 f. Orpheus wanders over 'the ice that lies beyond the North Wind, and the snow-bound Don'. The passage has many parallels, both in Greek and in Latin (see Pease's monumental note on 366); typical examples, on either side of Virgil, are Catull. 64. 154 ff. (Ariadne to the absent Theseus) 'quaenam te genuit sola sub rupe leaena,/ quod mare conceptum spumantibus exspuit undis,/ quae Syrtis, quae Scylla rapax, quae vasta Charybdis?', and Ovid, *Met.* vii. 32-33 (Medea to Jason) 'hoc ego si patiar, tum me de tigride natam,/ tum ferrum et scopulos gestare in corde fatebor': the former in its *naïveté*, the latter in its ingenuity, well illustrate what the Virgilian manner is and what it is not. Pease compares Tasso, *Gerusalemme Liberata* xvi. 56. 2 ff. 'te l'onda insana/ del mar produsse e 'l Caucaso gelato,/ e le mamme allattar di tigre ircana', etc.

horrens: to be taken closely with *duris cautibus*, the whole forming a kind of complex epithet ('beetling-flinty-cliffed').

367. Hyrcanaeque . . . tigres: Hyrcania was near the Caspian sea. Shakespeare was attracted by these tigers; see *Hamlet* ii. 2. 472, *Macbeth* iii. 4. 101, *3 Henry VI* i. 4. 153 'But you are more inhuman, more inexorable—O ten times more—than tigers of Hyrcania'; Milton speaks of 'the Hyrcanian cliffs of Caucasus' (*PR* iii. 317). Pease has a helpful note on ancient tigers.

admorunt: contracted from *admoverunt*, which would be a lumbering word for a hexameter; cf. *implessem, exstinxem*, 605-6.

368. nam . . . reservo?: 'for need I make pretence? Need I keep myself for worse blows?' Dido breaks off, to justify her anger with self-argument. *Nam* is used with questions, like γάρ, in lively or emotional conversation (e.g. *G.* iv. 445 'nam quis te, iuvenum confidentissime . . .?', *A.* ii. 373 f. 'festinate, viri! nam quae tam sera moratur/ segnities?'); the conversational origin of the use is clear from its frequency in Plautus and in such passages as Hor. *Epp.* i. 1. 76, i. 2. 37. The vivid indicative is used instead of the normal deliberative subjunctive, again colloquial; cf. iii. 367 'quae prima pericula vito?'

me: note the elided monosyllable; cf. 540, and see note on 570.

ad maiora: 'ad maiores scilicet iniurias' is the comment of Servius.

369 f. num fletu . . . amantem est?: 'when I wept, did he give any sigh? Turn his glance? Was he won, did he shed tears, was he sorry for me when I loved him so?' Dido continues her soliloquy (see Page's good note): she can hardly believe what she has heard and seen. The compound *ingemuit* implies momentary [action (cf. *intonare*, of a thunder-clap, *inlacrimare*, to burst into tears); *fletu* may be dative, though it could be an ablative of accompanying cause; forms in *-ui* are inconvenient for the hexameter, and datives in *-u* are quite frequent in Augustan poetry and in the prose of Caesar, Livy, Tacitus.

371. quae . . . anteferam? both *quae* and *quibus* are interrogative ('what first, what last'; *quid prius, quid posterius dicam* is Servius' comment): nothing matters now, one thing is no better than another.

   iam iam: cf. ii. 701 'iam iam nulla mora est'; the repetition gives an added urgency. Juno, her alleged protectress, and Jupiter (*Saturnius pater*) have forgotten all justice.

372. haec: 'all this', all that she is going through. The rhythm is unusual: the end of the second foot rarely coincides with the end of a word, because a caesura in the third foot can only be obtained, as here, by a following monosyllable, which causes a jerky effect avoided by Virgil, or by a line like 316 (see note there).

   aequis: the adjective is stressed by its unusual position (see note on 97); cf. *quietos*, 379, and ix. 209 'Iuppiter aut quicumque oculis haec aspicit aequis'.

373 ff. Heyne comments on these lines 'divina plane haec, sententiarum et verborum gravitate'; cf. Eur. *Med.* 476 ff.

373. nusquam . . . fides: 'nowhere can I safely put my trust.'

   eiectum . . . egentem: 'a stranded waif, destitute'; note the asyndeton, as her emotion rises (so too 375); *litore* is a local ablative, as in vi. 901 'stant litore puppes'; *eiectus* is often used of shipwrecked persons (e.g. Ter. *Andr*. 923 'Atticus quidam olim navi fracta ad Andrum eiectus est'), just as Dido herself had used it before when she felt pity for Aeneas, not scorn as now, sending a search-party to look for him, unknowing that he was really safe and near her (i. 576 ff. 'equidem per litora certos/ dimittam . . . / si quibus eiectus silvis aut urbibus errat'). Dido's egoism is clear here: what first strikes her in her misery is the blow to her pride; it is her own kindness to Aeneas that she casts up against him, just as in 320 ff. it is her own loss of self-respect that she stresses.

Her manner here to him is that of Iarbas towards herself (211 ff.).

375. Mackail notes the balance achieved by the assonance *amissam . . . a morte.*

376. **heu . . . feror**: cf. 110 'fatis incerta feror', and note.

nunc: this is the first of three stabbing gibes, as she flings back his 'authorities' at him. Here she begins to turn towards Aeneas again, but she does not address him directly till 380.

377. Dido repeats Aeneas' words of 356 (note the skilful adaptation and rearrangement), but in such a tone as to suggest that what he has said never really happened.

378. **horrida iussa**: 'orders at which he shivers' (cf. 280).

379 f. **scilicet . . . sollicitat**: 'Indeed! So the gods above are troubled about *this*! *This* worries and disturbs their calm!' *Scilicet* is ironical, as if a truth had suddenly been revealed; *is labor, ea cura*, by a common idiom, stand for *labor, cura de ea re.* Dido does not believe in Aeneas' divine mission: as if the quiet gods should be concerned for such things! Yet once she was ready enough to be convinced by a similar argument on Anna's lips (34 'id cinerem aut manis credis curare sepultos?'). She is made an Epicurean for the moment ('anachronistically', Pease solemnly remarks), picturing the gods as living in ἀταραξία, *placida cum pace quieti* (Lucr. vi. 73), and their calm tranquillity forms a fine contrast with her own raging passions. Note the emphasis thrown on *quietos* by its position.

380. **sollicitat**: the run-on is effective; Dido pauses, and then ends her soliloquizing, addressing Aeneas as abruptly as at the beginning of her speech.

refello: she will not chop logic with him, as he has done with her.

381. **i . . . undas**: 'go, seek your Italy on your winds, look for your realm over your sea.' *I* is scornful, as in *i nunc.* Should the pause follow *Italiam*, or *ventis*? The text as printed is in agreement with Quintilian, who quotes the words *i, sequere Italiam ventis* as a unit (ix. 2. 49), and this gives good symmetry, with effective emphasis on the two imperatives. The reader must make his own decision; but Quintilian probably knew what he was talking about.

382. **si . . . possunt**: 'if the powers of righteousness are of any avail.'

Pia is a bitter sneer; true *pietas*, as understood by heaven, will not be Aeneas' sort, but will punish villainy as it deserves. Again there is a poignant echo of happier days; see i. 603, where Aeneas says to Dido at their·first meeting 'di

tibi, si qua pios respectant numina, si quid/ usquam iustitia
est et mens sibi conscia recti,/ praemia digna ferant'. Page
has a good note on *pietas* at i. 10 (but he sadly misunderstood
pius in 393 below).

383. supplicia hausurum: 'that you will drain the full cup of
punishment'; Pease quotes a striking passage from Cowley's
Davideis (i. 16), 'I drove proud Pharaoh to the parted sea;/
He, and his host drank up cold death by Me'. Note the omission of *te* (as in 493, where *me* is omitted). This usage belongs
to good Latin of all periods, originating in colloquial speech,
as its frequent occurrence in Comedy and in Cicero's *Letters*
shows, although it is not confined to conversational style.
It occurs when the pronoun needs no stressing and can be
easily supplied; cf. ii. 432 f. 'testor, in occasu vestro nec tela
nec ullas/ vitavisse vices' (sc. *me*), Plaut. *Ps.* 565 'neque sim
facturus quod facturum dixeram' (sc. *me*), id. *Truc.* 204
'nondum advenisse miror' (sc. *eum*), Cic. *RA* 61 'confitere
huc ea spe venisse' (sc. *te*), Catull. 36. 4 ff. 'vovit . . . electis-
sima pessimi poetae/ scripta tardipedi deo daturam' (sc. *se*);
see my note on Cic. *Cael.* 58.

  Dido: this might be a Greek accusative form, but is more
probably a vocative; cf. *E.* vi. 44 'ut litus Hyla Hyla omne
sonaret', Prop. i. 18. 31 'resonent mihi Cynthia silvae'.
Mackail points out (on 335) that Virgil never uses an inflected
form of Dido's name. (In Ovid, *Her.* 7. 133 Palmer reads the
accusative form *Didon*.)

384 ff. sequar . . . adero: 'with dark flames I shall pursue you,
though I shall be far from you, and when icy Death has
sundered my body from its spirit, I shall be there, my ghost
shall be there, everywhere.'

  Dryden translates:

> Then shalt thou call on injur'd Dido's name;
> Dido shall come, in a black sulph'ry flame;
> When death has once dissolv'd her mortal frame,
> Shall smile to see the traitor vainly weep,
> Her hungry ghost arising from the deep,
> Shall haunt thee waking, and disturb thy sleep;

  Jodelle makes Dido say:

> . . . et, mesmes en mourant,
> Mon nom entre tes dents on t'orra murmurant,
> Nommant Didon, Didon, et lors, tousjours presente,
> D'un brandon infernal, d'une tenaille ardente,
> Comme si de Megère on m'avoit fait la soeur,
> J'engraveray ton tort dans ton parjure coeur.

Note the hissing sounds of Dido's words, and the slow deliberate rhythm: the ictus coincides with the word-accent (*sequar/ átris/ ígnibus/ábsens // ét cum/ frígida/ mórs* ...), more often than is normal, because here so few of the words spill over from one foot to another; cf. the solemn line vi. 127 *nóctes/ átque dies patet/ átri/ iánua/ Dítis.* The opening rhythm of 385 resembles that of 372 ('nec Saturnius haec ...'); but there *haec* is less closely attached to the preceding words than *mors* is here, and belongs rather in sense to what follows, whereas *mors* is isolated from what follows and so stands out sharply before the caesura. Note too the interpolation of *umbra* between *omnibus* and *locis*, natural but very effective.

Dido will haunt Aeneas like a Fury, just as Orestes was haunted and maddened by the mother whom he had killed, or just as Nero suffered (Sueton. *Nero* 34. 4 'confessus exagitari se materna specie verberibusque Furiarum ac taedis ardentibus', Stat. *S.* ii. 7. 118 f. 'pallidumque visa/ matris lampade respicis Neronem'); cf. ps.-Quintil. *Decl. mai.* x. 19 'nec tu, marite, nec tu timueris, ne ultricis umbrae vanis exagitere terroribus' (a theme concerning a *sepulcrum incantatum*), and *Decl. min.* 314 (p. 236 Ritter) 'sunt illa vera, quae extremo miseri spiritu dicebantur, "dabis mihi, scelerate, poenas; persequar quandoque et occurram"'. But any sensitive reader, as Servius saw, will think of the smoke blowing over the breakers from Dido's pyre (cf. v. 4), although she herself cannot have meant this. Editors have laboured much to explain the exact significance of Dido's threat (see Pease, ad loc., and Henry's long discussion): but is not mystery a prerogative of prophecy, and is not Virgil a poet?

386. **improbe**: the basic sense of this adjective is persistent lack of regard for others in going beyond the bounds of what is fair and right. So Virgil uses it of a greedy goose (*G.* i. 119), spoiling the farmer's work, of a snake (*G.* iii. 431), of a cruel eagle (*A.* xii. 250), of a wolf (*A.* ii. 356). The farmer's toil, remorseless as it is, is *improbus* (*G.* i. 146), the *cornix*, calling insistently for rain, is *improba* (*G.* i. 388); love is *improbus*, 'relentless' (412 below). A lion's slavering mouth is *improba* (x. 727). An avalanche of rocks, inexorably crushing everything in its path, is *mons improbus* (xii. 687). Aeneas is *improbus* in Turnus' eyes, as he ruthlessly hunts down the Rutulians (xi. 512, cf. xii. 261); Arruns, implacably hounding Camilla to her death, 'certam quatit improbus hastam' (xi. 767). In v. 397, the boxer Dares is termed *improbus* by an older man: the word sums up his greed for a prize without having to fight for it, his cruel pride in sheer strength, and the blustering caddishness which makes him frightened to fight when he sees what his challenge has to meet. Here, *improbe*

is something like 'heartless brute', though such a translation may shock traditionalists: in Dido's eyes, Aeneas has been completely selfish, and cruel in his selfishness.

See Henry and Page on ii. 356; Royds, *The Beasts, Birds and Bees of Virgil*, p. 35.

387. audiam: the elision of the final syllable of a cretic word (–∪–) is the only way in which a word of this pattern can be used in a hexameter, and it is very rarely found in Virgil (see on 684). Editors have again been worried by the 'illogicality' by which Dido is made to hear in her grave what her ghost is doing, and drastic rearrangements or omissions have been proposed (see Ribbeck, and the discussions of Henry and Pease). Virgil's imaginative picture deserves less frigid treatment.

fama: cf. Ovid, *Met*. xiv. 726 ff. 'nec tibi fama mei ventura est nuntia leti;/ ipse ego, ne dubites, adero praesensque videbor,/ corpore ut exanimi crudelia lumina pascas': Norden infers (on vi. 456 f.) that both Virgil and Ovid are following an Alexandrian tradition.

388 f. his . . . aufert: 'in mid-speech she breaks off her answer, flees in misery from the air of day, wrenches and sweeps herself away from his sight'; note the piling-up of words to show Dido's anger, grief, and scorn. The elision in *sermonem abrumpit* is a metrical picture of her action, and the rhythm of 389, with its onward rush to the fourth-foot caesura, further illustrates it.

390. Page well suggests that the line shows a 'stammering iteration'. But the fear that besets Aeneas is fear of himself; his logic is beginning to desert him, and he is fighting desperately against temptation.

parantem: M reads *volentem*; but *parantem* is far more graphic, and the alternative has no doubt come from *G*. iv. 501 f. and *A*. ii. 790 f. Both these passages depict an irrevocable parting in similar manner, the one when Orpheus loses his half-regained Eurydice, the other when Aeneas sees Creusa's ghost intangibly vanish into the unknown. In both there are words that can never now be spoken, upon the lips of a man who is left grieving for a lost and dear woman: can we really doubt that it was Aeneas' love that made him afraid here?

391. dicere: the run-on, and the pause, is characteristic and effective.

famulae: Virgil has *serva* twice only (v. 284, ix. 546), and never *servus*; he does not say in so many words that Dido faints, but *suscipiunt* lets us imagine it, and *conlapsaque membra* gives us the picture of what we have imagined; he

has the same technique in viii. 583 f. (Evander's farewell to
Pallas) 'haec genitor digressu dicta supremo/ fundebat:
famuli conlapsum in tecta ferebant'.

392. marmoreo . . . reponunt: 'they carry back her huddled
form to her marbled chamber, and set her tenderly upon a
couch.' Virgil has the epithet *marmoreus* elsewhere only of
a statue (*E.* vii. 35), of the sea (*A.* vi. 729), and of the dead
Orpheus (*G.* iv. 523); here, as Pease remarks, it presumably
refers to the beautiful African marbles which are so often
mentioned by the poets; but it is curiously otiose. The
dative *thalamo* is Virgil's favourite use, for *in* + accusative.
Page has a useful note at iii. 170 on the type of compound
represented by *reponunt* here ('duly place').

From now onwards Dido never leaves her palace again, and
this is the last memory that Aeneas ever had of her: he knew
that he had broken her heart, but he did not know that he
was to bring her death. In vi. 458, at their meeting in the
Underworld, he asks 'funeris heu tibi causa fui?', 'was it
death then that I brought you?', and in v. 5 he is shown as not
knowing the cause of the flames that rolled upwards from
Dido's pyre: a strange, remote insensitiveness, that surely
increased his ultimate misery.

393–415. *But Aeneas puts duty before desire, and he and his men
make the fleet ready to sail. All is bustle and excitement. But
Dido is in despair, and seeks to make a new attempt to touch
Aeneas' heart.*

393. at pius Aeneas: the words mark the crisis of the whole
book: they are of deep significance, and instinct with emotion.
'Virgil seems unmoved by his own genius, and begins the
next paragraph quite placidly *at pius Aeneas*!'—so Page, in
words that 'every schoolboy knows' and has echoed in examination answers for sixty years, words that are unjust and
quite misleading.

Virgil has not used this epithet of Aeneas before in this book:
the last occasion of its use was in i. 378, where Aeneas introduces himself to the unknown goddess who was, in fact, his
own mother, in the famous words *sum pius Aeneas*. If we
ask why Virgil has chosen to use it here, the answer is to be
found by looking at other places where it occurs.

It is used in i. 220, after the shipwreck; in i. 305, when
Aeneas goes out to explore the unknown land of Africa; in
v. 26, at a crisis in the voyage from Carthage, when owing to
a storm Palinurus proposes to turn the ship's course to Sicily,
and Aeneas is glad, because there his father lies buried; in
vi. 9, when Aeneas goes to find the Sibyl's cave; in vi. 176, as

he obeys the Sibyl's order to bury Misenus, and later (232) at the actual funeral; in vii. 5, after the burial of his old nurse Caieta. In all these passages we see Aeneas either bracing himself for some new ordeal, or doing some act of devotion to one whom he has loved, or simply with the thought of loved ones in his mind. Other passages show him as *pius* when he offers up a prayer: v. 685, at the crisis of the burning of the ships; viii. 84, in sacrifice to Juno; xii. 175, at the solemn pact with Latinus. In xii. 311 he is *pius* as he rallies his men at a crisis in the fighting, with an appeal to good faith (see Warde Fowler, ad loc.).

Another group of passages shows the epithet in a more complex setting. In x. 591 Aeneas is *pius* as he gibes at Lucagus, thrown from his chariot: in all this part of the fighting, his dominant emotion is misery at the death of Evander's son Pallas and his desire to avenge him, and in that context he / seems to feel that he is making atonement in some measure by cruelly killing an opponent. In x. 783 *pius Aeneas* is shown attacking Mezentius, the notorious *contemptor divum* (vii. 648), a byword for hideous cruelty (viii. 481 ff.). There is a revealing passage at x. 826: Aeneas stands over the body of the young Lausus, Mezentius' son, whom he has just killed, and into his mind there comes *patriae pietatis imago* (824), and he cries 'quid pius Aeneas tanta dabit indole dignum?' Here, *pius* contains not only his feeling that his own loyalties have been satisfied by the death of an enemy, but, much more, his sense of compassion ('it might have been my own son', he thinks) for one who had met death while coming to the aid of his own father: and the two opposing emotions unite in protest, as it were, at the mysterious inevitability of a pain that he has himself inflicted and cannot comprehend— he has done his duty, but it has brought him no happiness.

Pius, then, is a complex word, a sensitive symbol of adherence to a personal ideal of devotion, which may nevertheless bring pain and sorrow. Virgil never uses it lightly; and in this line it is neither perfunctory nor unintelligent. It is used here in the greatest crisis of Aeneas' life, as he braces himself to meet it and to win his victory; it means that he has been true to himself and done his duty at a dreadful cost; it is as if he has said, 'Get thee behind me, Satan.' The path of desire would have been so much easier and so much more comforting; *iussa tamen divum exsequitur* (396). The words *at pius Aeneas* here contain the same kind of protest as that of x. 826; a like protest to that which may be discerned, as W. B. Anderson points out (*CR* xliv, 1930, p. 4), in Aeneas' words at i. 378, where 'sum pius Aeneas' is 'not a

piece of smug complacency' but 'a poignant cry wrung from
a tortured heart'. In its own way, the *tamen* of 396 is as
moving as that other *tamen* spoken by Dido (329). In *at pius
Aeneas* here there is nothing 'placid', no 'glaring inconsistency' as Page supposed: the epithet is eloquent of struggle
and bewilderment and submission.

One of the difficulties in understanding Aeneas is Virgil's
very reticence. Dido is an open book: Aeneas we see only in
half-glances, half-revelations, such as *dulcis terras* (281),
optima Dido (291); here is another such glance, and all his
misery is there for us to pity. Heinze (op. cit., p. 123, note)
saw much that many have not seen.

Henry's long note on *pietas* at i. 14 is rewarding; and it
should be read with Warde Fowler to accompany it (*The
Death of Turnus*, pp. 146 ff.).

393 ff. at . . . revisit: 'but Aeneas recognized his duty. He
longed to comfort her and assuage her bitterness, to speak
and turn aside her misery; he gave many a sigh, and his
resolve was shaken by passionate love: but in spite of it all
he did as the gods had bidden, and went back again to his
ships.'

393. dolentem: so *dolor* is often better translated 'resentment'
than 'pain'.

394. solando: this is what his *pietas* would have him do—for one
aspect of *pietas* is tenderness to those we love—but he cannot.

395. multa gemens: *What a sigh is there! The heart is sorely
charged.*

animum: accusative of 'respect' after the passive participle
labefactus (cf. 217, and contrast 137).

396. classemque revisit: Aeneas goes back to the preparations
spoken of in 290. A less great poet might have shown his
further thoughts; Virgil characteristically allows the almost
mechanical act to help us to imagine them; cf. vi. 899 'ille
viam secat ad navis sociosque revisit' (after Aeneas' return
from the Underworld): Mackail comments 'here too, though
through no ivory gate, Aeneas returns to the task of life from
the interlude of a dream-Paradise'. Similarly, in ii. 804,
after the unbearable climax of the last hours of Troy, after
Aeneas has seen Creusa's ghost, and as he starts his preparation to cross the sea to an unknown home, Virgil ends with
moving simplicity 'cessi, et sublato montis genitore petivi'.

The following passage brings a very slight relaxation of
tension.

397 f. tum . . . navis: the heavy spondees show the ships being
dragged and shoved to the water's edge, and then the spondaic rhythm ends, and 'natat uncta carina'. The Trojans 'go

to it' (*incumbunt*—they work, in fact, like Trojans): the constant clash of ictus and accent marks their effort. The ships are *celsae* because of their high sterns; but the epithet is conventional, as in 554, i. 183, ii. 375, iii. 527, viii. 107, x. 261, and Virgil has it much like *Karthaginis altae* (97, where see note). *Litore toto* may be ablative after *deducunt* ('from the whole shore') or a local ablative ('all along the shore').

398. uncta carina: 'the pitchy hull'; *carina* is often used for 'ship', and *uncta* refers to the pitch on the timbers; Virgil has remembered an old phrase from Ennius (*Ann.* 478 V.) 'labitur uncta carina per aequora cana celocis'.

399. frondentis . . . remos: 'oars still sprouting leaves', tree-trunks to be made into oars (cf. *pinus*, of a ship). The words are explained by the appended *et robora . . . infabricata*, 'timber as yet unfashioned'. In their hurry to be off, the Trojans do not wait to have their oars shaped ready; presumably Virgil means a spare stock of oars, which they could prepare for emergencies during the voyage.

400. The unfinished line happens, by sheer accident, to be effective in its context (cf. note on 44). It clearly shows an incomplete passage, especially when taken in conjunction with the simile that follows, which is introduced by *ac velut* and then not completed by a *sic* clause; cf. ii. 623 ff., where an unfinished line is also followed by an uncompleted simile: see Mackail's note, and Sparrow, op. cit., p. 32. But here there is perhaps a further sign of accidental incompleteness, not deliberate effect: *fugae studio* forms a single rhythmic unit, cut off by the sense from *infabricata*, resulting in a singularly jerky effect, which could not have been cured even if the line were completed (the grouping *infabricata/ fugae studio/* would not easily lend itself to a rhythmic completion). I suspect that *fugae studio* is a mere jotting, to show the sense of what was needed to complete the line begun with *infabricata*.

401. migrantis . . . ruentis: 'you could descry them trekking and bustling along from every part of the city'; the vivid present subjunctive puts the distant scene actually before the reader's eyes as it happens. Mackail observes that this line could be transposed to follow 407, thus completing the simile, but that as the passage is in any case incomplete it had better be left where it is.

402. ac velut: *ac* cannot be translated, since it has no clause to complete it (see note on 400). Virgil uses *velut*, not *veluti*, before a vowel, as Wagner points out. See Norden on vi. 707 ff. for a suggestion that the combination *ac velut* has an archaic touch about it. In this graphic simile the Virgil of the *Georgics* is very plain to see; cf. *G.* i. 185 f. 'populatque ingentem farris acervum/ curculio atque inopi metuens formica senectae'. Pease remarks that it is 'probably suggested' by Apollonius Rhodius iv. 1452 ff.: but are we to allow the country-bred Virgil no observation?

403. hiemis memores: cf. *Proverbs* vi. 7–8 '[the ant] which having no guide, overseer, or ruler provideth her meat in the summer, and gathereth her food in the harvest', and Milton's 'parsimonious emmet, provident/ Of future, in small room large heart enclosed' (*PL* vii. 485). Royds points out (*The Beasts, Birds and Bees of Virgil*, p. 30) that grain-storing ants are peculiar to Mediterranean countries.

reponunt: a curious echo of 392, where the verb has the same content of care, but is used in so different a context. Cf. xii. 167 'sidereo flagrans clipeo' . . . 171 'admovitque pecus flagrantibus aris'; see Mackail, p. lxxx.

404 ff. it . . . fervet: 'across the fields tramps the black line, and over the grass they cart their spoils in a narrow lane: some heave and push with their shoulders at the monster grains; others dress the ranks, reproving the sluggard; the whole path is a seething, labouring mass.'

Servius records that the words *it nigrum campis agmen* were used of elephants by Ennius and of Indians by Accius, unfortunately without giving any contexts. Virgil's ants plod along with vivid determination; cf. *The Return of the Native*, p. 358 (Wessex edition), 'In front of her a colony of ants had established a thoroughfare across the way, where they toiled a never-ending and heavy-laden throng', etc.; Virgil and Hardy share much understanding. Pease quotes a critic who finds the short word *it* 'appropriate to the short legs of the ants', and comments seriously 'but this would not explain why the hemistich had been previously used of *Indi* and of elephants': fortunately Catullus' sparrow has not yet had its legs measured.

Note the solid spondees, and the conspicuous clash of accent and ictus (404 and 405 have an exactly similar rhythm), marking the difficulty of the work (cf. 397 f.). Virgil's choice of words is instructive: *praedam* supports *populant* and suggests the picture in *G.* ii. 60 'turpis avibus praedam fert uva racemos'; *convectant* implies manual labour (cf. Tac. *H.* iii. 27. 2 'paulum inde morae, dum ex proximis agris ligones dolabras et alii falces scalasque convectant'), as well as a co-operative effort; *grandia, trudunt, obnixae, umeris* all show Virgil with a secret smile, as he smiles at his bees in *Georgic* IV.

405. convectant: for the plural verb following *agmen* (the use

with *pars* is more common) cf. ii. 63 f. 'Troiana iuventus/
circumfusa ruit certantque inludere capto'.

calle angusto: cf. Aristotle *HA* ix. 38 (622ᵇ25) ὡς ἀεὶ μίαν
ἀτραπὸν πάντες βαδίζουσι.

grandia: cf. *G*. iv. 26 'et grandia conice saxa' (the *saxa* are
to give the bees a resting-place in mid-stream, and would
seem *grandia* to them).

406. agmina cogunt: a military phrase; the ants are not
allowed to straggle: *castigantque moras* is a variation.

407. moras: not necessarily equivalent to *morantes*. Cf. Pliny,
NH xi. 25 'mira observatio operis: cessantium inertiam
notant, castigant, mox et puniunt morte' (of bees: Pliny on
the bee is fascinating).

fervet: so *fervet opus* of the bees in *G*. iv. 169. Note how the
slow spondees have lessened in this and the previous line.
Here, presumably, there is a gap where Virgil would have
completed the simile introduced above by *ac*.

408. The apostrophe is effective, but it is partly due to Virgil's
wish to avoid inflecting Dido's name.

409. dabas: the tense shows the frequency of her cries.

fervĕre : cf. 567; this alternative form for *fervēre*, as if from
a third conjugation verb (like *stridĕre, fulgĕre*), is of some
convenience metrically; such variant forms are very common in Lucretius (see Bailey's edition, vol. i, p. 85). It is
possible that *fervere* here, after *fervet* in 407, shows that the
passage did not receive a final revision; Mackail remarks on
the 'awkward' repetition of *cogis* and *cogitur* (412, 414), and
he might have added *cogunt* in 406. But the Romans were
not as sensitive as we are on such matters (see my notes on
Cic. *Cael*. 3 and Quintil. xii. 1. 41), and it is not safe to infer
too much from these repetitions.

410. arce ex summa: Wagner notes that *ex*, not *e*, is used before a consonant in Virgil when the preposition follows its
noun, or as in *E*. vi. 19 'ipsis ex vincula sertis' (hence he
would read *bello ex tanto* in ii. 718).

411. misceri: cf. 160. The sea is a mass of confusion and noise.

412. improbe: 'relentless' (see on 386). Mackail regards the
line as 'feeble', and takes it as another sign of unfinished
work. Certainly a second apostrophe, so soon after 408, is
odd; but the line is in its own way not out of place, as a sudden piece of subjectivity, leading up to Dido's change of
front in what follows.

413. precando: for *precibus*, parallel with *lacrimas* (cf. *solando
. . . dictis*, 394).

414. animos: 'proud spirit', as often in the plural (cf. Mackail
on i. 149); note the juxtaposition with *supplex*.

415. ne quid . . . relinquat: 'lest she leave anything untried, and face her death when she need not.' Servius remarks '*frustra ex iudicio poetae est*', i.e. that it is an interpolated thought of Virgil's own, that if Dido could have found a way to touch Aeneas' heart and had not taken it, 'her death would have been wasted effort'; Pease compares the *moritura puella* of *G.* iv. 458, 'where *moritura* reveals the reflection of the poet rather than the consciousness of Eurydice herself'. But Dido has not yet planned her suicide (as is clear from 432–3); she only knows that without Aeneas she must die (cf. note on 308): and it is not necessary to take *frustra moritura* as other than part of Dido's own thought. See Mackail on xi. 741, where *moriturus* clearly is part of Tarchon's thought, not Virgil's subjective comment: Mackail remarks that in ii. 408 *periturus* 'conveys both implications'.

416–36. '*Anna*', she cries, '*they are in haste to go : and I must bear it. But do this one thing for me. Go to him—he will listen to you—and beg him to wait for fair weather. All I ask now is time to learn my lesson of sorrow; and if he is kind, he shall have his reward.*'

There is no introductory line before Dido begins to speak; this is unusual, but the situation as shown in 413–15 makes reasonable enough preliminary.

416. properari: 'the bustle.' The impersonal verb takes the place of a noun. This impersonal use of a passive verb is the oldest function of the Latin passive voice. It is a feature of conversational language, as is clear from its use in Comedy; e.g. Plaut. *Truc.* 368 f. 'sed dic mihi, benene ambulatumst?', *Pseud.* 273 'quid agitur, Calidore?'—'amatur atque egetur acriter'; in such passages, the important thing is the action or process, with the agent clear but subordinated ('walking been jolly?', 'love-making and being hard up'). In Ter. *Andr.* 129 'in ignem impositast: fletur', the impersonal *fletur* leaves the agent purposely vague, as Donatus saw: the act of weeping is what matters, not who is weeping (cf. Catull. 39. 4 f. 'si ad pii rogum fili/ lugetur'). In Juvenal's famous description of a house on fire at Rome (iii. 200 f. 'nam si gradibus trepidatur ab imis,/ ultimus ardebit quem tegula sola tuetur'), the vague, anonymous hubbub downstairs is contrasted with the unsuspected danger to a specific person who has most to suffer.

This idiom of the spoken language was taken over by the poets, and Virgil is particularly fond of it. Here, *properari* implies the general bustle, contrasted with the more specific *convenere*; cf. *E.* i. 11 f. 'undique totis/ usque adeo turbatur agris', of the general chaos all round, *A*. xi. 468 'ilicet in muros tota discurritur urbe', Livy ii. 45. 11 'totis castris undique ad consules curritur'. Other Virgilian examples are i. 700, *discumbitur* (see Conway); vii. 553, *pugnatur*; x. 355, *certatur*; vi. 179, *itur* (following *festinant . . . certant*); ii. 634 'ubi iam patriae perventum ad limina sedis' ('my journey brought me', where Virgil could have written *perveni*; cf. 151 above); i. 272 'hic iam ter centum totos regnabitur annos' ('the kingdom shall endure', Conway). The use corresponds to the French use of *on* or the Italian use of *si*: English is far less fond of the idiom.

See L.–H., pp. 543, 623, and especially J. Wackernagel, *Vorlesungen über Syntax* (Basel, 1926), i, pp. 144 ff.

417. Note the rhythm: formally there is a strong caesura at *vocat*, but the sense-pause divides the line at *convenere*, resulting in a rhythm of the Homeric pattern (see note on 164). The repeated hard consonants suggest the noise of the scene.

418. **et**: postponed (see on 33). This line is repeated from *G*. i. 304, where it refers to the safe arrival of a ship in port. Here, the garlands presumably show the sailors' joy at leaving a port where they did not want to stay (cf. 295 'imperio laeti parent'). Sparrow (op. cit., p. 97) attacks its appropriateness, and would regard it as a *tibicen* or temporary stopgap. But it seems perfectly reasonable in its context; and it even adds point to Dido's grief, that Aeneas' men should be so glad to go.

419 f. **hunc . . . potero**: 'this misery—this dreadful misery—if I had the power to foresee it once, I shall even have the strength to bear it now, my sister.' For this use of *sperare* cf. 292, xi. 275 f. 'haec adeo ex illo mihi iam speranda fuerunt/ tempore'; Dido seems to refer to her misgivings mentioned in 296 ff. Page regards her pleas as 'obviously unreal'; but she still thinks that in some way she *can* endure her pain, she still loves Aeneas (429), and is still concerned for his safety (cf. 309); she still has one last hope, and it is not till this fails that she gives up completely (450).

420. **tamen**: in spite of her resolve to be brave, there is one thing that she would like Anna to do.

Note in this line the rare elision at the transition from the fourth to the fifth foot (*miserae hoc tamen unum*); so ii. 658 'patrio excidit ore', vi. 622 'pretio atque refixit', viii. 96 'placido aequore silvas': see Norden, *Aeneis VI*, Anh. XI, p. 455. Note further the unusual end-pattern *hoc tamen unum* (cf. *hos regit artus*, 336, where see note): such endings are even less common if a monosyllable does not precede the two disyllables, e.g. x. 400 'morae fuit Ilo', x. 440 'medium

secat agmen', xi. 170 'magni Phryges et quam', where the
effect is very much harsher—these occur only. in the books
which can be shown to be of later composition. In Lucretius
such a pattern is far more frequent. See Norden, *Aeneis VI*,
Anh. IX. 4, a, pp. 446 ff., and an interesting note by Warde
Fowler, *CR* xxxiv, 1919, pp. 95 ff.; cf. Conway on i. 444.

421. nam: postponed (see on 33); the assonance in *solam nam* is
strange. In most examples of postponed *nam* in Virgil its
position in the line is the same as in this one (i. 518 *cunctis
nam*, iii. 379 *prohibent nam*, vi. 667 *medium nam*, x. 585
iaculum nam): here and in i. 518 it secures a clash of ictus and
accent in the fourth foot.

These lines refer to something that Virgil has not told us,
Anna must have been acting for Dido in some way: and Dido
says miserably (not necessarily out of jealousy) '*you* understand him, I do not; he would tell you things that he never
told me', a familiar situation. Cf. Heinze, op. cit., p. 135,
note 1, 393 f.

422. colere: 'would attend to', an infinitive of repeated or
characteristic action (cf. ii. 98, vi. 491, vii. 15, xi. 821 f. 'quae
sola Camillae/ quicum partiri curas'). This is found in Latin
from Plautus and Terence down to Apuleius and Fronto,
especially in the historians, but the label 'historic infinitive'
is too narrow and is often misleading. A single isolated instance is rare; it generally occurs in groups of several together (for an extreme instance of this see Fronto, p. 207 N.),
and is sometimes varied by an inserted imperfect indicative;
it is seldom found with passive forms. It is common with
frequentative verbs, and Tacitus likes to use it with inchoa-
tives; both Sallust and Tacitus have it in relative clauses,
and even after *cum*, *ubi*, *postquam*. Cicero has it often in his
letters, and in the *Verrines*, but seldom in his later speeches.
In late Latin it practically disappears, which accounts for the
absence of any trace of it in Romance languages. See Wölfflin,
ALL x, pp. 177 ff.; for a discussion of modern theories of the
character and origin of this infinitive see M. Schuster in
Festschrift für Paul Kretschmer, pp. 224–43. Wagner collects
Virgilian instances in *Quaest. Virg.* xxx.

422. arcanos: the word shows that Dido felt Aeneas' thoughts
to be some inner 'mystery', into which she was not initiated:
Virgil could have chosen no better word to hint at the gulf
between their minds.

423. viri: for *eius* (see on 3 and 479).

mollis aditus: just as Aeneas had hoped to find 'aditus et
quae mollissima fandi/ tempora.' (293 f.). How groping these
two were: Aeneas would have done far better to go in person

to Dido immediately after his decision to leave, instead of looking for ways and means to tell her; and if Dido had gone in person to him now, she might yet have won him back.

424. hostem: he is a 'foreign foe' now, and *superbus* at that (note the contrast with *supplex*, cf. 414), not now even a *hospes* (323). Yet Dido's heart is still torn, as 429 shows.

  adfare: a favourite Virgilian verb; Norden (*Aeneis VI*, p. 374) regards it as Ennian.

425. non ego: this suggests a reply to some remark by Aeneas (cf. note on 333). Dido has never shown herself a *hostis* to Aeneas; she has been kind to the Trojans, she is not like an Agamemnon who plotted against them.

  exscindere: the infinitive is analogous to that after verbs of purpose or desire.

426. Aulide: the assembly-point of the Greek fleet; here Agamemnon sacrificed his daughter Iphigeneia.

427. Dido has never committed sacrilege towards Aeneas by disturbing his father's grave. The reference is mysterious. Servius quotes a statement by Varro that Diomedes had violated Anchises' tomb (cf. Heinze, op. cit., p. 248, note 2); possibly Aeneas had told Dido of this: editors object that there was no time for it to have happened before Aeneas' arrival in Carthage, but since the reference in 425 f. is to fact, we should expect a reference to fact here, not a vague allusion to 'an imaginary crime of great atrocity' (Page). A. E. Raymond (*Phoenix* vi, 1952, pp. 66 ff.) connects the words with Aeneas' visions of Anchises in 351 f., an ingenious theory which would have more basis if Dido had included the reference in her speech to Aeneas (cf. 376 ff.). It is odd to find Dido saying 'patris Anchisae', unless it is an echo of Aeneas' own words as he told her the tale; though of course the lines contain a message from her to him, so that 'his father' is after all a natural phrase.

  cineres: a 'poetic plural' which occurs first here: the plural is preferable to *cinerem* (M) on grounds of euphony, and in fact Virgil only uses the singular accusative when the last syllable is elided, as in 34: see Maas, *ALL* xii, pp. 515 f.

428. cur . . . auris?: 'why does he refuse to let my words enter his stubborn ears?' This use of *nego* with a direct infinitive is poetic; so *G.* iii. 207 f. 'prensique negabunt/ verbera lenta pati et duris parere lupatis'.

429. amanti: cf. 370, 479. Note the *m*- and *f*-sounds in this and the next line, and the assonance in *det . . . exspectet . . . ventos . . . ferentis*.

430. For *-que . . . -que*, see on 83. *Ferentis* is used as in English, of a 'carrying' wind; cf. iii. 473 'fieret vento mora ne qua ferenti'; so φέρων ἄνεμος, *Od.* iii. 300. Contrast v. 832 'ferunt sua flamina classem'.

431. coniugium: cf. 172, and contrast 338. Dido has now torn away the last shreds of her self-pretence. Some editors think *antiquum* inappropriate; but it is all long past to Dido now; Mackail observes that the epithet means 'honourable' as well as 'old'.

432. pulchro: 'glorious' (cf. *G.* ii. 137 'pulcher Ganges', ibid. 534 'rerum facta est pulcherrima Roma'); it is ironical here— Latium is his fine fair love now. See Norden on vi. 821 for an interesting note on *pulcher* and καλός ('honourable') in con-nexion with the concept of *libertas*.

433 f. tempus ... dolere: 'it is time, a blank time that I ask, rest and respite for my passion, until my fortune schools me through defeat to sorrow.' *Inane* is compelling: it shows the utter void in Dido's life. *Spatium* alone would be difficult with *furori*, but *requiem spatiumque* combine to mean 'a resting-time'.

434. A terrible line, when we remember Dido's recent happiness, and her own unselfishness in helping others (i. 630 'non ignara mali miseris succurrere disco'). Note the triple initial *d*, and the *m*- sounds.

435. extremam ... veniam: 'this is the last indulgence that I implore.'

   miserere sororis: cf. 478 'gratare sorori', and see note.

436. quam ... remittam: the line is 'well known as the most difficult in Virgil' (Conington). Note the extreme difficulty of reading it aloud: *quam⌣mihi, cum⌣dederit, cumulatam⌣morte, morte⌣remittam*—there is no easy liaison between the words to make pronunciation easy, and the effect is intermittent and halting, as if the line were broken by sobs.

   The line is one of those for which Virgil himself may have left alternative readings (see Mackail, p. lvii). Servius knew both *dederit* and *dederis*: Tucca and Varius approved the second, he states, while others, less well ('male quidam legunt') read *quam mihi cum dederit cumulata morte relinquam*. The variant *cumulata* gives no sense, as Mackail observes; and *relinquam* is also meaningless (*remittam = reddam* or *re-feram*).

   Dederit, despite Servius' disapproval, gives the only reason-able sense. Dido is asking for a 'last favour' from Aeneas, through Anna (*extremam veniam* in 435 = *extremum munus* in 429), and she now says 'when he has granted it to me, *cumula-tam morte remittam*'. *Dederis* could only mean 'when you have procured it for me' (Mackail), which is very difficult; and then *tibi* must be supplied with *remittam*, which is harder still, since no one has ever explained why or how Anna should be made the recipient of a *munus* that Aeneas has provided, or how Dido could repay Anna by death, in whatever way *morte* is to be taken. Henry's notion that Dido will become Anna's 'guardian angel' is nonsense. Page thinks that with *dederit* the words *miserere sororis* become a 'weak and meaningless stopgap'; but this is not so: Dido means 'this is all I ask —I have come to this—see how I am fallen from happiness'.

Cumulatam seems clear: it must mean 'with interest added', good measure heaped up, as in Cic. *Phil.* xiv. 30 'ea quae promisimus studiose cumulata reddemus', *ad Fam.* ii. 6. 2 'nullam esse gratiam quam non . . . animus meus . . . in remunerando cumulare . . . posset' (see Pease). Dido says, 'when Aeneas has granted me this kindness, I shall repay him with interest, *morte*'.

Morte remains as a problem. Does it mean 'by dying', and does that mean 'by my suicide'? Or is it simply 'at my death'? The meaning 'suicide' can be quite ruled out (*a*) because it would be a strange 'reward', (*b*) because Dido has said above, very plainly, that she will be able to bear her grief (420—the future tense should be remembered), and that all she asks is time to get used to it. Ovid knew that Virgil did not mean 'by suicide', for in *Her.* 7. 177 ff. (clearly an echo of Virgil here) he says 'pro meritis et siqua tibi debebimus ultra/ pro spe coniugii tempora parva peto,/ dum freta mitescunt et amor, dum tempore et usu/ fortiter edisco tristia posse pati;/ *si minus*, est animus nobis effundere vitam': i.e. 'if he does *not* do me this kindness, I shall kill myself'. In fact, as Mackail has well pointed out, a *threat* here is quite inappropriate: Dido will repay Aeneas' kindness by her own kindness, and 'suicide' or mere 'death' is no way to reward him. The whole passage shows that she still hopes against hope; she has not yet taken her terrible decision.

I take *morte* as meaning 'at my death', or 'in my death', or 'when I die' (cf. 244). At her last meeting with Aeneas, she had threatened to haunt him vengefully (385 f.); she says now to Anna, 'tell him that if he is kind to me now, I shall be as kind or kinder to him when I die'—she will not haunt him, she will take back her curse, although it is more than he deserves (*cumulatam*).

The line then would mean 'and when he has granted this kindness to me, I shall repay it a thousandfold at my death'. But the fact that from Servius onwards scholars have discussed it endlessly (see Pease, ad loc.) tells its own tale; it is an outstanding example of Virgilian mystery, and any solution is bound to be subjective.

437–49. *But Aeneas is hard, and will not listen. He stands rooted like some Alpine oak which resists the battering of all the winds. He suffers, but he is not moved.*

437 ff. talibus . . . audit: 'in such words she kept beseeching, and such was the tale of tears that her sister sadly took and took again. But by no tears was he moved, he would not be managed and gave ear to no words.'

438. fertque refertque: see on 83.

439. aut: for *neque*; the force of the negative still applies.

   tractabilis: Aeneas will not respond to any handling or 'management'; the word is unusual (the only other passage where Virgil uses it is in 53 above, *dum non tractabile caelum*); cf. Ovid, *Rem. Am.* 123 f. 'impatiens animus, nec adhuc tractabilis arte,/ respuit atque odio verba monentis habet'. It suggests almost physical handling, as if an animal had to be tamed.

440. fata . . . auris: 'the Fates block the way, heaven stops his ears and keeps them at peace'; he is not allowed to hear what would have made him waver: Virgil makes it plain that Aeneas' implacability was not of his own wishing. *Placidas* (proleptic) implies 'undisturbed', 'soothed'; see Mackail here and on i. 521, and cf. note on 578. *Viri* again = *eius* (cf. 423). *Deus* is quite general ('voluntas deorum', Heyne).

441 ff. The following simile is no doubt from Virgil's own observation; *Alpini* suggests this, and the detail confirms it. A comparison with the oak-simile in Catull. 64. 105 ff. (where the tree stands on a foreign mountain) shows the distinction of Virgil's art. It is a type of simile that is normally used to illustrate a physical struggle (so *Il.* xii. 131 ff., xvi. 765 ff., Apoll. Rhod. iv. 1680 ff., Catullus, l.c.), as Virgil himself uses it in ii. 626 ff., v. 448 f., x. 693 ff.; but here it gains in vividness, for the struggle is one of the mind.

441. ac velut: taken up by *haud secus* in 447 (contrast 402). 'And just as when the northern gales of Alp, now on this side, now on that, battle among themselves to root up some sturdy oak whose timber is full of years, the sound of cracking grows apace, and as the trunk is battered the topmost leaves rain down upon earth—but the oak itself clings firm to its rock, stretching as far down to Tartarus with its root as it reaches to the winds of heaven with its top.'

   Stanyhurst begins: 'Thee winds scold strugling, the threshing thick crush crash is owtborne, /Thee boughs frap whurring, when stem with blastbob is hacked.'

   Note the compound description *annoso validam robore* ('sturdy-aged-timbered'); cf. 366.

443. eruere: a Greek type of infinitive, characteristic of elevated poetic style from Ennius onwards; the idea of effort in *certant* makes it natural; cf. *Il.* xvi. 765 f. ὡς δ' Εὖρός τε Νότος τ' ἐρι-δαίνετον ἀλλήλοιιν / οὔρεος ἐν βήσσῃς βαθέην πελεμιζέμεν ὕλην. Such infinitives are used by Livy and Tacitus in their poetically coloured prose, but not by Cicero. The rhythm of this and the next line, with their heavy spondees, well shows the battering of the stubborn tree.

it: rare in this way, with no word or phrase to show direction; cf. viii. 595 'it clamor' (in i. 725 Servius knew the reading *it strepitus* for *fit*).

stridor: Virgil uses this of ships' tackle creaking in a storm (i. 87), of the clank of fetters (vi. 558), of the whiz of a spear (xi. 863), of the buzz of swarming bees (vii. 65).

altae: not conventional here; the leaves at the top would feel the full force of the blast.

445. ipsa: the main bulk of the tree. The change from the tree as object in 441 to subject here, and the use of a pronoun to mark it, is highly characteristic of epic style in similes; cf. 70 ff. 'quam procul incautam . . . illa fuga', ii. 626 ff. 'ac veluti summis antiquam in montibus ornum . . .illa usque minatur', vii. 378 ff. 'turbo, quem pueri . . . exercent—ille actus habena . . .', Catull. 64. 105 ff. 'nam velut . . . quercum . . . illa . . .'; so too in Greek, e.g. Apoll. Rhod. iv. 1682 ff. ἀλλ' ὥς τίς τ' ἐν ὄρεσσι πελωρίη ὑψόθι πεύκη / τήν τε θοοῖς πελέκεσσιν ἔθ' ἡμιπλῆγα λιπόντες / ὑλοτόμοι δρυμοῖο κατήλυθον· ἡ δ' ὑπὸ νυκτὶ / ῥιπῇσιν μὲν πρῶτα τινάσσεται.

445 f. quantum . . . tendit: repeated from *G.* ii. 291 f. Page regards the exaggeration here as unnatural; but it clearly shows the contrast between the firm roots of Aeneas' purpose and the precarious, exposed position of his emotions. For the pattern of *auras/ aetherias*, contrasting with *Tartara*, cf. i. 546 f. 'vescitur aura/ aetheria neque adhuc crudelibus occubat umbris'; see Norden, *Aeneis VI*, Anh. III, B 1, pp. 399 f.

447. adsiduis: Dido's entreaties are 'always at his door'.

heros: probably deliberately used here, to magnify the picture of Aeneas' struggle, and his victory (it occurs nowhere else in this book).

448. tunditur: 'he is belaboured' by Dido's prayers; a vivid word, which suits the simile.

et magno . . . curas: 'and he feels the full force of suffering in his mighty heart.' *Magno* would be banal here if the context did not emphasize its importance (cf. *heros* above) *Curas* means primarily the sorrows of love, but it implies also all the sadness of his position in general (cf. 341).

449. mens . . . inanes: 'but his purpose stays steadfast; the tears stream down, but in vain.' A famous line, which F. W. H. Myers might well have added to his list of Virgilian universals (see note on 83). Whose are the tears? Virgil is purposely ambiguous, and why may he not remain so? The line is ruined by a chill analysis. Formally it must be argued that *mens* and *lacrimae* are not likely to refer to different persons; and St. Augustine, in his picture of the Stoic, plainly took the tears to be those of Aeneas (*de civ. Dei* ix. 4 fin. 'ita mens, ubi fixa est ista sententia, nullas perturbationes, etiamsi accidunt inferioribus animi partibus, in se contra rationem praevalere permittit: quin immo eis ipsa dominatur, eisque non consentiendo, sed potius resistendo regnum virtutis exercet. talem describit etiam Vergilius Aenean. ubi ait *Mens immota manet, lacrimae volvuntur inanes*'); cf. E. V. Arnold, *Roman Stoicism*, p. 391, 'in a happy phrase Virgil sums up the whole ethics of Stoicism' (see Warde Fowler, *The Death of Turnus*, pp. 44 f.). These tears could not be denied to Aeneas: but in the changing moods that repeated reading of Virgil always brings, few could withhold them for ever from Dido.

Two other Virgilian passages give and take away support for either view: x. 464 f. 'audiit Alcides iuvenem, magnumque sub imo/ corde premit gemitum lacrimasque effundit inanis'; xii. 398 ff. 'stabat acerba fremens ingentem nixus in hastam/ Aeneas magno iuvenum et maerentis Iuli/ concursu, lacrimis immobilis'.

450–73. *And now Dido is terrified and prays for death ; and grisly omens strengthen her purpose : she hears cries from her husband's tomb, she has ghastly dreams of herself on a lonely, endless road, hounded by a fiend—Aeneas.*

450. tum vero: the words mark a crisis (cf. 397); *now*, when all has failed, Dido's thoughts turn to suicide, and her final decision is shown in 475. Note the slow spondees to mark her misery, both in this line and the next.

fatis exterrita: she sees her doom clearly, and is terrified; nothing can save her, and she prays for the inevitable end.

452. quo magis . . . relinquat: 'the more to make her fulfil her resolve by leaving the light'; *inceptum* implies the resolve that she has now begun to form; *lucemque relinquat* explains and amplifies *inceptum peragat*. The vivid presents are used as if Virgil had intended to follow *orat* and *taedet* by another present; but in 453 he changes his mind and uses a past tense.

453. vidit: note the spondaic word, with no run-on to the second foot (cf. note on 185). Such words are generally a

natural spondee (i.e. a word like *stridens*, 185, *felix*, 657):
otherwise, if the second syllable of the word is only 'long by
position', as in *vidit* here, there is either a pause after it (as
here, or in ii. 80), or an enclitic *se* follows (e.g. i. 587 *scindit se
nubes*), or a proper name (e.g. i. 602 *gentis Dardaniae*); or
the word may itself be a proper name (i. 524 *Troes te miseri*),
or the preposition *inter* (*E*. viii. 13). See Maas, *ALL* xii,
pp. 515 f. (footnote), and Norden, *Aeneis VI*, Anh. VIII; cf.
also G. B. Townend in *AJP* lxxi (1950), pp. 22 ff.

turicremis: 'incense-flaming', a Lucretian compound, one
of the quite small group of picturesque compound adjectives
that gained Virgilian sanction (Ovid has it, *Her.* 2. 18, and
Lucan, ix. 989). No doubt Virgil was attracted to it by its
rich and stately sound. Cf. *ALL* xv, p. 229.

454. horrendum dictu: 'tale of grisly horror'; the hair stands on
end at the sight.

latices: an entirely poetic word, used of any liquid, often
simply of water (cf. 512), here either of wine, or perhaps (as
Pease suggests) of the water that was commonly mixed with
wine. The 'holy liquid' turns dark, like blood (cf. Ovid, *AA*
iii. 503 'nigrescunt sanguine venae', and the frequent use of
ater with *sanguis*).

455. The line amplifies and explains the previous one: *fusa
vina* particularizes *latices sacros*, and *in . . . cruorem* particularizes *nigrescere*. Page unnecessarily assumes a hendiadys.
If *latices* above means 'water', then there was a double
portent, as Pease remarks.

obscenum: 'gruesome', both disgusting and ill omened;
Virgil uses it of the howling dogs that portended Caesar's
death (*G.* i. 470), of the Harpies (iii. 241), of a Fury disguised
as a hag (vii. 417), of boding birds (xii. 876). Any Roman
reader would respect such omens: remember Livy.

vina: this plural nominative and accusative form is regular
in poetry (Virgil never uses the singular); yet for the genitive
and ablative *vini* and *vino* are regular. Löfstedt (*Synt.* i,
p. 48) explains this as due to a vague feeling about such
neuter plurals in *-a* that they had inherent in them the
original force of a collective feminine noun. See also Maas,
ALL xii, p. 521; he regards the predominance of the plural
as due largely to metrical convenience, since a form like
vinum was less mobile: but this seems to give too much
weight to the metrical argument.

456. Anna must not hear of this horror: she might suspect what
it portended.

457. in tectis: Dido is always within the palace-precinct. A shrine
to Sychaeus would be in accordance with Roman custom; cf.

Servius on vi. 152 'apud maiores . . . omnes in suis
domibus sepeliebantur, unde ortum est ut lares colerentur in
domibus . . . .inde est quod etiam Dido cenotaphium domi
fecit marito'. Somewhat similarly Lucan's widow Polla had
an image of him near her bed, guarding her when she was
asleep (Stat. *S*. ii. 7. 128 ff.).

458. antiqui: cf. note on 431. The *mirus honos* is explained in
the next line: the 'snow-white fleeces' (i.e. *vittae*) and the
'foliage of joy' show that Dido—until she met Aeneas—still
reverenced Sychaeus with a living love; contrast the altar to
the *manes* of Polydorus (iii. 64), 'caeruleis maestae vittis
atraque cupresso'. Page has a helpful note.

460 ff. hinc . . . voces: 'from here, it seemed, she caught the
sound of cries, words from her husband as he called to her,
when night held the world beneath its dark pall; and
solitary upon the roof-tops the eagle-owl made many a plaint
in melancholy moan, uttering his long-drawn moping
note.'

460. exaudiri: sc. *visae*. The compound implies sound caught
from a distance (cf. vii. 15 'hinc exaudiri gemitus iraeque
leonum'). Suetonius states, of Nero's imaginings after he had
murdered his mother, 'de Mausoleo, sponte foribus patefactis,
exaudita vox est nomine eum cientis' (*Nero* 46. 2). *Voces* are
indistinct 'noises', *verba* distinguishable sounds.

    vocantis: Ovid characteristically embroiders this (*Her.* 7.
101 f. 'hinc ego me sensi noto quater ore citari;/ ipse sono
tenui dixit "Elissa, veni"'), from which no doubt Pope de-
rived a passage in his *Eloisa to Abelard* (307 f.), 'Here, as I
watch'd the dying lamps around,/ From yonder shrine I
heard a hollow sound./ "Come, sister, come", it said, or
seemed to say.'

461. visa: Virgil likes to use *videre* of portents, even if 'seeing' is
not strictly apposite: see on 490 f.

    viri: 'husband' (contrast 423). Note the funereal spondees
and the alliteration of these lines. Norden (on vi. 110, cf. vi.
426, 833) suggests that alliteration of *v* was meant to express
pain and horror.

462. bubo: the eagle-owl; see D'Arcy Thompson, *A Glossary of
Greek Birds* (Oxford, 1936), s.v. βύας, and cf. his note s.v.
γλαῦξ for much interesting information. The many *u* sounds
in 461–3 strikingly represent the cry of the *bubo*, which is
particularly uncanny, as anyone who has heard Ludwig
Koch's broadcasts of bird-sounds will know; see 'Pliny, *NH*
x. 34 'bubo funebris et maxime abominatus publicis praecipue auspiciis deserta incolit nec tantum desolata sed dira
etiam et inaccessa, noctis monstrum, nec cantu aliquo vocalis

sed gemitu'. Pease collects owl-presages from Latin and
English; none is more grisly than Shakespeare's 'It was the
owl that shriek'd, the fatal bellman, which gives the stern'st
goodnight' (*Macbeth* ii. 2). Stanyhurst has 'Also on thee
turrets the skrich howle, lyke fetchliefe ysetled,/Her burial
roundel dooth ruck, and cruncketh in howling.'

463. longas . . . voces: a fine sound-picture. *Ducere* is used here
as it is with *gemitus* (ii. 288), or *suspiria* (Ovid, *Met*. x. 402),
or with *fletus* itself (Prop. i. 15. 40); but Virgil has invented a
fusion of this sense ('to draw' a sigh or groan) with that of 'to
prolong' (cf. ix. 56 'in longum ducis amores'), and has produced a notably observant picture. Cf. Tac. *Ann*. xi. 37
'lacrimaeque et questus inriti ducebantur', where a sense
of prolongation is also present. Another Virgilian owl-cry
occurs in xii. 862 ff. 'alitis in parvae subitam collecta figuram,
quae quondam in bustis aut culminibus desertis/ nocte sedens
serum canit importuna per umbras', again with melancholy
repetition of *u*.

464. priorum: Page and Mackail prefer *piorum*, the reading of
M, which Servius knew. But *priorum* has more point; as
Henry remarks, Dido remembers strange old prophecies, too
late. I cannot see any reason for rejecting it on grounds of
overdone alliteration; and the *pii vates* of vi. 662 is no parallel
to justify *piorum* here.

465. terribili . . . horrificant: 'make her shudder with their
ghastly warning.' The pause after *horrificant* precedes the
climax of horror: Aeneas, like a fiend, hunting her, not the
Aeneas she had known and loved.

  furentem: perhaps proleptic ('hounds her to madness'), or
simply 'she is mad, and there is Aeneas hounding her'.

466. in somnis: 'in a dream' (cf. 353); so, long ago, she had
dreamed of her murdered husband (i. 353 f. 'ipsa sed in
somnis inhumati venit imago/ coniugis ora modis attollens
pallida miris'). The rhythm well illustrates the remorseless-
ness of Aeneas' pursuit.

466 ff. semperque . . . terra: 'and she imagines herself always
left solitary and alone, always travelling an endless road, with
none beside her, searching for her Tyrians in a waste land': a
familiar nightmare. Dido's loneliness is overwhelming; she
has lost Sychaeus, lost Aeneas, lost her own people; she is
'like one who on a lonesome road Doth walk in fear and
dread, Because he knows some frightful fiend Doth close
behind him tread'. Compare the vivid lines in xii. 908 ff.
'ac velut in somnis, oculos ubi languida pressit/ nocte quies,
nequiquam avidos extendere cursus/ velle videmur et in
mediis conatibus aegri/ succidimus—non lingua valet, non

corpore notae/ sufficiunt vires nec vox aut verba sequuntur':
how superbly Virgil does these things.

469 ff. Dido in her distraught state is compared to the familiar
figures of Greek drama, in the *Bacchae* or in the *Eumenides*
(though Servius thought that Virgil had a play by Pacuvius
in mind). This is the only direct allusion in Virgil to stage-
representations (see Mackail). Some editors have criticized
him for comparing Dido to a 'stage-figure'; but there is
nothing stagy about the lines, and any Roman reader
familiar with Greek tragedy would find them a terrifyingly
real picture of Dido's condition. But there is more than a
literary allusion: Mackail notes a Pompeian wall-painting
(Pfuhl, *Malerei und Zeichnung der Griechen*, iii, plate 641),
showing Pentheus attacked by his mother Agave, with two
Furies in the background (this may explain the allusion to the
Furies here, for they are not otherwise connected with the
Pentheus-legend). Further, Pliny (*NH* xxxv. 144) mentions
a painting by the fourth-century Greek artist Theon of
Samos, depicting *Orestis insania*, as well as another artist's
painting of Orestes slaying his mother, and he adds that
some of the pictures he has listed were in Rome in his time;
so we may reasonably assume that Virgil's contemporaries
would have been familiar with his allusions here from art as
well as from reading or from the stage. The modern reader
will remember the terrible description of Athalie's dream
in Racine's play (Act II, scene 5).

469. Eumenidum: the Furies (the 'kindly-intentioned', a
placatory name, like the Euxine for the terrible Black Sea).
If Virgil has a painting in mind, an attendant Fury may well
have been a conventional detail even where the original
legend knew nothing of it (cf. the previous note): see D. L.
Page's introduction to the *Medea*, p. lix, where a figure, probably a Fury, is mentioned as appearing in a vase-painting of
Medea.

470. From Eur. *Bacchae* 918 f. καὶ μὴν ὁρᾶν μοι δύο μὲν ἡλίους δοκῶ, /
δισσὰς δὲ Θήβας.

471. Note the rushing dactyls. Virgil likes the resonant
epithet *Agamemnonius*; cf. iii. 54, vi. 838, and especially vi.
489 'at Danaum proceres Agamemnoniaeque phalanges', a
fine clanging line to describe the ghostly Greeks.

scaenis agitatus: 'hounded over the stage' (*scaenis* is a local
ablative). Ennius and others wrote tragedies on the Orestes-
legend, and Nero once acted the name-part in one (Sueton.
Nero 21) ; see Pease's note.

472 f. armatam . . . Dirae: 'fleeing from his mother—torches
and deadly dark serpents her weapons—while at the door are

posted the Fiends of Hell in vengeance.' Note the *a* and *i*
sounds; cf. vii. 324 'Allecto dirarum ab sede dearum'. The
Dirae (cf. 610) are the Furies; see Mackail on xii. 845: Warde
Fowler, however (*The Death of Turnus*, pp. 149 f.) thinks that
they are simply 'horrible creatures of ill omen', probably
known to the Romans through Etruscan art and lore. Here
Orestes' mother Clytaemnestra is represented as if she were
herself a Fury (cf. note on 384).

472. atris: not merely 'black' but 'ghastly'; cf. 384, 687, and
see Warde Fowler, *The Death of Turnus*, p. 92.

474-503. *Dido has taken her decision to die; but to gain time for
her plan, she calls her sister and pretends that by a sorceress'
arts she has found a way, either to win Aeneas back or to end her
passion for him. For this, she says, a pyre is needed; and Anna
unsuspectingly obeys her request to prepare it.*

474. ergo: the word sums up all the remorseless train of events
which have led to her final decision; it is as tremendous as the
great *ergo* of *G.* i. 489. 'Because of this, when she had
quickened the seed of madness within her, beaten to her
knees by agony ...'; *evicta* occurs again in 548, and elsewhere
in Virgil at ii. 630 only, in the simile of a tree which is battered
and struck 'vulneribus donec paulatim evicta supremum/
congemuit'.

475. decrevitque mori: the final resolve: only one course is left.

475 f. tempus ... exigit: 'all by herself in her secret heart she
works out the time and manner of it'; for *ipsa* cf. vi. 185
'haec ipse suo tristi cum corde volutat' (see Wagner, *Quaest.
Virg.* xviii, p. 468); *exigit* implies the perfecting of a detailed
plan (so *exactus* in Silver Latin often = *perfectus*).

476. dictis: in contrast to what she does not say, but keeps in
her heart.

477. consilium ... serenat: 'she masks her scheme with a cheerful look, and sets hope unclouded upon her brow.'

vultu: cf. i. 208 f. 'curisque ingentibus aeger/ spem vultu
simulat, premit altum corde dolorem'; the word often depends upon its context for its meaning; contrast, e.g., Catull.
64. 34 'declarant gaudia vultu' with Hor. *C.* iii. 3. 3 'non
vultus instantis tyranni'. This line must not be forgotten
when we read Dido's words to Anna.

spem fronte serenat: an imaginative phrase, showing the
bright untroubled appearance with which Dido masks her
dark thoughts. Mackail observes that Virgil uses *serenare*
elsewhere only in i. 255 (of Jupiter) 'caelum tempestatesque
serenat' (see Conway's note); in both passages, the verb implies not calmness, but brightness, absence of cloud.

For a sensitive discussion of the following passage see R. M. Henry in *CR* xliv, 1930, pp. 104 ff. He points out that although Virgil was deeply influenced by Apollonius Rhodius (iii. 616 ff., especially 802 ff.) in his introduction of the magic ritual, yet in Apollonius the magic is something 'normal and almost natural', whereas in Virgil it is 'a mysterious and secret rite to which the queen on the verge of madness turns as a last resource'; cf. Heinze, op. cit., pp. 141 f. The difference between Medea and Dido is that Medea belongs to the world of fancy, whereas Dido is a real and living woman.

478. **inveni . . . viam**: a subtle development of *spem fronte serenat*. Dido comes to Anna full of apparent excitement and hope: 'I have thought of a way,' she cries, 'it will all come out right'; and Anna believes her.

gratare sorori: a ghastly echo of *miserere sororis*, 435; Anna need pity her no more. For this type of parenthesis at the end of a line cf. vi. 399, xi. 408 'absiste moveri'.

479. **quae . . . amantem**: 'either to give him back in love to me, or to release me in my love from him'; *amantem* belongs to both *eum* and *me*. The order is significant; she puts first what she so much longs for, the alternative that in the dark horror of the next forty lines is never quite lost to view as a real possibility, however much it is primarily meant to deceive Anna.

This is a curious line, of deliberate near-prose. The poets use the nominative *is* comparatively seldom, and the oblique cases very rarely indeed: for Virgil cf. M. Hélin, *RÉL* v, 1927, pp. 60 ff.; for the elegists see Platnauer, op. cit., p. 116; and for a general examination of the practice of the Augustans and the Silver poets see Axelson, *Unpoetische Wörter*, pp. 70 ff. Virgil never has *eius* (cf. 3, note); *eum* occurs six times in the *Aeneid* and twice in the *Georgics*, *eam* once only (*Georgics*), *eo* twice and *ea* once (*Aeneid*), *eos* once in the *Aeneid* and once in the *Georgics*. The reason is that the pronoun is so colourless, with no independent existence apart from the noun to which it refers and for which it is a substitute. Yet in this one line we have *eum* and *eo* together.

Commentators seek to explain the pronouns here as a means by which Dido can 'avoid mentioning the hated name' of Aeneas (see Irvine and Pease). But in fact Dido's use of Aeneas' name is very infrequent. It occurs three times only: i. 576 'utinam . . . adforet Aeneas' (to the Trojan castaways, before she has met him), i. 617 'tune ille Aeneas?' (at their first meeting), and in line 329 of this book, where it is only an indirect mention of the name. She does not use it when she asks Aeneas to tell her the tale of Troy at the end of Book I, nor in her first speech to Anna (above, 9 ff.): here there is no question of a 'hated name'. She does not use it in her two speeches to Aeneas (except in 329), nor in her final curse (590 ff.): here her avoidance of it may be deliberate. It is clearly avoided in her last speech, on the pyre, where she says instead *Dardanium caput* (640) and *Dardanus* (662, where Virgil could have written 'Aeneas, nostraeque ferat secum omina mortis').

The fact is that Dido never has used Aeneas' name freely: it was not in the epic convention that she should do so (as may be seen from Apollonius Rhodius). 'Hatred' for it will not explain this line, which is not only remarkable for these pronouns but for the manner of their use: what ultimately gives the line its strangeness is that no person is named in close context to which they refer (as always elsewhere when Virgil has the pronoun). 'He' is not named; 'he' fills her whole life; Anna needs no telling who 'he' is. Dido is continuing a train of thought; but she is made to speak like this on purpose to seem casual and to put her sister off the scent. The line is a cleverly premeditated undertone, an elaborately matter-of-fact device to make her words in tune with an assumed expression of calm.

480 ff. Dido now changes her casual manner for a deliberately ornate description. She is at pains to stress the powers of the priestess-witch, and the suddenness with which the reader is transported to the world of magic is made even more eerie because Dido and Aeneas are such real persons. After 509 we hear no more of the witch; she has played her part. It is impossible to tell whether Dido brought her in to make her scheme for the pyre plausible, or whether she had really consulted her first; probably the former is the case, for it is plain that Dido had thought everything out very carefully (475). But even if at the start the witch was part of Dido's make-believe to trick her sister, in the end the sorcery became real to her for at least one moment: the Dido of lines 517–18 is herself deep in the world of magic.

Oceani . . . aptum: 'next to the bound of Ocean and the setting sun, there lies a place on the edge of the world, where the Ethiopians dwell; here Giant Atlas whirls upon his shoulder the vault of heaven, spangled with fiery stars.'

Dido begins with an ἔκφρασις, in a traditional manner (see Heinze, op. cit., pp. 396 ff.): *locus est*, or more commonly *est locus*, is a conventional opening of such a passage (cf. i. 159, 530, vii. 563, Ovid, *Met.* ii. 195, viii. 788, etc.); elsewhere it is varied by the naming of the place or object described (i. 441 'lucus in urbe fuit', viii. 597 'est ingens gelidum lucus . . .',

Ovid, *Met.* i. 168 'est via sublimis', etc.). It is an epic mannerism, which goes back to Homer (e.g. *Il.* vi. 152 ἔστι πόλις
Ἐφύρη μυχῷ Ἄργεος ἱπποβότοιο, xiii. 32 ἔστι δέ τι σπέος εὐρὺ βαθείης
βένθεσι λίμνης).

481. ultimus Aethiopum: i.e. a place belonging to the Ethiopians, which is *ultimus* (cf. Catull. 11. 11 f. 'ultimosque
Britannos'). In Homer the 'blameless Ethiopians' were the
holiday entertainers of the Olympian gods. They were
thought of vaguely as living across Africa, from east to west
(cf. Stat. *Th.* x. 85 'Aethiopasque alios', of the western
Ethiopians).

482. axem: often of the sky, but here with the actual 'axis' implied too. *Aptum* is a true participle ('fitted with'), as often
in Lucretius. The splendid line is not all Virgil's imagining;
its brilliant glow goes back ultimately to Ennius (*Ann.* 159
'caelum suspexit stellis fulgentibus aptum', 339 'hinc nox
processit stellis ardentibus apta'), and Lucretius shares in
it too (vi. 357). Virgil repeats it in vi. 797 (cf. Sparrow,
op. cit., p. 100). Fanshawe translates: 'Where on great
Atlas' neck the heaven thick set/ With glorious diamond-
stars hangs like a carcanet.'

483. hinc: a notable mannerism of ἔκφρασις, going back to
Homer. In every such description, the opening *locus est*,
etc., is taken up (sometimes after a considerable interval)
by a word of this type; so i. 441 *lucus in urbe fuit* . . . 446 *hic
templum*, ii. 21 *est in conspectu Tenedos* . . . 24 *huc*, ii. 713 *est
urbe egressis tumulus* . . . 716 *hanc ex diverso sedem*, vii. 563
est locus . . . 565 *hunc*, viii. 597 *est ingens gelidum lucus* . . . 603
haud procul hinc, Ovid, *Met.* i. 168 *est via* . . . 170 *hac iter est*,
viii. 788 *est locus* . . . 790 *illic*. Similarly, in the two passages
quoted above (on 480 ff.) from Homer, there is a following
ἔνθα in each; cf. Apoll. Rhod. iii. 927 ἔστι δέ τις . . . 928 αἴγειρος
. . . 929 τῇ. The point is discussed by E. Fraenkel, *De Media
et Nova Comoedia Quaestiones Selectae*, diss. Göttingen, 1912,
pp. 46 ff. (a reference which I owe to Mr. G. W. Williams): it
is there shown that the mannerism passes from epic to the
tragedians, in places where they are close to epic style, e.g. in
messengers' speeches (Aesch. *Pers.* 447 νῆσός τις ἐστὶ . . . 450
ἐνταῦθα, Eur. *Hipp.* 1199) or in descriptions of places (Eur. *El.*
1258 ἔστιν δ' Ἀρεώς τις ὄχθος . . . 1264 ἐνταῦθα); Aristophanes
parodies it in *Av.* 1473 ff., 1553 ff. The trick reappears in
Latin Comedy (e.g. Ter. *Heaut.* 902 f., *Ph.* 88 ff.). Cf. Vahlen's
edition of Ennius, footnote to p. cl.

Massylae gentis: i.e. Numidian (cf. 132), a useful variant
(cf. *Nomadum*, 320, and Norden on vi. 59). Dido has had the
sorceress 'pointed out' (*monstrata*) as 'coming from there',

i.e. from Ethiopia: a nice circumstantial detail. Stanyhurst renders: 'From thence came a mayd priest, in soyle Massyle begotten,/ Seixteen of Hesperides Sinagog, this sorceres used,/ For to cram the dragon.' Gavin Douglas calls the *sacerdos* 'ane haly nun, ane full grete prophetes'.

484. Hesperidum: the 'daughters of Evening', who had the golden apples in their garden; *templi* is probably used of the precinct (τέμενος), not the temple-building. Dido is at once precise and romantic; the sorceress had apparently retired from her responsible post (cf. *dabat, servabat*, 485), perhaps, as Pease gravely suggests, because Hercules had killed the dragon whom she guarded. Heinze well points out (op. cit., p. 142) that the elaborate account of her powers is designed to elevate the furtiveness of magic to something worthy of a heroic tale.

484 f. epulasque . . . ramos: this particularizes her duties as *custos*; the relative *quae* is out of place, the grammatical order being *quae dabatque epulas draconi et sacros servabat . . . ramos*, as Mackail notes (*-que . . . et* joining the two verbs); the sense is 'she, I mean, whose task it used to be to feed the dragon, protecting the holy boughs upon the tree'—by feeding the dragon, the priestess herself took part in guarding the fruit.

486. spargens . . . papaver: 'sprinkling oozy honey and the poppy's load of drowsiness.' A magnificent and lovely line, of the 'Homeric' type (see on 164): it begins with a single cut-off spondaic word (cf. 185, note), and *umida* in its turn occupies the second foot, with no run-on to the third, a most unusual effect; there is no strong caesura anywhere, only a weak pause in the third and fifth foot; the whole rhythm is dreamy and dropping, full of 'all the drowsy syrops of the world', even sleepier than 81 or ii. 9 or v. 856. Irvine compares vii. 711 'Ereti manus omnis oliviferaeque Mutuscae'; other unusual rhythmic effects which in some degree approach it are xii. 619 'confusae sonus urbis et inlaetabile murmur', xi. 851 'antiqui Laurentis opacaque ilice tectum' (note, in a rather similar context, xii. 419 'ambrosiae sucos et odoriferam panaceam').

Servius comments on the line: 'incongrue videtur positum ut soporifera species pervigili detur draconi', and successive commentators have echoed him, claiming that if the priestess wanted to keep the dragon fit for its work, she had no business to make it sleepy. But Virgil cannot have written such a deliberately languorous line without meaning what he says, and *soporiferum* cannot be dismissed as a 'gradus-epithet' (the phrase is Page's). Mackail remarks 'even a dragon has

to be kept in a good temper', and the priestess did this by
giving it a special treat (cf. Pliny, *NH* xix. 168 'candidum
[papaver] cuius semen tostum in secunda mensa cum melle
apud antiquos dabatur'). Henry claims that this mixture of
honey and poppy was no narcotic but 'the sweetest sweet and
greatest delicacy known before the invention of sugar', and
thus describes it as he himself ate it in the Tyrol: ' Honey and
ground poppy-seeds are mixed together so as to form a paste
of the thickness of jam. A dessert-spoonful of this conserve is
wrapped round with a dough made of wheaten flour, butter,
eggs, and milk. Thus little dumplings or patties are made,
each about the size of a joint of the thumb. These are baked,
not in the oven, but in a pan with melted butter, and are
eaten on feast-days as a delicacy.' It was this that was
smuggled into the Spartan lines by divers, when they were
blockaded in Sphacteria (Thuc. iv. 26. 8 ἐσένεον δὲ καὶ κατὰ τὸν
λιμένα κολυμβηταὶ ὕφυδροι, καλῳδίῳ ἐν ἀσκοῖς ἐφέλκοντες μήκωνα μεμε-
λιτωμένην) ; and Trimalchio had dormice for dinner, dressed
with the same sweet (Petron. 31. 10, where Burman pleasantly comments 'conveniente scilicet gliribus condimento,
utrumque enim somnum facilem dat').

What then of *soporiferum*? Virgil's use of it, and his deliberate rhythm, must be all part of the ' magic' atmosphere; the
witch was able to make the dragon take a nap after a good
dinner and wake him up if an emergency threatened. Heinze
(p. 142, note 3) compares the sorceress in Tibullus i. 2. 52,
who was said 'sola feros Hecatae perdomuisse canes', and
suggests that Virgil means primarily to show the special
power of the Massylian witch.

A quite different explanation was proposed by A. I. Tran-
noy in *Revue Archéologique*, 5 sér., 27 (1928), pp. 136 ff. He
takes 486 not as an expansion of *epulas* in 484 (because then
et . . . ramos interrupts the connexion), but as referring to the
libations made to the invisible spirits of the air whose power
might break the branches: he points out that in all mythology sacred trees must not be cut or touched in any way, and
further that among the powers of sorcery claimed by Medea in
Ovid, *Met.* vii. 202 is that of driving off the winds. Thus he
takes Virgil to mean that the sorceress fed the dragon to
guard against human attack, and kept asleep the powers of
the air so that the branches on the tree might be safe. This
is ingenious, but seems to rest on no real evidence, while it
ignores the very Virgilian style of 485, which surely shows *et
. . . ramos* to be no interruption but an extension and am-
plification of *epulasque . . . dabat*.

I should prefer to accept the view that Virgil wishes to show

the great powers that the witch possessed, and her know-
ledgeable treatment of dragons; I wonder, however, if the
mixture was intended medicinally, when the dragon was ill;
Pliny (*NH* xx. 201 f.) explains that poppy-seed mixed with
rose-oil was good for headache and ear-ache, and in *NH*
xxii. 108 that honey similarly mixed was good for ear-ache:
enough (even without the rose-oil) to suggest that both
honey and poppy-seed could be used effectively as medicine
by a powerful sorceress. But *quousque tandem*? Virgil has
drawn a fascinating, mysterious picture of magic powers:
why destroy the illusion?

mella: Virgil does not use the form *mel*; it occurs twice in
Ovid, and nowhere else in Augustan poetry; probably the
singular was avoided for the sake of euphony (see Maas, *ALL*
xii, p. 522; analogous plurals are *tura, farra, aera*, though the
singular forms of these are rather less avoided).

487. haec: this takes up *sacerdos* (483) just as *hinc* (483) takes up
locus est (481), a duplication of the mannerism noticed on 483.
carminibus: 'charms', 'spells', ἐπῳδαί.

488. ast: cf. vi. 315 f. 'navita sed tristis nunc hos nunc accipit
illos,/ ast alios longe summotos arcet harena'. The form is
archaic; Virgil uses it only before a vowel (generally before
ille or *alius*) for metrical convenience, except in x. 743 (*ast de
me*); see Norden on vi. 316.

489 f. sistere . . . manis: 'that she makes the river-water stop
still, and turns the stars backward; she conjures up the midnight souls of the dead.' These are all the conventional
powers of magic; cf. Apoll. Rhod. iii. 532 f. καὶ ποταμοὺς ἵστησιν
ἄφαρ κελαδεινὰ ῥέοντας, / ἄστρα τε καὶ μήνης ἱερῆς ἐπέδησε κελεύθους,
Tibullus i. 2. 43 ff., Ovid, *Am.* ii. 1. 23 ff., etc. (see Pease).

489. fluviis: either dative ('for rivers') or a local ablative.

490. nocturnos: cf. 303, and see note on 118.

490 f. mugire . . . ornos: 'you will see earth rumbling beneath
your feet, and ash-trees come marching down from the moun-
tains'; cf. 460, vi. 256 f. 'sub pedibus mugire solum et iuga
coepta moveri/ silvarum, visaeque canes ululare per umbram',
iii. 90 'tremere omnia visa repente'. Sound and movement
are so welded that both can be 'seen'; cf. Prop. ii. 16. 49
'vidistis toto sonitus percurrere caelo', Aesch. *Sept.* 103
κτύπον δέδορκα: contrast ii. 705 f. 'et iam per moenia clarior
ignis/ auditur'. Shakespeare laughs in the same idiom (*MND*
v. 1. 195 f. 'I see a voice: now will I to the chink, To spy an I
can hear my Thisby's face'). See Norden on vi. 256.

491. ornos: one of Virgil's ways of avoiding the metrically intractable *arbores* is to specify a kind of tree (but *arbusta* is a
frequent substitute).

492 f. testor . . . artis: 'Dear, I make the gods my witness, yes, and you, my sister, sweet one, that I do not willingly arm myself with magic arts.' Dido has recourse to black arts only when all else has failed—a line of much significance.

493. dulce caput: like φίλον κάρα ('dear heart' would be our idiom); see note on 354, and cf. 613, 640.

accingier: used with a direct object, like a Greek middle (see on 137, and cf. ii. 510 f. 'inutile ferrum/ cingitur'); the subject *me* is omitted (see on 383). This form of the passive infinitive belongs to very old Latin; it occurs in the XII Tables, and in legal formulae such as Cicero quotes in *Caec.* 95, in Cato, and often in Plautus; Ennius and the tragedians gave it the sanction of high poetry, and from them it passed to Lucretius and Virgil (who is fond of it), Catullus, Horace, and some of the Silver Latin poets. As a museum-piece it appears as late as the fourth-century Ausonius and the poem *de cupiditate* by Sebastus (Baehrens, *PLM* iv. 119).

494. tu: the pronoun emphasizes the command (cf. the mock-solemn 'tu regibus alas/ eripe', *G.* iv. 106 f.). *Secreta* implies both 'going apart' and 'secretly', elaborated in *tecto interiore*; no one but Anna must know of her dealings in sorcery. For all these preparations see note on 498.

tecto: used loosely here, as *sub auras* ('towering skyward') shows (cf. 692); strictly it means the covered part of the building.

495. viri: for *eius* (see on 3, 479); there is surely no question here of avoidance of Aeneas' name, only a matter of poetic usage. By *arma* Dido seems to mean the sword mentioned in 507 and 646, presumably a present that she had had from Aeneas, and which she kept in her room.

496. impius: 'no thought of duty then', a bitter gibe: Aeneas had forgotten his *pietas* towards the gods when he loved her enough for this, just as now in his callousness he has forgotten his *pietas* towards her.

exuvias: 'the things he wore', cf. 507, 651. Virgil has it of a snake's cast-off skin (ii. 473), a lion's hide (ix. 307), spoils taken from an enemy (ii. 275, x. 423), all different aspects of the act expressed in *exuere*. But it is specially used of the clothes or other belongings of a person on whom sympathetic magic is practised (cf. *E.* viii. 91 'has olim exuvias mihi perfidus ille reliquit'); here it is some personal thing that Aeneas had worn or had given to Dido, or something that she had secreted as belonging to him, now symbolic of himself; cf. Theocr. 2. 53 f. τοῦτ' ἀπὸ τᾶς χλαίνας τὸ κράσπεδον ὤλεσε Δέλφις, / ὠγὼ νῦν τίλλοισα κατ' ἀγρίῳ ἐν πυρὶ βάλλω. Readers of *Emma* will find a good example of *exuviae* in the court-plaister and the pencil-end that Harriet Smith so cherished as having belonged to Mr. Elton (ch. 40).

que ... que: this is not 'double *-que*' (see on 83), as the first is a true coordinate.

496 f. lectumque ... perii: 'and the marriage-bed which has brought me my doom'; *iugalem* shows that Dido still clings to her self-deception (cf. 172).

497 f. abolere ... sacerdos: 'it is my will to blot out everything that recalls that man whom I abhor, and the priestess points the way.' In *abolere* Dido uses a word that brings an echo from i. 720 f., where Cupid, disguised as Ascanius, 'paulatim abolere Sychaeum/ incipit'.

nefandi: very strong; so the Cyclops are *gens nefanda* (iii. 653), and the swords that Sinon has escaped (ii. 155) are *nefandi*. Here Dido will not name Aeneas, and the *viri* of 495 is not enough; she must let Anna think that he is a man whom she hates and would like to injure—Anna must not know that life without him is unendurable. And yet, in 479, she has said that she loves him.

498. monimenta: anything that calls a person to memory; so in iii. 486 Andromache gives Ascanius a cloak as a 'souvenir' of her (*manuum ... monimenta mearum*), in v. 571 f. we hear of a horse 'quem candida Dido/ esse sui dederat monimentum et pignus amoris', in xii. 945 f., when Aeneas sees Turnus wearing Pallas' belt, 'oculis ... saevi monimenta doloris/ exuviasque hausit'. In a wider sphere the Alps are 'Caesaris monimenta magni' (Catull. 11. 10), the sea round Actium is 'Iuleae pelagus monumenta carinae' (Prop. iv. 6. 17). Catullus uses *mnemosynum* similarly (12. 13).

iuvat: like *placet*. It is Dido's considered decision (cf. 660). The primary MSS. vary between *iuvat* and *iubet*; but *monstrat* following *iubet* would be very weak. Mackail and Sparrow (op. cit., p. 145) regard the passage as incomplete, with *monstratque sacerdos* added as a stopgap from 483. But it is hard to see why an interpolator should have added just these words if he really had 483 in mind, and in fact that line affords no real parallel. The line seems reasonably satisfactory as it stands: Dido says 'this is what I have decided to do, and this is how the priestess tells me to do it'; she ends with a reference to the *sacerdos* on purpose to put Anna off the scent; *monstratque* is certainly a little abrupt, but no more so than *monstrat amor verus patriae* in xi. 892.

Throughout this speech, Dido has been working out a careful plan to carry out her purpose while deceiving Anna. She has invented (or asked the witch to invent) an ambiguous ritual (cf. 479, and see Heinze, op. cit., p. 142, note 1). The general situation resembles that of Theocritus' second Idyll, where some of Simaetha's prayers are for Delphis' love, others seem intended to harm him: Gow comments (p. 40) that the latter may also aim 'not at injuring Delphis, but at reawakening a consuming passion'. Dido's words in 497 f., *abolere nefandi cuncta viri monimenta*, might likewise be taken either to ensure Aeneas' destruction and her freedom, or that he will be consumed with love for her. Dido leaves Anna to decide for herself the meaning of the rite. The whole thing is, and must be, ambiguous. And in fact the epithet *nefandi* points one way, but in the actual rite that follows it is the hope of winning him back that is uppermost (the *effigies* of 508, not mentioned previously, suggests this, and also the mysterious *matri praereptus amor* of 516). Only Dido herself knows that the ritual is to end in neither of the two ways that she has pretended in 479: she is *haud ignara futuri* (508). Yet who can say whether, by the time all the sorceries were prepared, she was not herself deluded, in her unbalanced state, into thinking for a moment that the magic might really work, and even work in her favour?

S. Eitrem has discussed the following passage in *Festskrift til Halvdan Koht*, Oslo, 1933, pp. 29-41, in a paper entitled *Das Ende Didos in Vergils Aeneis*. He remarks on certain aspects of the ritual which suggest that it could never have succeeded, as Virgil describes it, and was never meant to succeed. (1) The pyre (itself an unusual object in such a ritual) is elaborately constructed, but never kindled: the incantations are made (510), but nothing is burnt and the *effigies* remains untouched; (2) the magic ingredients are not ready, but have to be fetched (513 f.) just when one would have expected the rite to be consummated; (3) an essential condition for success in such a rite is that the central figure in it desires success; but Dido has no such wish—her intention is to die, and the sorceress never has her full confidence; she is ashamed in her heart at her recourse to magic, and she prays not to the chthonic deities but to the *conscia fati sidera* (519 f.).

Eitrem concludes that Virgil's main purpose is to show Dido's own mental conflict, her *furor*, and that the details of the ritual are never clearly conceived as such, but serve only as a backcloth to the death-scene to come. He sees lack of revision in the various inconsistencies and difficulties (e.g. 513 ff., and the epithet *soporiferum* in 486, which he thinks untenable), and notes the obscurity of *monstrata piacula* in 636 and of Anna's words in 680 f. *patriosque vocavi voce deos*,

which look as if she herself had taken part in the ritual
meant for her deception. He advances the theory that Virgil
introduced this pseudo-magic to please the taste of con-
temporary literary circles, and perhaps also to show another
aspect of 'fraus Punica' in Dido's treatment of her sister.
Both these points seem to me irrelevant: high tragedy is not
written like that. Eitrem further thinks that Virgil found the
combination of magic (his own idea) with the story of Dido's
suicide on the pyre (the tradition of his sources) too difficult
to manage successfully, and that he has botched the whole
thing. This seems to me quite wrong. It is this very ad-
mixture that gives the passage its *color*, deepening the
tragedy and increasing our pity and terror. Nor can I
think that Virgil would have changed any essentials in a
revision. Eitrem is on surer ground when he stresses the
poetic imagination which kept the final death-scene always
in mind. For the poet in Virgil is in complete control. He is
not, as in the eighth *Eclogue*, specifically describing a magic rite
which is complete in itself and is concerned with a pitiful but
familiar situation of ordinary life. He confronts us with a
deeper sorrow, the dark mystery of human behaviour in the
shadow of madness, in which details are of no individual
significance and it is the sum of them alone that matters—
and in his depicting of that sum Virgil shows a firm and
masterly control of his material. Heinze well remarks of the
contrast between the eighth *Eclogue* and this passage, 'das ist
die bäuerliche Alltagszauberei im Gegensatz zur heroischen'
(op. cit., p. 143, note): the darkness of Dido's rite casts heroic
shadows.

499. effata: she has 'told her mind' (cf. 30, 76); she has been
quite firm and collected, and the effort of it is shown in *pallor
simul occupat ora.*

500. tamen: Anna does not notice her sister's ghastly looks, and
'never thinks that it is death that her sister cloaks by these
strange rites'; for *praetexere*, cf. 172.

    funera: Virgil uses this plural form of a single death here
only; Lucretius has it before him (vi. 1199, 1234, of death by
plague); perhaps the Greek use of θάνατοι (see on 694) provides an analogy.

502. concipit: with *mente*; Anna 'never dreams of such wild
madness' (contrast *concepit furias*, 474); devoted as she is to
Dido, she is not very perceptive, and thinks that in the end
Dido will suffer no more than she did at Sychaeus' death—
and yet, that must have been agony enough.

503. The broken line is perhaps a note, to remind Virgil that an
insertion was needed (cf. note on 44).

504–21. *The pyre is raised, and Dido sets Aeneas' sword and an image of him on it; the priestess chants her mysteries, and mixes her horrid brew; and Dido prays.*

504. at regina: cf. 1 and 296; Dido's thoughts were very different from Anna's.

penetrali in sede: 'in the inmost heart of her home', a careful adaptation of 494.

505. ingenti . . . secta: 'piled huge with pinewood and logs of holm-oak', a complicated set of ablatives (*erecta* must be taken closely with *pyra* as an ablative absolute).

Note the curious assonance in *erecta . . . secta*; see note on 55, and cf. 542; other striking lines of this type are i. 266 'ternaque transierint Rutulis hiberna subactis', ii. 353 'incensae: moriamur et in media arma ruamus', iii. 540 'bello armantur equi, bellum haec armenta minantur'.

506 ff. intenditque . . . futuri: 'she hangs the place with garlands, and crowns it with the foliage of death; above she sets the things he wore, the sword he left, and an image of him upon the couch. Well she knew what was to be.' The verbs *intendit* and *coronat* are correlated by *-que . . . et*, as in 484–5. Virgil inverts the normal construction *serta loco intendit*.

507. funerea: emphatic; how different this is from the *festa frons* with which Dido had adorned Sychaeus' shrine (459). Virgil probably means cypress-boughs; compare the description of Misenus' burial (vi. 214 ff.) 'principio pinguem taedis et robore secto/ ingentem struxere pyram, cui frondibus atris/ intexunt latera, et feralis ante cupressos/ constituunt'. Such a preparation might surely have made Anna suspect something of the truth. We are not told whether she was with Dido at the performance of the ritual (but cf. 680, and note on 498); one would not have expected her to be there, for the ordeal was Dido's alone, though she presumably superintended the erection of the pyre.

super: adverbial. In what follows, the first *-que* is a true connective, joining *ensem* with *exuvias*.

508. effigiem: presumably of wax; as it melts, so the lover will melt—a familiar type of sympathetic magic. It is strange that there has been no mention of this before; but it surely shows that part of the ritual really is an attempt to win back Aeneas, or at least to make Anna believe this. In Dido's last speech, when she addresses the *exuviae* on the pyre (651), the image is not mentioned either, but by then all need for deception has gone. Cf. Theocr. 2. 28 f. ὡς τοῦτον τὸν κηρὸν ἐγὼ σὺν δαίμονι τάκω, / ὡς τάκοιθ' ὑπ' ἔρωτος ὁ Μύνδιος αὐτίκα Δέλφις (see Gow's note), and Virgil's imitation of it in *E.* viii. 80 f.

haud . . . futuri: Dido knows her purpose (cf. 475), but no one else knows it, or must know it.

509. The priestess begins her invocation to the Powers of Darkness. Her hair is loosed (*effusa*, 'middle', with *crinis* as direct object, cf. 137), because in magic there must be nothing bound or knotted; so Medea is 'nuda pedem, nudos umeris infusa capillos' (Ovid, *Met*. vii. 183), and Canidia in Hor. *Sat.* i. 8. 24 is 'pedibus nudis passoque capillo'.

510. ter centum: of any large number (see Wölfflin, *ALL* ix, pp. 177 ff.). The compound of three is part of the magic (see Gow on Theocr. 2. 43); cf. *E*. viii. 73 ff. 'terna tibi haec primum triplici diversa colore/ licia circumdo, terque haec altaria circum/ effigiem duco; numero deus impare gaudet'. In the magic practice described by Hardy in *The Return of the Native* (Wessex edition, pp. 443 ff.), the Lord's Prayer is repeated backwards three times, while the image of Eustacia Vye slowly melts; cf. Joshua Sylvester's lines

> Thrice toss these oaken ashes in the air,
> And thrice three times tie up this true love-knot;
> Thrice sit thee down in this enchanted chair,
> And murmur soft 'She will' or 'She will not'.
> Go burn these poisoned weeds in that blue fire,
> This cypress gathered at a dead man's grave;
> These screech owl's feathers and this pricking briar,
> That all thy thorny cares an end may have.

In such a ritual, it was essential to list the names of any divinities who might be in any way concerned, so as to comprehend all possibilities and eliminate any chance of failure through negligence. Many such lists occur in the extant magic papyri; see also some of the spells in Audollent, *Defixionum Tabellae* (Paris, 1904), and the introduction, p. lix. This principle was not confined to 'black' magic; in all ritual it was proper to give the god or gods the choice of name or function that pleased them most; see Catull. 34, where after listing Diana's various functions and names, Catullus ends 'sis quocumque tibi placet/ sancta nomine', and the great prayer to Zeus in Aesch. *Ag*. 160 ff., beginning Ζεύς, ὅστις ποτ' ἐστίν, εἰ τόδ' αὐτῷ φίλον κεκλημένῳ, τοῦτό νιν προσεννέπω (where see Fraenkel).

tonat ore: cf. 680 f. 'patriosque vocavi/ voce deos' (see note).

Erebumque Chaosque, etc.: Virgil names particular powers included in the general *ter centum deos* (here there is a triple correlative -*que*, cf. 83). He is not concerned with any technical formula; he wishes merely to invest the horrid ritual with all possible mystery and terror. But even in such a context he shows all his familiar care for detail in matters of worship; the names of both Erebus and Chaos occur in existing magical papyri (cf. Preisendanz *PGM* i. 120 Χάος ἀρχέγονον, Ἔρεβος, φρικτὸν Στυγὸς ὕδωρ). Hecate naturally occurs frequently; note Audollent no. 243 (an inscription from Carthage, third century A.D.) ὀνόματα Ἑκάτης τριμόρφου μαστει-γοφόρου δεδούλου λαμπαδούχου χρυσοσανδαλιαιμοποτιχθονίαν . . . .

511. tergeminam: 'three-fold'; so *septemgeminus* (vi. 800), *centumgeminus* (vi. 287). At Seven Springs, near Cheltenham, a reputed source of the Thames, an inscription runs 'hic tuus o Tamesine pater septemgeminus fons'. Hecate is the chthonic counterpart of Diana and the Moon (cf. Catull. 34). In art she was shown as a triple figure, with the three faces in different directions (cf. Frazer on Ovid, *F.* i. 141).

512 ff. sparserat . . . veneni: 'and she had sprinkled water feigned to come from the springs of Hell; and potent herbs she goes to fetch, herbs cut by a sickle of bronze beneath the moon, oozing black poisonous milk.' The horror rises to a climax. For the postponed *et* in 512, 513, 515, see on 33.

512. simulatos: Servius comments 'in sacris . . . quae exhiberi non poterant simulabantur, et erant pro veris': the counterfeit is regarded as equivalent to the reality for the purposes of the magic rite, just as an effigy is equivalent to the actual person. Cf. A. D. Nock in *CR* xxxviii, 1924, p. 169.

Averni: the lake which gave entrance to the underworld (vi. 126); cf. Hor. *Epod.* 5. 25 f. 'at expedita Sagana per totam domum/ spargens Avernalis aquas'.

513. falcibus . . . aenis: cf. Ovid, *Met.* vii. 227 'partim succidit curvamine falcis aenae' (of Medea). Macrobius discusses this passage (*Sat.* v. 19. 7 ff.) and quotes a fragment of Sophocles as Virgil's alleged source.

Bronze is universal in such a connexion. Iron was taboo; it was 'a new and uncanny discovery at the end of the bronze age' (C. Bailey, *Phases in the Religion of Ancient Rome*, p. 24 —see the whole chapter), a 'stranger' that might upset tradition. So bronze is used to drive away ghosts at the Lemuria (Ovid, *F.* v. 441, where see Frazer, and cf. *F.* ii. 577), and to counteract an eclipse of the moon (Ovid, *Met.* vii. 207 f.); bronze nails were used in *defixiones* (curse-tablets). Pliny mentions various plants, especially those used in magic rites, which must be cut *sine ferro*: thus (*NH* xxiv. 103) he says of *selago*, used by Gaulish Druids 'contra perniciem omnem', 'sine ferro, dextra manu per tunicam operta, sinistra eruitur velut a furante, candida veste vestito pureque lautis nudis pedibus'.

ad lunam: probably 'by moonlight'; so Pliny says (*NH* xxiv. 12) that mistletoe is said to be more efficacious 'prima luna collectum e robore sine ferro'.

quaeruntur: from the witch's store; but why were these things not ready from the first? See note on 498.

514. **pubentes**: cf. xii. 412 f. 'dictamnum genetrix Cretaea carpit ab Ida/ puberibus caulem foliis'. The meaning may be simply 'downy', or it may imply potency. Servius notes 'sciendum inter homines et herbas esse reciprocam translationem: sic enim *pubentem herbam* dicimus, quemadmodum *florem aetatis*'. It looks like a ritual use.

lacte: defined by *nigri veneni*; *cum* = 'containing' (cf. L. & S., s.v., II. B).

515 f. **quaeritur . . . amor**: 'she goes to fetch too a love-charm, ripped from the brow of a foal as it comes to birth, torn away before the mother can seize it.' This is the grisliest of all the witch's gatherings. The traditional explanation is that Virgil means the *hippomanes*, a growth on the head of a foal, which the mother bites off unless she is prevented; see Pliny, *NH* viii. 165 'equis amoris innasci veneficium hippomanes appellatum in fronte, caricae magnitudine, colore nigro, quod statim edito partu devorat feta' (Irvine quotes Philemon Holland's delightful translation). The legend goes back to Aristotle (*HA* vi. 572ª19 ff., 577ª7 ff.). If Virgil means this growth—and the connexion of the tradition with sorcery can be seen from many passages listed by Pease—then *amor* is used here in a startling sense, 'a piece of love' as it were, which Mackail denies to be possible; but in this context it is bold to say that such a Virgilian experiment is impossible (Pease compares the use of στέργημα in Soph. *Tr.* 1138).

Virgil appears to follow a quite different tradition in *G.* iii. 280 f., where he uses the actual word *hippomanes*, and says of it 'lentum destillat ab inguine virus', again, however, in a context of miracles and magic spells. Now there its properties are connected with madness in horses; and in Theocr. 2. 48 the same properties are ascribed to it, and the specific name given, but the thing is termed a plant, φυτόν, on which Gow comments 'it would seem to be connected with some plant having a more or less milky juice'. Does not this suggest the *herbae nigri cum lacte veneni* of 514? Can Virgil have thought of *hippomanes* at first in its Theocritean sense (it is in fact inconceivable that he did not have Theocritus' lines in mind here), and then have begun a passage about it in its traditional form as Pliny describes it, which he did not complete? In that case Mackail is probably right in regarding

515–16 as 'a tentative note for an alternative to the couplet 513–14'.

The passage is clearly unfinished; this is shown not only by the incomplete line 516, but by the difficult transition to 517 (see below), and perhaps also by the curiously repetitive *sparserat et, falcibus et, quaeritur et*, so close together. Mackail holds that *quaeritur* has no subject, and that *et matri praereptus amor* is in loose apposition to the missing subject. In spite of his view that *amor* cannot mean a 'love-charm', it is hard to reject the sense that tradition has given it, however we suppose the passage would have appeared in its final shape. In any case the chance that has left the lines unfinished has added to their mysterious horror. The real world has been left far behind, and the figure of Death deepens the shadows of despair. The opening of Act IV of *Macbeth* has its match here.

517 ff. ipsa ... precatur: 'Dido herself, beside the altars, carrying the holy meal with reverent hands—bared of its bonds one foot, her robe ungirt—calls upon the gods her witnesses, she whose purpose it is to die, and upon the stars that share the secrets of fate. And then, to whatsoever power has charge of those who love on terms that match not, a just power, a mindful power, she says her prayers.'

In contrast with the preceding passage, with the witch and her horrid mumbo-jumbo, Dido seems calm and collected; she performs her self-imposed ritual and prayer with dignity and tragic composure; she has the strength which her dreadful purpose gives her, *haud ignara futuri* as she is.

517. mola: the *mola salsa*, meal (*far*) and salt, sprinkled on the altar at a sacrifice (a ritual word); cf. v. 745 'farre pio et plena supplex veneratur acerra', xii. 173 'dant fruges manibus salsas', *E.* viii. 82 'sparge molam'.

Mola is the reading of F and of Servius; M and P have *molam*, which many editors retain, either supplying *sparserat* from 512 (surely impossible), or (with Mackail) assuming a lacuna before the line. Mackail objects that *mola manibusque piis* is 'hardly sense' with *testatur*. But the words can perhaps be taken as a very loose 'accompanying' ablative, showing the manner in which Dido performed the rite, the two nouns together meaning 'with a reverent offering of the holy meal' (cf. Pliny, *NH* xviii. 7 'Numa instituit deos fruge colere et mola salsa supplicare atque . . . far torrere').

piis: the word applies to *mola* also. But it seems like a horrible parody of the familiar *piae manus, far pium* in orthodox worship; cf. *pia vitta*, 637.

518. unum exuta pedem: the participle is middle, with *pedem* as

direct object (cf. 137). The bare foot and the loosened robe
are of the essence of magic ritual (cf. 509, note); Pease observes that leather (the skins of dead animals) was taboo in
sacred rites (cf. Frazer on Ovid, *F.* i. 629), while with the feet
bare the performer was in direct contact with the earth and
the chthonic powers. Pease has a large collection of examples
of the baring of the feet, but here one foot only is bared:
Servius explains 'quia id agitur ut et ista solvatur et inplice-
tur Aeneas', the shod foot keeps Dido free of the spell, the
bare foot works the spell against Aeneas. The line, like all
the rest of the passage, is instinct with all the primitive
power of folklore; see Irvine's note, and his reference to
Frazer, *The Golden Bough*[3], vol. iii, pp. 310 ff.; he well terms
this 'a complex act which possibly loses more than it gains by
too close inspection'.

veste: in the ablative, the singular form predominates in
Augustan poetry (*vestibus* occurs first in Ovid, *Met.* v. 601),
whereas in the dative the plural is regular and the singular
occurs once only (Ovid, *Met.* iv. 117): see Maas, *ALL* xii,
pp. 527 f.; he thinks that a trochaic form like *veste* had
greater mobility within the line, whereas the spondaic *vesti*
was less mobile than the plural form (a somewhat doubtful
argument).

519. moritura: here at last the word has its full and conscious
meaning.

deos: see note on 498; as Eitrem points out, it is not the
chthonic deities to whom Dido prays, as one would have expected if she had felt no shame at her magic practice.

520 f. si quod . . . numen: a good example of the type of precautionary clause referred to on 510: in case she has omitted
any power who ought to be named, she adds an invocation to
whatever (unknown) Spirit is concerned with the fate of such
as she (cf. Bailey, *Religion in Virgil*, p. 62).

non aequo foedere: i.e. lovers whose love is not on an equal
footing, each to each.

521. iustumque memorque: see on 83, and for the rhythm see
on 59. Dido appeals to any Spirit who will right her un-
doubted wrongs. The line is most moving in its simplicity;
amid all the dark mysteries of magic, Dido is shown at the
end as 'saying her prayers' like a puzzled child who has been
hurt.

Virgil leaves the magic rite, with the tension of it unre-
solved. We never know whether Dido still had some lingering
hope left in practising it, though it is clear from what follows
that her resolution to die has a final wavering. It is a passage
of subtle poetic art: Dido's uncanny calm, the mysterious

witch, the gruesome ritual, the suspense—all this deepens the colouring and adds to the horror of the suicide to come.

522-52. *It is night, and all the world of nature sleeps ; but Dido cannot sleep. Her heart is a turmoil of love and anger, and she turns over and over again many an argument with herself; yet there is no other thing that she can do but die. She turns on Anna and blames her for everything : it is all Anna's fault that she has been faithless to the dead who had faith in her.*

522 ff. nox . . . silenti: 'it was night; and all over earth tired creatures were enjoying the calm of sleep. The woods and the wild seas had sunk to rest, and it was the time when the stars slide midway in circling course, when every meadow is quiet, quiet the beasts and patterned birds, those that haunt the pools' clear expanse and those that dwell in the shrub-roughened fields, wrapt in sleep, protected by the silent night.'

Heyne well remarks of these lovely lines, 'suavissima noctis descriptio, quae ipsam rerum quietem spirare videtur': note the sustained mastery of alliteration and assonance (*placidum, soporem, corpora; nox, fessa, terras, silvae, saeva ; quierant, aequora ; volvuntur, lapsu, lacus liquidos ; dumis, rura ; tenent, silenti*). Dryden is at his fine best in his version of them:

'Twas dead of night, when weary bodies close
Their eyes in balmy sleep, and soft repose:
The winds no longer whisper thro' the woods,
Nor murm'ring tides disturb the gentle floods.
The stars in silent order mov'd around,
And peace, with downy wings, was brooding on the ground.
The flocks and herds, and parti colour'd fowl,
Which haunt the woods, or swim the weedy pool;
Stretch'd on the quiet earth securely lay,
Forgetting the past labours of the day;

and Henry quotes Tasso, *Gerusalemme Liberata*, ii. 96:

Era la notte, allor ch' alto riposo
Han l'onde e i venti, e parea muto il mondo.
Gli animai lassi, e quei che'l mar ondoso,
E de' liquidi laghi alberga il fondo,
E chi si giace in tana o in mandra ascoso,
E i pinti augelli, nell' obblio profondo,
Sotto 'l silenzio de' secreti orrori,
Sopian gli affanni, e raddolciano i cuori.

They can be paralleled many times from Virgil himself and throughout Greek and Latin poetry; Pease collects a host of

passages, one of the finest of which is Apoll. Rhod. iii. 744 ff.,
where Medea cannot sleep for love of Jason. Yet here we
have more than a description of the calm of night, more even
than the contrast between Dido's stormy heart and the tranquillity all around her: there is the contrast between the
natural and the unnatural, the normal life of man and the
abnormality of dark witchcraft; and all the while there is
another sleep awaiting Dido.

522. carpebant: here and in the next two lines the fourth foot
ends with a word-ending ('diaeresis'), which adds to the
smoothness of the rhythm and suggests something of the
monotony of the routine of sleep. It is a rhythm that Virgil
is careful not to use in excess (cf. note on 185); contrast,
e.g., Catullus 64 where seven of the first ten lines have this
rhythm, or the practice of Lucretius or of Cicero in his
Aratea.

523 f. saeva . . . aequora: cf. Stat. *S.* v. 4. 5 f. 'occidit horror/
aequoris, et terris maria acclinata quiescunt' (see the appendix to the *Oxford Book of Latin Verse* for a translation of
this poem, with sonnets to Sleep added for comparison, by
Sidney, Daniel, Drummond, Wordsworth, Keats, Hartley
Coleridge).

524. cum . . . lapsu: a fine picture of tranquil movement.

525. cf. P. Gerhardt's lines: 'Nun ruhen alle Wälder,/ Vieh,
Menschen, Stadt und Felder,/ Es schläft die ganze Welt.'

   tacet: the voice of the fields is silent, though by day they
are alive with sound. *Tacent* must be supplied with what
follows (but see on 528).

   pictae: 'gay', like *varius* (cf. 202); so στικτός; cf. Milton,
PL vii. 433 f. 'From branch to branch the smaller birds with
song/ Solaced the woods, and spread their painted wings',
and the *variae volucres* of Lucr. ii. 344 f.

526. liquidos: *late* must be taken closely with it; the word
means clear, as well as smooth-flowing (cf. Tennyson's 'The
shining levels of the lake').

527. rura: the plural form is far more frequent than the singular in poetry, and occurs in prose also (see Maas, *ALL* xii.
p. 522, note).

   somno: either modal, or a local ablative; *sub* is probably
'under the protection of' night, which acts as a sheltering
cover for the sleeping world.

528. This line is wanting in the best MSS., and Servius ignores
it. It is generally regarded as an insertion from ix. 225 'laxa-
bant curas et corda oblita laborum'; yet it rounds off the
metrical paragraph well and in Virgil's manner (see Mackail,
introd. pp. liii ff.), while *corda oblita laborum* has a poignancy

here that is lacking in ix. 225. Page regards it as 'certainly unnecessary', but Henry and Irvine defend it stoutly. If it were not for the lack of MS. support, I could see no reason for deleting it as superfluous in itself; if it is retained, the stop after 527 must be omitted, and *tacent* need no longer be supplied with *pecudes*, etc. in 525.

lenibant: so *nutribant, insignibat, vestibat* (vii. 485, 790, viii. 160). The normal imperfect forms are impossible in hexameters.

529 ff. at non . . . accipit: 'but the Queen of Carthage, with doom in her heart, rests not, nor ever looses her limbs to sleep, nor in eyes or breast takes night to herself.' A verb such as *tacet* or the like must be supplied with *at non*, and with this punctuation (or with a comma after *Phoenissa*, which many editors print) *neque* connects *solvitur* with this unexpressed verb. But in G. iii. 349 f., iv. 530, there is a similar use of *at non* in ellipse, and in those passages the phrase so introduced stands alone with nothing linked to it; and Professor W. S. Watt has suggested to me that this would be a more effective arrangement here also, with a colon after *Phoenissa*, giving the sense 'but not so the Queen of Carthage, with doom in her heart: she never looses her limbs', etc. With this punctuation, *neque* introduces an independent sentence, amplifying what precedes, and *neque . . . ve . . . aut* are used in correlation (a poetic use, as in Ovid, *Tr.* iii. 10. 13 'nix iacet, et iactam nec sol pluviaeve resolvunt'; see L.-H., p. 664).

529. infelix animi: see note on 203 (*amens animi*), and cf. *inops animi* (300).

Phoenissa: here a noun, as in i. 714 (but an adjective in i. 670, vi. 450).

530 f. Editors compare Tennyson, *The Marriage of Geraint*, 'She found no rest, and ever fail'd to draw/ The quiet night into her blood'.

531 f. ingeminant . . . aestu: 'doubled is all her anguish, and once more love swells up to rage, and tosses in a vast tide of angry thoughts.' Note the assonance in *curae, rursus, resurgens, fluctuat, aestu*.

532. irarum: for the plural see on 197. Dido's passion comes surging back, and combines with her angry misery to make her once more irresolute, even though her decision has been taken. A change of subject is usually assumed with *fluctuat* (Mackail points out, on vii. 211, that such a change is a favourite Virgilian artifice); but it is more vivid to keep *amor* as subject, and the phrase becomes Catullus' *odi et amo* in starker form. Cf. viii. 19, xii. 486.

533. sic adeo . . . volutat: 'this is the way she dwells upon her thoughts, and this is what she turns and turns again in her secret heart.' *Sic* and *ita* both refer to what follows; *adeo* emphasizes *sic* (cf. 96), 'thus, just thus'.

insistit: generally taken as 'she starts to speak' (cf. xii. 47 'sic institit ore'). But she is not speaking, she is thinking to herself; in xii. 47 an actual speech follows, and *ore* makes the sense plain. Here, *insistit* ought to be, and is, explained by *secumque . . . volutat*: she 'persists' in her troubled thoughts. *Sic* acts for *in his sententiis*, just as *ita* acts instead of an object to *volutat*. Dido wearily goes over argument after argument (see on 547), and it is not surprising that at the end of all her sleepless ramblings she illogically blames Anna for everything.

534. en: this interrogative use is common in Plautus and Terence, in the formula *en umquam* (cf. *E.* i. 67, *A.* vi. 346 'en haec promissa fides est?', where Norden quotes Donatus on Ter. *Ph.* 348, *en habet vim indignationis post enarratam iniuriam*); see L.-H., p. 650. 'See', or 'Lo!' in English does not really bring out its force, which is a mixture of exasperation and despair.

quid ago: Maas points out (*ALL* xii, p. 513, note) that Virgil nowhere else has *ago* without a following elision (cf. x. 675 'quid ago? aut quae . . .?', xii. 637 'nam quid ago? aut quae . . .?'; *E.* i. 13, ix. 37). He thinks that Donatus' reading *agam* here is probably correct. The parallel passages with *en* suggest that *ago* should not be taken as deliberative, as some editors assume; the meaning is 'what *am* I doing?', i.e., 'where is my hesitation leading me?'. Dido's self-questioning is like that in Soph. *Ai.* 457 ff., Eur. *Med.* 502 ff., Catull. 64. 177 ff., etc.; the rhetorical colouring can be seen from the fragment of C. Gracchus quoted by Cicero in *de or.* iii. 214 'quo me miser conferam? quo vertam? in Capitoliumne? at fratris sanguine madet. an domum? matremne ut miseram lamentantem videam et abiectam?'

534 ff. rursusne . . . maritos?: 'Shall I then turn back and sue my wooers of other days, a laughing-stock? Shall I grovel and beg a husband from the Numidians, though time and again I have disdained marriage with such as they?' *Rursus* does not mean 'once more', for Dido has never sought them; she argues 'shall I give up my plan for the alternative (*rursus*) of finding a husband here?'

534. inrisa: Stanyhurst has 'a castaway milckmadge'.

535. Nomadum: not contemptuous, as Page thinks; see on 320.

536. sim: concessive; *maritos* is used as in 35.

537. igitur: she dismisses the first possibility and comes to a second.

ultima: this may perhaps imply slavery, but need not be more than 'uttermost'. Henry vigorously comments: 'The queen and founder of Carthage, the noble, generous, high-minded Dido, coolly deliberates whether or not to accompany a foreigner and refugee she knows not whither, in the capacity of *serva* and *pellex*! Fie on the interpretation! Fie on the reader who, accepting it, does not lay down the book, closed for ever on Dido and her shame! . . . No, no; unhappy Dido, fallen as thou art, thou art not fallen into the pit of ink into which commentators represent thee to have fallen.'

538 f. quiane . . . facti?: 'what, because they are glad that in other days I raised them up by my help? Because gratitude for past kindness stands firm in hearts that do not forget?'

538. quiane: *-ne* belongs, not to *quia*, but to a question that is not formally expressed ('shall I do this, because . . .'), a colloquial usage; cf. Catull. 64. 180 'an patris auxilium sperem? quemne ipsa reliqui?' (where *quemne* = *eumne quem*). *Scilicet* would have shown the same turn of incredulity—the Trojans can have no real gratitude to her. Cf. x. 673, where *quosne* is used similarly. See L.-H., p. 648.

539. bene: either with *memores*, or with *stat*, or with *facti*.

540 f. quis me . . . accipiet?: 'again—suppose me willing—who will suffer me, who will take me aboard his proud ship, the woman they hate?'

540. autem: this carries her argument a stage further—'I may be willing, but who will want me?'

fac velle: sc. *me*; *fac* = 'imagine', a conversational turn; cf. Cic. *RA* 97 'fac audisse statim', *ad Fam*. vii. 23. 1 'fac quaeso qui ego sum esse te', Ovid, *Met*. ii. 290 'sed tamen exitium fac me meruisse'. The omission of *me* is also colloquial; see note on 383.

superbis: not otiose; Dido thinks of the tyranny of a foe to a slave.

541. invisam: note the juxtaposition with *superbis*, and the run-on. Mackail prints *inrisam*, the reading of the second hand in M, surely less good, in spite of *inrisa* in 534; the eagerness of the Trojans to go has left Dido with no illusions.

nescis: an effective self-apostrophe, to avoid the metrically intractable first person of the verbs.

542. Laomedonteae: i.e. perfidious (a reference to *gratia facti* above). Laomedon of Troy employed Apollo and Neptune to build its walls, and then refused payment, a debt which Virgil felt took long enough to pay (*G*. i. 501 f. 'satis iam pridem sanguine nostro/ Laomedonteae luimus periuria Troiae'), but which his generation had at last paid. For the prosody *-ēae*, see on 6.

sentis . . . gentis: a curious rhyme (cf. notes on 55, 505); it faintly foreshadows the pattern of much medieval hexameter-writing.

543. quid tum?: a further stage; suppose she is taken, how shall she go?

sola . . . ovantis?: 'alone, in flight, to keep the company of jubilant sailormen?' Mackail notes the antithesis of *sola fuga* and *ovantis*, 'a lonely fugitive among their triumphant array'. A Roman reader would think of the *ovatio* that a victor received; Dido will attend a Trojan triumph.

544. Tyriis: this instrumental ablative is normal with *stipatus* and *comitatus*; cf. Conway on i. 312, and see my note on Cic. *Cael.* 34.

545. inferar: 'shall I go to join them' (cf. 142 *infert se socium*); the meaning 'attack', which some editors prefer, is absurd in this context.

quos . . . revelli: an objection appended to her own argument, as in 536 and 538, though by a different construction. She had had trouble enough in persuading her people to sail from Tyre to Carthage; it was not likely that they would be ready to uproot themselves again.

547. Dido's argument has now come full circle. She has said to herself: 'Can I expect to marry a Numidian prince? No: I have alienated them all. Shall I go with the Trojans, hoping that they will remember my past services? No: no-one will want me, they do not know gratitude. Suppose they do allow me, shall I go alone? No: the sailors will be rough to me. Shall I take a Tyrian bodyguard? No: they would not come.' In the rambling, hopeless argument, Virgil has clearly shown Dido's weary agony, and her despair is summed up in 547: only one course remains, to die.

quin . . . dolorem: 'no, no, die—it is all you deserve—turn sorrow back with the sword.' For *quin* see note on 99.

ut merita es: Dido's wandering thoughts now turn to her own desertion of Sychaeus: she has brought it all on herself. And then she irrationally turns against her sister and blames her for the whole calamity, a strange and horrible climax to a fine and subtle passage.

548 f. tu . . . hosti: '*you*, no, no, die—it is all you deserve—turn tears, *you*, my sister, first set this load of ills upon me to madden me, first cast me into a foeman's path.' For *evicta* cf. 474. Dido has forgotten all logic now.

prima: almost 'in the beginning' (see on 169). *Furentem* is proleptic.

549. oneras . . . obicis: Anna was the original cause, and still remains as the cause, so Latin uses the present tense; see note on *vindicat*, 228. Note Dido's use of *hosti*; cf. 424.

550 f. A most difficult passage, to which Henry devotes twelve pages. We must not forget Dido's state of mind as she comes painfully to this final conclusion of her self-torment; she is scarcely coherent now, and it is as if we overhear the mutterings of delirium.

The main problems are three: (a) the meaning of *non licuit*, (b) the sense and construction of *thalami expertem*, (c) the implications of *more ferae*.

As regards (a), the context seems to connect *non licuit* with Dido's blame of Anna; the two previous lines are left in the air if this passage is not closely connected with them. I would therefore take the sense as 'You would not let me' (i.e. *non licuit per te*), not as a general statement meaning 'I had no right'.

As regards (b), editors generally take *thalami expertem* as 'unjoined in lawful wedlock'. This view is based largely upon an interpretation of an unfortunate remark of Quintilian, who says (ix. 2. 64) 'est emphasis etiam inter figuras cum ex aliquo dicto latens aliquid eruitur, ut apud Vergilium *non licuit thalami expertem sine crimine vitam degere more ferae*. quamquam enim de matrimonio queritur Dido, tamen huc erumpit eius affectus ut sine thalamis vitam non hominum putet sed ferarum'. For this interpretation see Henry, and M. B. Ogle in *TAPA* lvi, 1925, pp. 26 ff. I think it means 'unmarried', but not in Horace's sense of *nuptiarum expers* (*C*. iii. 11. 11), or in Statius' sense of *expers conubii* (*Th*. x. 62): I would take *thalami* to refer to the past that is now lost, and interpret *thalami expertem* (i.e. *thalamo carentem*) as equivalent to *non nuptam*, in the particular sense of 'a widow'. That *non nupta* could be used in this sense is shown by Cic. *Cael*. 49; and in Apul. *Apol*. 27 *non nupserit* means 'was a widow'. This interpretation leads naturally on to the mention of Sychaeus in 552. There seems no more difficulty in this than in the use of the word *vidua* to mean an unmarried woman, which is clear from Juv. 4. 4, and from Statius' application of *viduos annos* to an unmarried girl (*S*. i. 2. 168); similarly, Catullus uses it of an 'unmarried' vine (62. 49). Fanshawe was near the truth when he translated the lines: 'Why might not I, alas! have mourn'd away/ My widow'd youth, as well as turtles do?'

As for the construction, it seems more reasonable to understand *me* with *expertem*, than to take the adjective with *vitam*, as some editors have suggested.

As regards (c), Quintilian has again obscured the issue; he

has been adduced as proving *more ferae* to mean 'beast-fashion' in the sense of 'promiscuously'. But his explanation must be read in the light of its purpose, i.e. to illustrate the figure *emphasis*, 'cum ex aliquo dicto latens aliquid eruitur': he clearly takes the surface meaning to be a 'complaint against marriage' by Dido (which is in itself not true), and deduces the real meaning to be that living unmarried (*sine thalamis*) is not a thing for men but for beasts—i.e. that without a husband life is intolerable, and one might as well not be a human being at all. Nothing here indicates that Quintilian necessarily took *thalami expertem* as 'without lawful wedlock', or that by *vitam ferarum* he meant promiscuity. It is true that he took *expertem* with *vitam*, but this is for the purpose of the 'hidden meaning' that he professes to deduce (see Henry, p. 796).

The sense of *more ferae* is far more probably something like 'in simple innocence'; as Conington and Mackail observe, it is well illustrated by Virgil's own picture of Camilla in xi. 570 ff. or Ovid's of Daphne (*Met.* i. 474 ff.); and Henry adduces a number of passages which show a contrast between the wickedness of man and the simplicity of the beasts of the field (e.g. Cic. *RA* 150 'inter feras satius est aetatem degere quam in hac tanta immanitate versari', Ovid, *F.* ii. 291 f., of the Arcadians, 'vita feris similis, nullos agitata per usus;/ artis adhuc expers et rude vulgus erat'). It must, however, be admitted that the normal implication of *more ferae* would be bestiality, not innocence (cf. Livy iii. 47. 7 'pecudum ferarumque ritu promisce in concubitus ruere', and other passages cited by Pease): and if Virgil has used it to mean 'in simple innocence,' he has certainly been an innovator here. Yet perhaps it is relevant to remember that the simple, innocent, tame fawn of vii. 489 is still a *ferus*. And I should prefer to believe that Virgil was using *more ferae* in his own original way, than that he was guilty of the tasteless exaggeration of making his noble Dido speak of herself as 'promiscuous'. Lastly, if *sine crimine* does not imply 'innocence', what does?

My interpretation of the passage is, therefore: 'You would not let me live my life in widowhood, innocently, like a woodland creature, without tasting the bitterness of love like this.' I cannot think that Dido is concerned with indicting her passion for Aeneas as adulterous: what fills her mind completely in the end, almost delirious as she is, is primarily the thought of Sychaeus' trust in her, which she has broken on Anna's advice. However, this is one of those passages which will have a different message for every reader of Virgil:

Mackail well remarks 'the broken inconsequence of lines 548–52, and the note on which Dido breaks off, are among the masterpieces of Virgilian art'; and in such a moment neither dogma nor pedantry has any place.

551. nec: postponed (see on 33); by *curae* Dido means the whole complex of her misery, caused by her love for Aeneas.

552. non . . . Sychaeo: 'I have not kept my word, the word I gave to the ashes of the dead, the word I gave to Sychaeus'; the line is echoed by Dante (*Inferno*, v. 61 f.), 'L'altra è colei che s'ancise amorosa,/ E ruppe fede al cener di Sicheo'. Editors generally take *Sychaeo* as an adjective; Mackail compares iii. 602 'Danais e classibus', vi. 118 'lucis . . . Avernis' (cf. Conway on i. 686 'laticemque Lyaeum'). Henry takes it as a noun, in apposition to *cineri*, which seems to me preferable: the use of an adjective formed from a proper noun is too artificial in this context, where it is Sychaeus as a person who is uppermost in Dido's mind. The reading is not quite certain: *Sychaeo* is a correction added by a second hand in P (from *Sychaeies*, perhaps for *Sychaei est*—cf. the reading of M in 632), while M has *Sychaei*. But the sound of *cineri . . . Sychaei* seems to tell against the genitive.

As Dido's passion had begun with her self-searchings over her pledge to Sychaeus (15 ff.), so now her tortured mind brings her back to it.

553–83. *But Aeneas is asleep, on his ship, now that all is ready. And he dreams of Mercury, warning him of danger if he delays: he wakes in alarm, calls out his men, and in great haste the fleet puts to sea.*

In contrast to Dido Aeneas' struggle with conscience is over, or seems so. The quieter tone of this passage comes as a relief to the tension of the past hundred lines.

553. tantos . . . questus: 'such were the terrible grievings that she kept pouring out within her heart'; for the (poetic) transitive use of the verb cf. *rumpere vocem* (ii. 129, iii. 246, etc.); *suo pectore* is an elaboration of *secum*.

554. Aeneas: in antithesis with *illa*, with no particle expressed. The slow rhythm of this and the next line suggests deep calm.

certus eundi: a poetic construction, used also by Tacitus, on the analogy of the genitive after adjectives expressing knowledge or ignorance; contrast *certa mori* (564).

555. carpebat somnos: a clear echo of 522. But Aeneas' will is not as firm as he imagines (just as Dido has shown irresolution in spite of the decision taken in 475), and the new apparition of Mercury is needed to harden it to final action. It would still have taken very little, even yet, for Aeneas and Dido to save their love: but *fata obstant*.

556 f. huic . . . somnis: 'to him there came, in a dream, the shape of a god coming a second time in like appearance.' This is not an actual visitation (as in 265 ff.), but a vision in a dream (cf. 353).

558 f. omnia . . . iuventae: 'like in every way to Mercury, in speech as in complexion, in his golden hair, in his body that wore youth's lovely grace.'

558. omnia: an adverbial accusative of reference after *similis* (so ix. 650 f. 'omnia longaevo similis, vocemque coloremque/ et crinis albos et saeva sonoribus arma'). This use of *omnia* is an invention of Virgil's, by analogy with πάντα, and was seldom imitated (cf. Stat. *Ach.* ii. 9 f. 'omnia visu/ mutatus rediit', Nemesianus *Cyn.* 114 'omnia magnum'); it is foreign to prose (Livy xxi. 34. 5 is not an example of it). See Wölfflin, *ALL* ii, pp. 95 ff., 615; L.-H., p. 379; Kroll, *Wissenschaftliche Syntax*, p. 36. The corresponding use of *cetera* (τἆλλα) is common in poetry, especially after *similis*, *nudus*, etc., and is found in Sallust, Livy, the elder Pliny, and Tacitus. See Wölfflin, l.c., p. 91, and also *ALL* xii, p. 478. Both uses are generalizing examples of the poetic accusative of 'respect' after adjectives, used especially of parts of the body (so *vocem*, *colorem* here, particularizing *omnia*), an entirely Greek mannerism, first imported to Latin by Virgil and widely adopted by the poets after him. The first certain prose example of such an accusative is Tac. *Ger.* 17 'nudae bracchia' (so *Ann.* vi. 9 'clari genus'); see Landgraf, *ALL* x, pp. 209 ff., Kroll, l.c., and cf. Conway on i. 320.

vocemque coloremque: for double *-que* see on 83. The line is hypermetric, with elision between the second *-que* and *et* at the beginning of the next line. Virgil has a number of examples of this hypermetric *–que*, and most of them occur with this correlated use of double *-que* (e.g. i. 332, ii. 745, *G.* ii. 344, 443). No special effect seems intended here, unless perhaps Virgil wishes to show the close fusion of the less tangible aspects of the god with his physical attributes. Elsewhere the device is used for a dramatic metrical picture, as in 629; so vi. 602 (of an overhanging rock) 'quos super atra silex iam iam lapsura cadentique/ imminet adsimilis' (see Norden), *G.* i. 295 f. 'aut dulcis musti Volcano decoquit umorem/ et foliis undam trepidi despumat aeni' (where the hypermetric syllable shows the exciting point at which the liquid rises to the top of the pan and nearly but not quite boils over). It occurs in Lucilius (547 M.), Lucretius (v. 849), and Catullus (34. 22, 64. 298, 115. 5) before Virgil (all with *-que*, except

Lucr. l.c.); but it was Virgil who first used it for artistic purposes. Neither Lucan nor Statius uses it. There are no examples in Homer, and its only occurrence in dactylic Greek poetry is Callim. *Ep.* 41. 1 f. ἥμισύ μευ ψυχῆς ἔτι τὸ πνέον, ἥμισυ δ' οὐκ οἶδ' / εἴτ' Ἔρος εἴτ' Ἀΐδης ἥρπασε, πλὴν ἀφανές.

559. flavos: the epithet is characteristic of gods or heroes (see Pease on 590).

iuventae: so P, and Servius; *iuventa*, M (cf. ix. 365 'galeam Messapi habilem cristisque decoram'). For the rhythm of the line see on 58. Mercury's young grace recalls i. 589 ff. (of Aeneas) 'ipsa decoram/ caesariem nato genetrix lumenque iuventae/ purpureum et laetos oculis adflarat honores'.

560. nate dea: this form of address to Aeneas is common (Dido herself uses it in i. 615), but here it is surely meant to make him conscious of his *pietas*. Mercury goes at once to the point, as in 265.

ducere: the word suggests the length and soundness of Aeneas' sleep (note the repeated *u* sound); 'can you sleep so sound when a hazard like this is near?'

561. deinde: note the (normal) scansion *deīnde* for *deĭnde*. Mackail takes it as used adjectivally with *pericula* ('dangers-to-come'), cf. *late liquidos*, 526; see his note on i. 13, where he compares iii. 609 'hortamur quae deinde agitet fortuna fateri'. But it need not mean more than 'presently' here. Virgil avoids placing *deinde* at the opening of a line (see Mackail on i. 195), and so does Statius. Note the monosyllabic staccato of Mercury's words (cf. note on 16).

562. demens: Mercury is deliberately rough with Aeneas (cf. *heia age* below). The word is strongly emphasized (see on 185).

Zephyros: while Aeneas has been asleep, a miraculous favouring west wind has sprung up—the winter storms are over—and he is still delaying. For the repeated *s* sounds see on 305 f.

563. illa: there is no need to name Dido; cf. *G.* iv. 506 (of Eurydice) 'illa quidem Stygia nabat iam frigida cumba'.

dirumque nefas: this particularizes *dolos*. Mercury's business is to represent Dido as desperate to the point of attacking Aeneas: how far she was from such a plot may be judged from her unhappy gropings in 534 ff.

564. certa mori: 'resolute to die.' Mercury means that she will have vengeance even at the cost of her life, and this is how Aeneas takes it: his ignorance of her death in vi. 458 is not inconsistent with this passage. This use of an infinitive after an adjective, explaining the sphere or purpose of it ('epexegetic'), is one of the many ways in which the poets found the infinitive so convenient metrically: contrast *certus eundi*

(554); the pattern *ĕŭndī* could be used nowhere else in the line but at the end, while an infinitive is far more mobile.

variosque . . . aestus: 'and is working up changeful tides of storming anger'; for the plural *irarum* cf. 532.

565. non . . . potestas?: 'and hurry you not from here in hot haste, while haste is yours to have?' The present *fugis* adds to the urgency of Mercury's tone; note the quick dactyls, and the excited alliteration of these lines.

566 f. iam . . . flammis: 'soon you will see the ocean a turmoil of moving timber, will see the grim glow of torches, and the shore seething with flame.'

turbari trabibus: Mackail takes this as 'a welter of timbers', after a Carthaginian attack which would break up Aeneas' fleet. But it more probably refers to the assembling of the Tyrian ships (cf. 410 f.). The use of *trabs* for 'ship' goes back to Ennius (cf. *carina, abies, pinus*; see Kroll, *Studien zum Verständnis der römischen Literatur*, p. 252). For *fervēre* see on 409.

568. his . . . terris: the *dulces terrae* of 281.

569 f. heia age . . . femina: 'up, up, break your lazy ways! A shifty thing, a changeful thing is woman, always.'

569. heia age: cf. ix. 38 'hostis adest, heia!', in a like context of danger. *Heia* belongs to colloquial language, and Mercury's use of it suits his deliberate roughness to Aeneas. For a like abrupt manner cf. vi. 388 ff., where Charon is made to speak in character.

rumpe moras: cf. viii. 443 'praecipitate moras', ix. 13 'rumpe moras omnis'. Virgil has the plural accusative ten times in the *Aeneid*, the singular twice (once in elision, and once—x. 428—balancing another singular).

varium et mutabile: Stanyhurst has 'A windfane changabil huf puffe/ Always is a woomman'. The position of *femina* gives it great emphasis; Mercury wishes to leave it ringing in Aeneas' ears. Dryden oddly calls these famous words 'the sharpest satire, in the fewest words, that ever was made on woman-kind' (*Dedication of the Aeneis*, vol. xiv of the 1808 edition, p. 175). But Mercury is lying, as he lied in 563, and Virgil makes it clear that his Dido was the sport of the gods. In spite of her wild moods she had never ceased deep within her to love Aeneas, and she had no plots against him to do him personal injury. Henry comments: 'Dido in particular was unchangeably and devotedly attached to Aeneas, whom, if she did not pursue with fire and sword, it was not that *his* inconstancy did not so deserve, but that *her* magnanimity disdained, and *her* still-subsisting passion forbade.'

Note that Mercury vanishes on a single word at the beginning of a line, as in 276 (see note); cf. Norden on vi. 155, 886.

570. sic ... atrae: 'so he spoke, and vanished commingling with the pall of night.' Note the elision of *se* (cf. 278), a metrical representation of Mercury's disappearance. For elision of monosyllables in Virgil see Norden, *Aeneis VI*, Anh. XI, pp. 456 ff.; the most frequent elisions are of *me, te, se, iam*, and there is a higher percentage of such in the *Eclogues* (the influence of Catullus is seen here) than in the *Georgics* or the *Aeneid*; it belongs especially to informal verse, as is shown by its much greater relative frequency in Lucilius, Catullus, and Horace's *Satires*. Note *se* elided before a short syllable in i. 455, and *te* similarly in xii. 439 (where Mackail's note is inaccurate); *iam* is elided before a short syllable in vi. 629. In xii. 582 the reading of the second hand in M would give an elision of *iam* twice in one line, and Page prints this text.

571. tum vero: cf. 450; here in his turn Aeneas realizes at last the full truth of his position.

  subitis . . . umbris: one would expect this to refer to the sudden 'apparition' of Mercury (not the god himself, but *forma dei*), rather than to any sudden darkness as the vision disappears, as some editors take it: for even if the god had a supernatural brightness about him (cf. 358, note), there is no reason why the sleeping Aeneas should have been frightened by darkness. But the plural is odd, and cannot easily be explained on metrical grounds (see Norden, *Aeneis VI*, p. 409, where this passage is among those listed as having the plural to avoid hiatus), for Virgil could well have written *subita conterritus umbra* (cf. iii. 597 'aspectu conterritus haesit'). Nor are the parallels quoted by editors entirely helpful, for the context in all shows that the reference is to the spirit of a dead man in the grave (e.g. v. 81, vi. 510, Ovid, *Am*. i. 13. 3), where the plural can presumably be explained by analogy with *manes* (cf. Prop. ii. 8. 19 'exagitet nostros Manis, sectetur et umbras'). A rather nearer parallel is perhaps Livy xl. 56. 9 'curisque et vigiliis, cum identidem species et umbrae insontis interempti filii agitarent, exstinctum esse', where *species* shows that an actual 'apparition' is meant. Possibly Virgil felt that the singular would have been more appropriate to describe a ghostly visitation from the dead (as in ii. 772), and that the plural was needed to show that this was the dream-form of a living god. I do not regard this as a very satisfactory explanation; but I cannot believe in the interpretation of *umbris* here as 'darkness'. There is a close parallel to the general situation in iii. 172 ff. (where Aeneas dreams that his *Penates* spoke to him) 'talibus attonitus visis et voce deorum/ . . . corripio e stratis corpus', where *talibus attonitus visis* is not unlike the *subitis exterritus umbris* of this passage.

572. corripit . . . corpus: 'wrenches his limbs from sleep' (cf. iii. 176, just quoted); Lucretius has a fine picture of a man waking suddenly from sleep (iii. 925) 'cum correptus homo ex somno se colligit ipse'. In vi. 472, Dido 'tandem corripuit sese atque inimica refugit', after her stony silence when Aeneas pleaded with her in the Underworld.

572 f. sociosque . . . praecipitis: 'and he gives his men no peace till they come tumbling up.' At last Aeneas is more anxious than his men to be off. *Praecipitis* is proleptic; some editors, however, including Mackail, read a vocative *praecipites*, with *vigilate*, as part of Aeneas' speech. Mackail holds that *vigilate* alone would mean 'keep watch', not 'awake', but cf. Ovid, *Her.* 10. 9 'incertum vigilans, a somno languida', *Ex Pont.* i. 10. 21 ff. 'somnus/ non alit officio corpus inane suo;/ sed vigilo, vigilantque mei sine fine dolores'. Mark the rush of dactyls in all this speech; Irvine well notes the energy and haste of words and metre.

574. citi: adverbial; cf. 118, note. The usage is a feature of poetic style from early times, and as such occurs in the prose of Livy and Tacitus; but it has roots in conversational language (cf. Plaut. *Stich.* 391 f. 'ego huc citus/ praecucurri'): see Löfstedt, *Synt.* ii, pp. 368 ff.

574 ff. deus . . . instimulat: 'a god—sent down from high heaven —a god, see, once more pricks us on to speed our flight, sundering the twisted cable-strands.' The infinitive *festinare* is used as if after a verb of command (cf. Page on ii. 64). The cables would not normally be cut, unless there was danger about; so in iii. 666 f., after the encounter with Polyphemus, 'nos procul inde fugam trepidi celerare recepto / supplice sic merito tacitique incidere funem'.

576. sancte: Aeneas recognizes the authority of the god; he does not doubt that the god is Mercury, but adds *quisquis es* in the usual precautionary way (cf. ix. 22): see note on 510.

577. iterum: this may be taken closely with *imperio*, as Mackail observes (i.e. *iterato imperio*, 'the renewal of command'); but it might simply refer to their previous obedience in 295.

ovantes: 'exultant' (cf. 543); they are cheerful as they do the god's bidding; as Irvine remarks, they go from Carthage *dis auspicibus*.

578 f. adsis . . . feras: 'O be thou near, and give us thy kindly help, bring us stars of grace across the heavens.' The interjection *o* marks a heightening of tone (cf. 31), as Aeneas makes his solemn prayer.

578. placidusque iuves: cf. iii. 265 f. 'di, talem avertite casum/ et placidi servate pios'; these are the only two passages where Virgil has *placidus* as a personal adjective; otherwise he applies it to sleep, death, the sea, night, peace, the winds, places, or to a person's heart or face or voice (cf. 440). Mackail suggests 'gracious' or 'benign'; the sense is that nothing is to ruffle the favour of heaven.

579. vaginaque ... ensem: perhaps a reminiscence of Ennius; cf. vi. 260, and Norden's note.

580. fulmineum: emphatic; it suggests brightness, speed, sharpness.

retinacula: the *torti funes* of 575. Note the dactyls here and in 581-2, and the unusual run of three successive lines with a weak caesura in the third foot, with a verb in the same position in each (but the rhythm of 582 differs from that of 580-1).

581. rapiuntque ruuntque: the Trojans 'hurry and scurry'; see on 83.

582. litora ... aequor: 'they make a desert of the beaches, the sea cannot be seen for ships.' *Deseruere* marks instantaneous action (cf. 164); one moment the ships are still beached, the next they are manned and putting out to sea. The rhythm is that of 164, 417: there is a strong caesura after *latet*, but the sense marks the real pause in the weak position after *deseruere* (see note on 164). As Hardie remarks (*Res Metrica*, p. 8), the rhythm is Homeric; contrast v. 140 'haud mora, prosiluere suis, ferit aethera clamor', a quite different effect because the main pause follows *suis*, not *prosiluere*.

583. adnixi ... verrunt: 'they tug and churn the foam and sweep the deep'; the dactyls now give place to heavy spondees, with marked clash of ictus and accent (cf. Norden, *Aeneid VI*, p. 423), showing the steady IN, OUT, IN, OUT of the rowers; compare the fine rhythms of the start of the boat-race in v. 136 ff. This line occurs also in iii. 208, where the Trojan crews have sighted land and have taken to the oars for the last part of the distance; but the contrast here with the swift launch makes it more effective now.

spumas: Virgil has this plural five times, *spumam* once only (iii. 567, with elision); in three instances a vowel follows, once the form is followed by *s* (i. 35, plainly for sound-effect), once by *m* (*G.* iii. 449, cf. note on *cineres*, 427). He does not use the nominative plural. See Maas, *ALL* xii, p. 516.

584-629. *In the glimmering dawn, Dido sees the ships moving out, and cries out in passion : 'Shall he escape, and mock me? Attack him with flame and steel! But no, it is too late : I should have torn him in pieces first, burnt his ships and destroyed him*

*and his son, perished myself in the flames . . . O Sun, and all
avenging Gods, hear my prayer. If he must reach Italy, let it be
with a cruel curse upon him and upon all his name ; and let
there be war between my people and his people, for ever.'*

584 f. Virgil describes dawn in Homeric fashion; the lines are
repeated in ix. 459 f. (cf. 129, and see note on 6).

586. regina: cf. 1, 296, 504. Dido has been looking from a
watch-tower (*e speculis*) even before the first whitening of
dawn. The setting, but not the context, recalls a Shakes-
pearian picture: 'In such a night/ Stood Dido with a willow
in her hand/ Upon the wild sea-banks, and waft her love/ To
come again to Carthage.' Cf. xii. 595 'regina ut tectis venien-
tem prospicit hostem' (of Amata, see Mackail, Appendix B).

587. aequatis . . . velis: 'the fleet moving forward in even line
of sail'; note the separation of epithet from noun, to avoid
the two ablative forms together (cf. Norden, *Aeneis VI*,
Anh. IV). Virgil draws a vivid picture of the Trojan ships in
company (see Page); note the smooth, ordered rhythm;
the rowing has now ceased, and the sails are hoisted (the reverse process to that described in iii. 207).

588. litoraque . . . portus: 'and realized that the shore was desert,
the harbour empty, no rowers left.' *Vacua* must be supplied
with *litora*; note the pleonasm of *sine remige* (Wagner compares Sil. It. x. 582 'vacuum sine corpore nomen'); see note
on 284.

589 f. terque . . . comas: 'three times, four times, she struck her
hand upon her lovely breast, and tore her bright hair.' For
terque quaterque see on 83. The participles are middle, with
virtually a present force, and are followed by a direct object:
contrast *G.* iv. 357 'percussa nova mentem formidine mater',
where *percussa* is a true passive (since the blow is not of
Cyrene's own striking, but comes from the external *formido*)
and *mentem* is accusative of 'respect'; cf. Page on ix. 478.

589. decorum: so Lavinia in xi. 480 is 'oculos deiecta decoros';
cf. xii. 155 (of Juturna) 'terque quaterque manu pectus per-
cussit honestum'.

590. flaventis: Dido's hair is the colour of most heroines' in
mythology; but Pease's note here makes the reader forget its
beauty. Chaucer shows her (in a different context) pleading
with Aeneas, 'dischevele, with her brighte gilte here'. Fanshawe translates: 'Seeing the fleet sail smoothly on, she
knocks/ Three or four times her breast of ivory,/ And tearing
piteously her amber locks . . . .'

These physical manifestations of emotion are common in
the poetry of the Mediterranean world (cf. 673); that they are

not imaginary is shown by Plutarch's account of Cleopatra's
self-disfigurement after Antony's death, made even more
graphic in North's horrifying paraphrase (Plut. *Ant.* 82 ἐκ
δὲ λύπης ἅμα τοσαύτης καὶ ὀδύνης—ἀνεφλέγμηνε γὰρ αὐτῆς τὰ στέρνα
τυπτομένης καὶ ἥλκωτο—πυρετῶν ἐπιλαβόντων, ib. 83 εἰσιόντι δ' αὐτῷ...
προσπίπτει, δεινῶς μὲν ἐξηγριωμένη κεφαλὴν καὶ πρόσωπον, ὑπότρομος
δὲ τῇ φωνῇ καὶ συντετηκυῖα ταῖς ὄψεσιν· ἦν δὲ πολλὰ καὶ τῆς περὶ τὸ
στέρνον αἰκίας καταφανῆ).

The speech that follows must surely rank with the most
magnificent of any poet in any language. It begins abruptly,
with Dido's anger characteristically at full pitch; her irresolution has gone, and she calls wildly on her Tyrians to pursue
the Trojan fleet. Then the tone changes (595), and in a brief
soliloquy she reproaches herself for her own folly, then in
a passage of heightened rhetoric she mocks Aeneas' *pietas*,
and in hissing anger rages in self-recrimination at her own
cowardice in not treating him as he deserved. At 606 there is
a sustained pause. The fury and the hot utterance leaves her,
and her words ring out deliberately and clearly in measured
tones of cold and deadly hate; it is not only Aeneas now
whom she will hunt and haunt, but the whole Trojan people;
and as the terrible words rise inexorably to their tremendous
climax, foreshadowing her as yet unknown avenger Hannibal
(625) and the death-struggle of Rome and Carthage, the
speech has a Roman quality of implacable pride and command and purpose—a Cato might have spoken so against
Dido's own Carthage.

This is the only one of Dido's speeches in which she shows
no turning back to her love for Aeneas, no weakening anywhere. But the passionate hatred in it does not mean that
Mercury's words in 560 ff. were justified: there was never any
danger to Aeneas from Dido while he stayed; it is his departure, now irrevocable, that has precipitated the storm, and it
will be seen that even so she is not prevented from remembering her love for him at the end of all.

590 ff. pro Iuppiter . . . remos!: '"By God, and shall he go, this
man?", she cries, "and shall it prove that he has flouted our
royal power, vagabond that he is? Will no-one out with
their arms, stream out from all Carthage, hound him down?
None tear the ships from the sheds? Go, quick, bring fire, get
me weapons, strike on your oars!"'

590. pro Iuppiter!: an angry oath, striking in its abrupt in-
tensity.

591. hic: deictic; she flings her arms seaward.

   inluserit: the future perfect implies 'shall his mockery be
an accomplished fact?'; cf. ii. 581 'occiderit ferro Priamus?

Troia arserit igni?' ('shall this really happen, and Priam be
killed, Troy burnt?'), ix. 281 f. 'me nulla dies tam fortibus
ausis/ dissimilem arguerit', x. 333 f. 'non ullum dextera
frustra/ torserit in Rutulos', ix. 783 ff. 'unus homo . . ./ . . .
tantas strages impune per urbem/ ediderit? iuvenum primos
tot miserit Orco?' It is the tense that one would use to
translate the colloquial English 'to get away with doing
something'.

advena: Aeneas is an interloper, an upstart, a newcomer
with no status as compared with Dido's royal power (note
nostris here); so in xii. 261 the Rutulian augur Tolumnius
calls Aeneas *improbus advena*. Dido herself had seemed such
to Iarbas (211). Stanyhurst has 'Shal a stranger give me the
slampam?'

592. **expedient . . . sequentur**: the subject *alii* is omitted, with
notable effect; in her wild fury Dido calls indiscriminately
on anyone near.

593. **deripient**: this is Heinsius' emendation of MSS. *diripient*,
but it is unnecessary, and Mackail does well to return to the
MSS. reading. Dido thinks of no orderly launching, and uses
a wild, exaggerated, vivid expression: her men are to 'fall
wildly upon the ships in the sheds', in their haste to attack
Aeneas; cf. i. 211, and Warde Fowler on xii. 283. Somewhat
similarly Suetonius, speaking of the eagerness of the public to
get copies of Persius' book, says (*vit. Pers.* ad fin.) 'editum
librum continuo mirari homines et diripere coeperunt'; and
cf. Quintil. vi. 1. 47 'pueris in epilogum productis talos iecit
in medium, quos illi diripere ("scramble for") coeperunt'.
For *navalia* cf. Ovid, *Met.* xi. 455 f. 'protinus eductam
navalibus aequore tingi/ armarique suis pinum iubet
armamentis'.

594. **citi**: see on 574. Note the excited haste of the line, with
the hard rattle of *t* sounds, and the almost stammering effect
of *ferte citi* and *date tela* (cf. ix. 37 'ferte citi ferrum, date tela,
ascendite muros').

595. **quae . . . mutat?**: 'what is this madness that makes my
purpose falter?'; cf. xii. 37 'quo referor totiens? quae mentem insania mutat?' Dido's mood changes, as she realizes
how useless such an attack is now; this line is muttered to
herself, in contrast with her imperious cry in the preceding
lines, but her tone is gradually raised again from *en dextra
fidesque* onwards.

596. **infelix . . . tangunt**: 'poor luckless Dido, and is it now that
your godless deeds come home to you?' She apostrophizes
herself, as in 541 (note the slow spondees here, and contrast
593–4). By *facta impia* she means her lack of *pietas* to

Sychaeus, and perhaps also her failure in her duty to her own people; it is nonsense to refer the words to Aeneas, as some editors do.

597. decuit: sc. *tangere*; the force of *dabas* is 'you were for giving'; cf. 374, and i. 572 f.

597 ff. en dextra . . . parentem: 'see, behold his right hand, his pledge of honour! The man who (the tale so runs) carries with him the Penates of his home! The man who (so they say) bore up on his own shoulders his old, weary father!' Note the alliteration, the hard consonants *p, c, t*, and the series of *s* sounds that continues with increasing effect to 606.

597. en: a good example of the 'indignant' *en* (see on 534); Virgil was the first to use this demonstrative *en* with a nominative (see Köhler, *ALL* vi, p. 45).

598. aiunt: the only occurrence of the form in Virgil; it implies that Aeneas' *pietas* was all a traveller's tale; with *quem*, a genitive must be supplied as antecedent. (Note the curious *fama est* of xii. 735, and cf. note on 204.)

599. subiisse umeris: cf. ii. 707 f. 'ergo age, care pater, cervici imponere nostrae;/ ipse subibo umeris, nec me labor iste gravabit', words which are entirely Virgilian in their moving simplicity. Ovid (*Her.* 7. 77 ff.) much embroiders the *aiunt* of this passage.

600 ff. non potui . . . mensis?: 'could I not have torn him away, rent him asunder, strewn his limbs over the sea? Or murdered his men with the sword, yes, butchered Ascanius himself and served him at his dear father's table, a fine feast?' Dido means that she should have treated Aeneas like some victim in a Greek tragedy (so Medea killed her brother Apsyrtus and flung him overboard, and Atreus killed Thyestes' sons and served them to him at table); but the allusions are secondary to the high and undisguised rhetoric. Note the *p* and *s* sounds, and the parallel position of *absumere, ponere*.

600. abreptum: the verb is often used of 'haling away' for punishment, e.g. Ter. *Andr.* 786 'hanc iam oportet in cruciatum hinc abripi', Cic. *Phil.* iii. 31.

601. absumere: so iii. 654 (with *leto*), ix. 494 (with *ferro*); Catullus has the verb first in this sense (65. 14), in a somewhat similar reference; cf. 'the deep damnation of his taking off'. The meaning is frequent in Livy, Sallust, Tacitus.

602. patriis . . . mensis: *this* is what Aeneas' 'pietas' deserves.

603. verum . . . fuisset!: 'ah! but it had been a perilous issue: suppose it *had*!' *Verum* introduces an objection, like *at* or *atqui*: Dido's disjointed thought makes her point out possible danger in the course that she should have followed, and then she answers the objection in *fuisset*.

fuerat: the indicative is put vividly for the normal subjunctive (*si fecissem* must be understood), to make the risk more apparent; the construction is like that of ii. 54 f. 'si mens non laeva fuisset,/ impulerat ferro', and of the familiar examples in *G*. ii. 132 f., Hor. *C*. ii. 17. 27 ff.; the indicative in the apodosis marks the near-reality of the fact or action, the subjunctive in the protasis (here absent) marks it as hypothetical. If Virgil had used the normal construction here, he could not have followed it by the concessive *fuisset*.

604 ff. quem . . . dedissem: 'whom did I fear, with death so soon to come? I should have flung fire on his encampment, filled the gangways with flame, slain son and father and all their kind, and cast myself, my very self, upon the pile.'

604. A very good example of the type of line already noted in 164, 417, 582: the effective pause follows the weak caesura in the third foot, and the strong caesura after *faces* is scarcely noticeable.

castra : the stockade round the ships; cf. ix. 69 f. 'classem, quae lateri castrorum adiuncta latebat/ aggeribus saeptam circum et fluvialibus undis'.

tulissem: this and the following pluperfects are 'past jussives', a retrospective command (cf. 678), as in Cic. *Verr*. iii. 195 'quid facere debuisti? . . . rettulisses . . . solvisses . . . ne emisses . . . sumpsisses'. For the sound and feeling of the lines, cf. ii. 585 ff. (Aeneas' thoughts at seeing Helen) 'exstinxisse nefas tamen et sumpsisse merentis/ laudabor poenas, animumque explesse iuvabit/ ultricis flammae et cineres satiasse meorum'.

605. implessem: this, and *exstinxem* below, is a type of contracted form that Virgil likes; they enable him to use words that would otherwise be metrically intractable (e.g. *implevissem*, *exstinxissem* here) or impossible (so *repostum* for *repositum*, i. 26): note *accestis*, for *accessistis*, i. 201, *traxe*, for *traxisse*, v. 786. So Lucretius has *confluxet* (i. 991), *remosse* (iii. 69), *consumpse* (i. 233), *abstraxe* (iii. 650). Norden (on vi. 57) regards such forms as a mark of archaizing style; Horace has them in the *Satires* only, Ovid has only one example.

606. memet: Virgil has this emphatic form once only elsewhere (vii. 309); *egomet* occurs in iii. 623, v. 650, vi. 505, *vosmet* i. 207. Such forms (which occur a number of times in Horace's *Satires*) appear not to have been used by later epic poets; Norden (on vi. 505) regards them also as a mark of archaizing. The conjunction of *memet* with *ipsa* is characteristic of Latin; *ipsa* stresses Dido's own responsibility as subject, whereas *ipsam* would have put undue stress on herself as object; thus, *se ipse interfecit* means 'he caused his own death', but *se ipsum* *interfecit* would mean 'it was himself he killed' (not someone else); see my note on Cic. *Cael.* 11.

607 ff. The tone now changes, after a pause, and Dido rises to a supreme effort as she denounces Aeneas and all his race. Notice the great art with which Virgil varies the position of the main pauses: after *preces* (612), *haeret* (614), *funera* (618), *harena* (620), and then again (after a single summing-up line in 621), after *munera* (624); the ultimate command is rapped out in a short staccato sentence in 624 (*nullus . . . sunto*), and then the last five lines come surging up with scarcely a pause; the speech ends with a remarkable hyper-metric line (see note on 629); see Knight, *Accentual Symmetry in Vergil*, pp. 80 ff., for an analysis of its rhythms. The passage makes the tale of Dido part of Roman history, as if it were Virgil's justification for including it in his epic; cf. Heinze, op. cit., p. 438.

Sol . . . preces: 'O thou Sun, who dost light up in fiery progress all the works of earth: and thou, who hast helped to set these sorrows upon me and knowest them all, thou Juno: and thou Hecate, whose wailing worshippers fill cities at the midnight crossways: and ye Fiends of vengeful Hell: and all ye Gods of dying Elissa—hear this, and turn your power upon my ills, the power that they have deserved, and give ear to my prayer.'

Note the solemn spondees, the alliteration, the long *a* sounds (*terrarum, harum . . . curarum . . . ululata*), and especially the intricate vowel-arrangement of 610.

Jodelle has (Act v):

Toy, Soleil, qui regardes
Tout cecy; toy, Junon, qui, las! si mal me gardes,
Coulpables de mes maux; toy, Hecate hurlée
De nuict aux carrefours; vous, bande eschevelée,
Qui pour cheveux portez vos pendantes couleuvres,
Et dans vos mains les feux vangeurs des lâches œuvres;
Vous (dy-je), tous les Dieux de la mourante Elise,
Recevez ces mots-cy.

Compare Aeneas' prayer in xii. 176 ff., 'esto nunc Sol testis et haec mihi Terra vocanti', etc., a close parallel; the invocation to the Sun has its counterpart in numerous passages of Greek tragedy (see Pease's note), especially Soph. *Ai.* 845 ff.

607. lustras: see on 6.
608. interpres: cf. 356. Juno as the goddess of marriage (cf. 166) had been 'intermediary', as it were, between Dido and Aeneas, and so had full knowledge of the *curae* which she herself had helped to cause.

609. nocturnis : see on 118. For the worship of Hecate at the crossroads cf. her cult-title *Trivia* (Τριοδῖτις), vi. 13, 35, etc., Catull. 34. 15.

ululata: this may refer either to the cries of worshippers, or to the howling of dogs; cf. vi. 257 f. 'visaeque canes ululare per umbram/ adventante dea', as Hecate approaches. Note the passive use of a participle of an intransitive verb; cf. Stat. *Th.* iii. 158 f. 'nulloque ululata dolore/ respexit Lucina domum'; so *regnata*, vi. 793 (cf. *regnandam*, vi. 770, where see Norden), *bacchata*, *G.* ii. 487, *triumphatas*, *G.* iii. 33. No doubt the use originated as the poets experimented in synonyms (*triumphatus* for *victus*, *ululatus* for *clamatus*, see L.-H., p. 377), helped by the impersonal passive idiom (see on 416): it is easy to see in *ululata* here an impersonal sense ('Hecate in whose worship there is a wailing'), just as *triumphatas . . . gentes* (*G.* iii. 33) suggests 'races over whom there has been a triumph'; from this it is a natural step to the use of such participles with an agent expressed, as in *G.* ii. 487, *A.* vi. 793, etc. This seems to me preferable to Norden's view that the construction is a Grecism, based on such uses as βασιλεύεσθαι, θριαμβεύεσθαι. See Lejay in *Revue de Philologie* xli, 1917, pp. 215 ff., and cf. Page on iii. 14.

610. A singularly haunting line; besides the intricate vowel-pattern, note the slow drop of the monosyllables *et di*, and the assonance with *et Dirae*. For *Dirae* see on 472 f.

di morientis Elissae : whatever gods there be who can and must hear the dying Elissa, on these she calls—the common precaution (cf. 519 ff., and notes), in a new and awful form. Dido is *moritura* no more.

612. The invocation runs smoothly and firmly to its end in mid-line (cf. viii. 574 'et patrias audite preces. si numina vestra . . .'), and then Dido pauses before she begins her curse upon the Trojan people and all their descendants.

613. infandum caput: 'this abhorrent being' (cf. 354, 493, 640); she will not name Aeneas (see on 479). Virgil no doubt had in mind the passage in *Od.* ix. 534 ff., where Polyphemus curses Odysseus (ὀψὲ κακῶς ἔλθοι, ὀλέσας ἄπο πάντας ἑταίρους, / νηὸς ἐπ' ἀλλοτρίης, εὕροι δ' ἐν πήματα οἴκῳ), but how different the two settings are, and how Virgil's lines are instinct with the complex memories of history.

adnare: the word suggests a difficult passage (cf. i. 538, vi. 358).

614. fata Iovis: cf. vi. 376 'desine fata deum flecti sperare precando', and see Norden's note (*fata = voluntas*). See Bailey, *Religion in Virgil*, pp. 229 f.

hic terminus haeret: 'this is a bound that stands embedded': there is no means of passing the boundary-stone set by Fate, 'a truly Roman image of immovability' (Page). Virgil has adapted Lucretius' *alte terminus haerens* (used of the finite power of things, i. 77, &c.—one of Lucretius' great signature-phrases, like *flammantia moenia mundi*); cf. xii. 897 ff. 'saxum antiquum, ingens, campo quod forte iacebat,/ limes agro positus, litem ut discerneret arvis;/ vix illud lecti bis sex cervice subirent'. For a somewhat similarly planned passage cf. ii. 659 ff.

615 ff. at bello ... harena: 'but let him be harried by sword and spear of a valiant people, let him be an exile far from home, let him be wrenched from the embrace of his Iulus, and go on his knees for help, and see his own folk perish in shame. And when he has surrendered to the terms of a peace that bears hard upon him, may he never enjoy his realm or the light he longs to see: but may he fall untimely, with none to bring him burial, on the open shore.'

'Among the Romans a Poet was called *Vates* ... whereupon grew the worde of *Sortes Virgilianae*, when, by suddaine opening *Virgils* booke, they lighted vpon any verse of hys making: whereof the histories of the Emperors liues are full, as of *Albinus*, the Gouernour of our Iland, who in his childe-hoode mette with this verse, *Arma amens capio nec sat rationis in armis*; and in his age performed it' (Sir Philip Sidney, *An Apologie for Poetrie*). These famous lines of Virgil were lighted upon by Charles I when he consulted the *Sortes*, traditionally in the Bodleian Library, though Archbishop Sancroft's papers place it at Windsor, and John Aubrey states that it occurred at Carisbrooke. The date is similarly uncertain: one account says that the consultation was suggested by Lord Falkland, who fell on Newbury Field in 1643 (and that when he in turn tried to remedy the evil *sors*, he opened the book at xi. 152 ff., Evander's lament for his dead son Pallas); but Aubrey gives the date as 1648, and that it was Abraham Cowley who suggested the *Sortes* to the King ('Mr. Cowley alwaies had a Virgil in his pocket'). See Macray, *Annals of the Bodleian* (1890), pp. 70, 96, and H. A. Loane in *Classical Weekly* xxi, 1928, pp. 185 ff.

615. at: in strong contrast; if this must be, at least let it happen thus.

audacis populi: the Rutulians. Aeneas never returned to Troy (*finibus extorris*); he had to leave his son and implore Evander's help, and he witnessed the 'cruel deaths' of so many of his Trojan people.

616. Note the elision in *complexu avulsus*, a metrical picture of

the violence suffered; *complexu raptus* would have been possible, but would have been less metrically vivid.

617. Irvine quotes from Trevelyan's *Life and Letters of Lord
Macaulay*, ch. xiv, Macaulay's horror at seeing an inscription
'ultimus suorum moriatur', 'an awful curse'.

618. Note the spondees, the triple monosyllable (cf. note on
132), and the fourth-foot rhythm *sub leges* (see on 522): all
combine to produce slow relentless deliberation.

pacis iniquae: the bargain by which Italian and Trojan
races should mingle, but the name of Troy be lost; cf. xii.
826 ff., especially 834–7.

619. Aeneas' reign is said to have lasted for three years only;
Servius preserves a tradition that his body was never found
(see Pease's quotations).

optata luce: i.e. the happiness of a long life; the fourth-
foot rhythm is the same as in 618.

620. The famous words toll like a knell.

ante diem: to die in one's prime, and to die unburied—
these were the most dreadful things that a man could suffer
in ancient times; burial is 'solus honos Acheronte sub imo'
(xi. 23); Turnus bestows on Pallas 'quisquis honos tumuli,
quidquid solamen humandi est' (x. 493); Nisus prays that if
he should be killed 'sit qui me raptum pugna pretiove
redemptum/ mandet humo' (ix. 213 f.); it is the *inops in-
humataque turba* that yearns to cross the Styx (vi. 325); it is
Misenus' unburied body that pollutes the fleet (vi. 150). So
Teucer in Sophocles' *Ajax* (1175 ff.) prays εἰ δέ τις στρατοῦ / βίᾳ
σ' ἀποσπάσειε τοῦδε τοῦ νεκροῦ, / κακὸς κακῶς ἄθαπτος ἐκπέσοι χθονός, /
γένους ἅπαντος ῥίζαν ἐξημημένος, and the whole setting of the
Antigone tells the same tale.

621. haec ... fundo: 'this is my prayer: this is my last utterance, and with it goes my life-blood.' Note the elision in
vocem extremam, as if Dido's voice falters for an instant; but
the rhythm is insistent, with its marked clash of ictus and
accent, and no pause till the fourth foot.

622 ff. tum vos ... nepotesque: 'and then do you, my Tyrians,
hound with hate and hate again all his stock and all his race
to be, sending to my ashes these gifts in dedication. Let there
be no love nor any bond between my people and his people.
And O do thou rise up, thou someone who shall avenge me,
arise from my bones to harry the Dardan settlers with fire
and blade, to-day, to-morrow, whensoever the power shall be
thine to do it. Shore with shore in battle-grip, sea with sea
and sword with sword—this is my curse upon them: let
them be locked in war, they and their sons' sons.' Dryden
has:

These are my prayers, and this my dying will;
And you my Tyrians, ev'ry curse fulfil.
Perpetual hate, and mortal wars proclaim,
Against the prince, the people, and the name.
These grateful off'rings on my grave bestow;
Nor league, nor love, the hostile nations know:
Now, and from hence in ev'ry future age,
When rage excites your arms, and strength supplies the
    rage:
Rise some avenger of our Libyan blood,
With fire and sword pursue the perjur'd brood:
Our arms, our seas, our shores, oppos'd to theirs,
And the same hate descend on all our heirs.

622. Tyrii: contrast i. 735 'et vos o coetum, Tyrii, celebrate faventes', spoken by Dido when she welcomed the Trojans to her feast.

623. exercete: see on 100, and cf. *G.* iv. 453 'non te nullius exercent numinis irae'. The plural *odiis* (note that Virgil might have written *odio*) is used for repeated acts of hatred; cf. v. 785 f. 'non media de gente Phrygum exedisse nefandis/ urbem odiis satis est'; see note on 197.

623 f. cineri . . . munera: so Catullus at his brother's tomb brings offerings to the dead *tristi munere*, after travelling far, 'ut te postremo donarem munere mortis/ et mutam nequiquam alloquerer cinerem' (Catull. 101. 3 f.). But instead of wine and oil, it is revenge that will be Dido's *munus* in the grave. *Haec* refers both to what has preceded and to what follows. *Mittere* is the usual word for dedicating offerings, as in vi. 380 'et statuent tumulum et tumulo sollemnia mittent', *G.* iv. 545 'inferias Orphei Lethaea papavera mittes'.

624. munera: cf. vi. 886, where *munere* occurs in a like position of emphasis. Virgil cannot have been unaware of the echo from *funera* (618), in the same position in the line, and with a like pause, though less marked, after it: the *funera* of the Trojans are to be the *munera* that Dido's own people shall give to her.

nullus . . . sunto: there is a world of passion concentrated in this short staccato sentence, placed in its elaborate context. Once Dido welcomed the Trojans, saying 'Tros Tyriusque mihi nullo discrimine agetur' (i. 574).

sunto: the solemn formal imperative (cf. vi. 153 'ea prima piacula sunto'), which Virgil uses as an archaism; it belongs to the language of laws from the Twelve Tables onwards, and may be seen *passim* in Cato's *de agri cultura*, from which Virgil adopts it for his didactic manner in the *Georgics* (e.g. ii. 197, 408-13).

625. This was the line that Filippo Strozzi of Florence wrote with his own blood upon his prison-wall in 1537 (cf. Myers, *Essays Classical*, p. 116). Dido prophesies the rise of Hannibal (note the repeated *s* sounds): but she does not know' his name, he is simply *aliquis* to her. The second person *exòriare* in which she addresses the unknown is remarkable and very moving; cf. i. 327 ff. 'o quam te memorem virgo? ... / ... sis felix nostrumque leves, quaecumque, laborem', on which Mackail comments 'in both passages Virgil puts what was perhaps in Latin also a colloquialism to strikingly noble use'. In Aesch. *Ag.* 1279 f., Cassandra says οὐ μὴν ἄτιμοί γ' ἐκ θεῶν τεθνήξομεν· | ἥξει γὰρ ἡμῶν ἄλλος αὖ τιμάορος, lines from which Fraenkel thinks Virgil consciously borrows here, adding that his admiration for the great Greek poets is characteristically shown by 'the loving care with which Virgil chooses ornaments from Greek tragedy to adorn the last speeches of Dido'.

626. Note the dactyls, and the rare end-rhythm (see on 58), and the assonance in *ferroque sequare colonos*: the effect well shows the continuity of the harrying for which Dido prays.

627. The rhythm is again remarkable. Technically a strong caesura is present after *dabunt*; but the reflexive *se* is attached so closely to *dabunt* that there is no real pause, and so there is present in the fourth foot an effect like that at the end of a line (just as *ferroque sequare* above gives the same effect in the fifth foot); it bears a certain resemblance to *G.* i. 514 'fertur equis auriga, neque audit currus habenas', where there is a like context of ruthlessness. (A line with a very curious fourth-foot effect is ix. 57 'arma viros, sed castra fovere. huc turbidus atque huc', where *castra fovere* gives an end-of-line rhythm followed by a strong pause, barely covered by the elision before *huc*.)

628 f. Nothing could better express the interlocked struggle of Rome and Carthage than these two lines, with their juxtaposition of repeated nouns in different cases. Lucretius could have written *fluctibu' fluctus*, and perhaps Virgil regretted that his stricter code forbade this. But the crowning effect is the hypermetre of 629, on which Wagner comments 'haud scio an Virgilius ipsa hypermetri ratione aptissime adiuverit impetum irae in hanc extremam exsecrationem erumpentis'. Other hypermetric lines are closely bound to their following context, even where the hypermetre concludes a sentence (as in x. 895, *G.* ii. 443); but this is the end of a speech, and the redundant syllable is left to die away in the pause that follows. There is something nearly comparable in vii. 470, where a hypermetric line ends a piece of reported speech, but

the high drama is absent there. Dido seems to leave the two
peoples locked for ever in their enmity. And would not the
Roman reader have thought also of that other struggle, the
Civil War?

Marlowe quotes these two lines (without the final -*que*) in
a different context (see note on 651).

628. **litoribus** : this plural dative serves metrical necessity as
well as the sense (Virgil has it only once elsewhere, vii. 1); in
the ablative, he uses the singular *litore* alone: see Maas, *ALL*
xii, p. 497.

630–50. *Dido now seeks to end her sufferings. She sends for
Sychaeus' old nurse, and bids her tell Anna to come with all that
is needed to complete her sacrifice to the Powers of the Underworld. And then, flushing and paling she climbs the pyre ; and
she unsheathes a sword, a Trojan sword ; but as she catches
sight of the relics of the man she has loved, she pauses to weep
and remember ; and then she says farewell.*

630 f. **et partis . . . lucem**: 'and she whirled her heart now this
way, now that, looking for the first moment to cut off the
light of life that she so loathed.' Note the stressed position
of *invisam*, and the pictorial elision in *primum abrumpere*.

abrumpere lucem: cf. viii. 579, ix. 497 'crudelem abrumpere vitam', where there is also an elision before *abrumpere*.
Lucan embellishes the idea into 'extremae momentum
abrumpere lucis' (iv. 483).

632. **Barcen**: Jodelle makes her a principal character in this
play. The nurse as confidante goes back to Eurycleia in the
Odyssey (Pease has a long list of ancient nurses); but here it
is Dido's dead husband's nurse to whom alone she can turn—
the ghost of her past is always near: and now there is a fresh
person whom she must deceive.

633. **namque . . . habebat**: 'for her own lay in the dark dust of
her homeland of long ago.'

suam: a sense-construction is evident here; it is as if
Virgil had intended to say 'suam enim non adfari potuit,
quia eam cinis ater habebat', and *suam* is retained irregu-
larly although the construction of the sentence is rearranged.
It is so natural in the context that the reader is hardly conscious of a departure from formal grammar; and it enables
Virgil to avoid the form *ipsius*. It is eased by the fact that
there was a tendency to use *suus* colloquially where *eius* might
have been expected; cf. Cato *de agri cult.* 31. 2 '(materies)
tum erit tempestiva, cum semen suum maturum erit', Ovid,
Met. xv. 818 f. 'ut deus accedat caelo templisque colatur,/ tu
facies natusque suus'. See L.-H., p. 470.

cinis . . . habebat: yet the nurse's body is itself the ash. Mackail observes that the phrase is unique, pointing out that vi. 362 (of Palinurus) 'nunc me fluctus habet' is not parallel.

634. Annam . . . sororem: 'Anna—dear nurse, please bring her here—my sister.' It is not very profitable to dispute whether *mihi* belongs to *cara*, or whether it should be taken with *siste* as an 'ethic' dative; personally I do not think the latter is possible. But it might be better to omit the commas which the Oxford text shows after *Annam* and *mihi*, so that either possibility remains open.

Dido is very quiet now. Her paroxysm is past, and the way to death clear. Just as it was Anna who had made the arrangements for the pyre, so now she is to bring the ritual offerings for the pretended sacrifice. But the need for pretence is nearly over: Dido really needs Anna to come in time to comfort her as she dies—but her sister must not yet suspect the true reason for her summons.

635. dic . . . lympha: 'tell her to be quick and sprinkle herself with river-water.' Virgil again uses the language of ordinary Roman ritual at an act of chthonic worship (cf. Bailey, *Religion in Virgil*, p. 284); water was used in purification; so, after the burial of Misenus, Corynaeus 'ter socios pura circumtulit unda/ spargens rore levi et ramo felicis olivae' (vi. 229 f.).

636. monstrata piacula: 'the atonement-offerings that have been prescribed' (presumably by the priestess-witch, cf. note on 498). The *pecudes* and the *piacula* are probably identical (cf. vi. 153 'duc nigras pecudes; ea prima piacula sunto'); Bailey compares Lucr. iii. 51 ff. 'parentant/ et nigras mactant pecudes et manibu' divis/ inferias mittunt'.

637. sic veniat: 'this is how she must come.'

pia . . . vitta: cf. *manibusque piis*, 517; but the 'garland of holiness' is a ghastly detail here, when Dido is herself to be the sacrifice.

638. Iovi Stygio: Pluto, Ζεὺς χθόνιος; cf. vi. 138 'Iunoni infernae dictus sacer' (of the Golden Bough, sacred to Proserpine).

rite incepta: Dido has always been careful to use the proper ceremony; but perhaps she says this deliberately, because of her shame at having recourse to magic and in order to legitimatize it as much as possible.

639. perficere: a ritual word (cf. vi. 637 *perfecto munere divae*, and Norden's note).

finemque: -que is a true copula here, not correlative with the following -que.

640. Dardaniique . . . flammae: 'giving over to the flame the

Dardan creature's pyre'; -*que* appends an explanation of *finem imponere curis*. For *Dardanii capitis* (not much more than 'the Dardan'), cf. 613, and see note on 479 (again she does not name Aeneas); cf. xi. 399 f. 'capiti cane talia demens/ Dardanio rebusque tuis' (said by Turnus to Drances). The form *Dardanii* here is one of the three Virgilian examples of the genitive in -*ii*, which is not pre-Augustan; the others are iii. 702 (*fluvii*) and ix. 151 (*Palladii*, in an interpolated line); see Mackail on iii. 702, and Maas, *ALL* xii, pp. 510 ff.

641. illa . . . anili: 'the nurse went hurrying away with an old dame's anxious care'—a graphic picture (*studio* is nearly 'fuss'), which would be almost amusing if the old woman's errand were not so dreadful. Stanyhurst has 'Shee trots on snayling, lyk a tooth shaken old hagge'.

celebrabat: this reading seems difficult to defend. Servius *auct.* gives it as an alternative to *celerabat*, 'quia antiqui hoc verbum in velocitate ponebant', and illustrates the meaning from a line of Accius 'celebri gradu gressum adcelerate'; the primary MSS. vary between the two. But Virgil nowhere uses the verb in such a manner (see Mackail's note), and I should prefer to abandon it for *celerabat* (so Mackail), which is supported by several parallels in later writers (see Pease).

anili: there is a variant *anilem*, not so well attested, and giving a less imaginative picture; *gradus anilis* is good, but *studium anile* is better. Statius embroiders Virgil (*Th.* vii. 479 ff.) 'hinc atque hinc natae, melior iam sexus, anilis/ prae-cipitantem artus et plus quam possit euntem/ sustentant' (where *plus quam possit euntem* is itself a good touch). In a very different context, Homer depicts the old nurse Eurycleia (Od. xxiii. 3) thus, γούνατα δ' ἐρρώσαντο, πόδες δ' ὑπερικταίνοντο.

642 ff. at trepida . . . usus: 'but shivering, a wild thing in her monstrous design, Dido—her bloodshot eyeballs rolling, her quivering cheeks here, there, stain-flecked—paling with death so surely near—Dido burst into the inner dwelling of the palace, and up the high stair she climbed in frenzy, and un-sheathed a sword, a Dardan sword, a gift she had never sought for such an end.'

Dido's time is near; her purpose is *immanis*, horrible, un-canny, shocking, and she is fevered and beside herself, but yet steadfast and unflinching. The dreadful description is in the manner of high tragedy; it is as if we were listening to a Messenger's speech. Dryden begins:

The nurse moves onward, with officious care,
And all the speed her aged limbs can bear.
But furious Dido, with dark thoughts involv'd,
Shook at the mighty mischief she resolv'd.

> With livid spots distinguish'd was her face,
> Red were her rowling eyes, and discompos'd her pace:
> Ghastly she gaz'd, with pain she drew her breath,
> And nature shiver'd at approaching death.

642. *Trepida, immanibus, effera*, all contribute to the sum of horror.

643. volvens: here 'rolling' is appropriate (cf. note on 363); so vii. 399 (of the maddened Amata) 'sanguineam torquens aciem'.

aciem: the pupil of the eye (concrete for the abstract sense of 'sharpness of vision'); cf. Stat. *Th.* x. 166 ff. (of a prophet's frenzy) 'nudusque per ora/ stat furor, et trepidas incerto sanguine tendit/ exhauritque genas—acies huc errat et illuc', a typical example of 'silver' writing, which shows Virgil's stature.

644. interfusa: a 'middle' use, with *genas* as direct object; the *maculae* were caused by her own fever. Henry compares Milton, *PL* x. 1007 ff. 'She ended here, or vehement despair/ Broke off the rest; so much of death her thoughts/ Had entertain'd as dyed her cheeks with pale'.

pallida morte futura: cf. viii. 709 (of Cleopatra) 'pallentem morte futura'. Lucan develops the idea (vii. 129 f.) into 'multorum pallor in ore/ mortis venturae faciesque simillima fato'.

645. interiora . . . limina: cf. 494; Anna had carried out her orders carefully. *Limen* is used for one of the parts of the palace-buildings, much as *moenia* is sometimes used for the 'buildings' of a city.

646. The rhythm of the line, with no strong pause in the third foot, is steady and purposeful.

gradus: this is the reading of the second hand in P, a correction from *radus*. Mackail follows the Oxford text in preferring it to *rogos* (M, Donatus). I cannot agree: *gradus* has surely been brought into the text from 685, where it is in place (see note): here, a word for 'pyre' is plainly needed. With *gradus* we have to picture Dido 'climbing the high stair' and unsheathing the sword before she reaches the pyre; *hic* in 648 will mean 'then', the mention of the *vestes* and the *cubile* must be understood to mean their presence on the pyre, and we are not told that Dido climbed on to it: it is surely more dramatic, as well as more sensible, to read *rogos* here, leaving to the imagination her ascent to the turret on which the pyre was placed (this can be easily understood out of *interiora domus inrumpit limina*). Possibly the plural form *rogos* gave a copyist trouble. Virgil seems first to have used the plural here of a single pyre (cf. Maas, *ALL* xii, p. 525, note);

Ovid may have had this very passage in mind in *Her.* 7. 193
'nec consumpta rogis inscribar Elissa Sychaei' (cf. *Met.* xi.
333, *F.* iii. 546, *Ex Pont.* i. 9. 48, etc.); Propertius has it (ii.
8. 20 'insultetque rogis calcet et ossa mea'), and it occurs in
Statius (e.g. *Th.* vi. 194, xii. 124), while its Virgilian origin is
strongly supported by its presence in the *Declamationes
Maiores* attributed to Quintilian (x. 4, 5, pp. 192–3 in Lehnert's
text) which have many echoes of Virgil's language (cf. note on
664 f.). An analogous innovation is Virgil's use of the plural
poli for *polus* in i. 90, an experiment which he did not repeat,
but in which later poets imitated him (see Mackail, ad loc.).

647. Dardanium: emphatic; it was not any sword, but a Trojan
sword that brought death to Dido—and that too a sword
that she herself had begged as a gift. But it is mere pedantry
to be concerned about the occasion of the gift, or whether it
was the same sword as that mentioned in 507.

648 ff. hic . . . verba: 'and here she caught sight of the Trojan
dress, the bed she knew; and she stayed a little in tears and
remembrance; and then she flung herself upon the couch, and
spoke her last farewell.' The influence of Greek Tragedy is
again clear; cf. Eur. *Alc.* 175 ff. κἄπειτα θάλαμον ἐσπεσοῦσα καὶ
λέχος, / ἐνταῦθα δὴ 'δάκρυσε καὶ λέγει τάδε· / 'Ω λέκτρον, ἔνθα παρθένει'
ἔλυσ' ἐγὼ / κορεύματ' ἐκ τοῦδ' ἀνδρός, οὗ θνῄσκω πέρι, / χαῖρ'· οὐ γὰρ
ἐχθαίρω σ'· ἀπώλεσας δ' ἐμὲ / μόνην. (See Heinze, op. cit., p. 137,
note 2.)

648. Iliacas vestis: the *exuviae* of 496 and 651.

649. lacrimis et mente: the ablatives are probably causal.

650. novissima verba: cf. vi. 231 'lustravitque viros dixitque
novissima verba' (Corynaeus at the funeral of Misenus). But
here Dido bids herself her own *ave atque vale* (cf. xi. 97 f. 'salve
aeternum mihi, maxime Palla, / aeternumque vale', Catull.
101. 10 'atque in perpetuum, frater, ave atque vale').

651–71. *Dido prays for the end : 'In life I have been great' she
says ' and in death I shall still be great. I have built a noble city,
I have avenged my murdered husband. If but Trojan ships had
never come to Carthage, happiness had been mine. I shall die
with none to avenge me, but die I must, and death is my choice.
May the Trojan see the flames of this pyre, and be haunted by the
presage of my death'. She falls back dying, and a great lamentation arises, as if an enemy were within the gates.*

Marlowe (Act **v**) fuses this speech with Dido's words in 628–9:

Now, Dido, with these relics burn thyself,
And make Aeneas famous through the world
For perjury and slaughter of a queen.
Here lies the sword that in the darksome cave

He drew, and swore by, to be true to me;
Thou shalt burn first; thy crime is worse than his.
Here lies the garment which I cloth'd him in
When first he came on shore: perish thou too.
These letters, lines, and perjur'd papers, all
Shall burn to cinders in this precious flame.
And now, ye gods, that guide the starry frame,
And order all things at your high dispose,
Grant, though the traitors land in Italy,
They may be still tormented with unrest;
And from mine ashes let a conqueror rise,
That may revenge this treason to a queen
By ploughing up his countries with the sword!
Betwixt this land and that be never league;
Litora litoribus contraria, fluctibus undas
Imprecor, arma armis ; pugnent ipsique nepotes!
Live, false Aeneas! Truest Dido dies;
Sic, sic iuvat ire sub umbras.

651 f. dulces . . . curis: 'sweet things that once were his, sweet
so long as fate and heaven so willed, take this my spirit, and
loose me from these sorrows.' Dido's love comes flooding
back, and all she remembers now is that he and she were once
happy together. Chaucer has a beautiful version:

A cloth he lafte, and eek his swerd stonding,
When he fro Dido stal in her sleping,
Right at her beddes heed, so gan he hye
Whan that he stal a-wey to his navye;
Which cloth, whan sely Dido gan awake,
She hath hit kist ful ofte for his sake;
And seide, 'O cloth, whyl Jupiter hit leste,
Tak now my soule, unbind me of this unreste!
I have fulfild of fortune al the course'.

653 ff. These are infinitely noble lines: 'echt römischer Hero-
ismus' is Heinze's comment (op. cit., p. 137, note 2). Several
commentators have remarked on their lapidary quality (see
especially E. Fraenkel in *Glotta* xxxiii, 1954, pp. 157 ff.),
comparing the inscriptions on the tombs of the Scipios;
Propertius caught something of their mood in his elegy on
Cornelia (iv. 11. 45 f. 'nec mea mutata est aetas, sine crimine
tota est:/ viximus insignes inter utramque facem'), and in
Camilla's dying words 'hactenus, Acca soror, potui' (xi. 823)
there is a like nobility. But here an English reader may
think rather of Cleopatra's words, 'Give me my robe, put on
my crown: I have/ Immortal longings in me', or of Othello's,
'I have done the state some service, and they know't.'

653. vixi: not necessarily 'my life is done', but 'I have lived a full life'; see Sen. *de ben.* v. 17. 5 'illud in confesso est: quis sine querela moritur? quis extremo die dicere audet: *vixi et quem dederat cursum fortuna peregi*? quis non recusans, non gemens exit? atqui hoc ingrati est, non esse contentum praeterito tempore', where Seneca's interpretation is clear. Similarly, Horace's famous 'vixi: cras vel atra/ nube polum Pater occupato/ vel sole puro'/ is followed by 'non tamen irritum,/ quodcumque retro est, efficiet neque/ diffinget infectumque reddet/ quod fugiens semel hora vexit' (*C.* iii. 29. 43 ff.). As *felix* below shows (it is a word that occurs nowhere else in this book), Dido would have been well content to die, in the knowledge of what she had achieved, if Aeneas had not shattered all her happiness: *vixi* here is full of pride, not of resignation.

654. et . . . imago: 'and now a glorious ghost of what I am shall go beneath the earth.' Note that Dido says not *mea*, but *mei*: she is supremely conscious that her name will live, and the personal pronoun shows this; *mea* would have conveyed a different sense (Virgil might have written 'magnaque sub terras mea nunc descendet imago'). Cf. Nepos vi. 1. 1. 'Lysander Lacedaemonius magnam reliquit sui famam' (where *suam* would have been impossible), Tac. *Ann.* ii. 13. 1 'adsistit tabernaculis fruiturque fama sui' (where *sua* would have had a different shade of meaning), ibid. ii. 54. 3 'adito Ilio quaeque ibi varietate fortunae et nostri origine veneranda' (where *nostri* has something of the same pride that *mei* has here). Dido will be welcomed by the Shades, as Turnus knew that he would be (xii: 648 f. 'sancta ad vos anima atque istius nescia culpae/ descendam magnorum haud umquam indignus avorum'); cf. Warde Fowler, *The Death of Turnus*, p. 115.

Heyne's footnote here (p. 704 of the fourth edition, vol. ii) deserves recording: 'perlato ad nos, dum haec in manibus sunt, gravissimo nuntio de morte *Munchhusii*, immortalis viri, cum perculsus ingenti luctu animus vix ulterius progredi in opere potest, dolori nostro vel alieno loco paullum indulgere liceat. *Vixit* et Is, *vixit*, et *cursum*, at quam gloriosum! quam ad omnem posteritatis memoriam memorabilem! *peregit*', etc., a piece of *pietas* towards a fellow scholar which is typical of the age, like Buttmann's tribute to Spalding on Quintil. xii. 3. 6.

655. urbem . . . statui: a poignant echo of i. 573 'urbem quam statuo vestra est'. Note the structure of these lines, with a self-contained spondaic word in the first foot in 651, 657, 658, as well as here (see on 185).

656. ulta ... recepi: 'I took vengeance for my husband, exacting punishment from the brother who was my foe'; cf. i. 343 ff., and see Mackail.

658. Note the smoothness and simplicity of the line, aided by the structure of the first and fourth feet (cf. note on 522); the only clash between ictus and accent is caused by *Dardaniae*; the versification here should be compared with the violence of Dido's speech in 590 ff. The *motif* goes back to the opening of Euripides' *Medea*, which Ennius in his turn imitated; but Virgil has used it with greater art, and in a more sublime context.

659 ff. dixit ... mortis: 'and with the words she buried her lips in the bed, and cried "We shall die, with none to avenge us; but let death be ours. This way, yes, this, I am resolved to take my shadowy path. Let his eyes drink deep of this flame, the Dardan, heartless, from over the sea, and let him carry with him an omen, the omen of our death."'

659. os impressa toro: again a middle participle, with direct object.

inultae: but an *ultor* will one day arise (625).

660. moriamur: the reflection caught and carried on from *moriemur* (note the royal plural), the mood of command echoing the mood of fact, is one of those haunting effects of an inflected language that is out of reach in English. There is a pale imitation in Propertius ii. 8. 17 f. 'sic igitur prima moriere aetate, Properti? / sed morere: interitu gaudeat illa tuo'.

sic, sic: Servius comments 'et hoc eam se loco intellegimus percussisse', and some modern editors also hold that with the words Dido twice stabs herself. But it is not in Virgil's way to let us see such horrors. Dido means 'this shall be the manner of my dying' (for *iuvat* cf. 498),—'by her own hand, with that very sword, on that very bed, and on that pyre' (Henry), and, we may add, unavenged, and famous, and still loving Aeneas, and with the flame of her pyre to haunt him.

Irvine records a suggestion that Othello stabs Desdemona when he says, 'I that am cruel am yet merciful; I would not have thee linger in thy pain. *So, so.*'

iuvat: it is her decision; but it is hard not to think that the word means also that death is kind.

661. crudelis: reproachful, not in hatred; cf. 311, 681, and Euryalus' mother's cry in ix. 481 ff. 'tune ille senectae/ sera meae requies potuisti linquere solam / crudelis?' For *ab alto* ('far out at sea') see Conway on i. 34.

662. Dardanus: the form is an alternative for *Dardanius* (cf. ii. 618, vi. 57, xi. 287). Here in the nineteen lines that Dido has spoken just before her death, she has used this synonym for

'Trojan' three times; and *ensem Dardanium* in 646 f. reflects
her thoughts. She has not used it before in the book, except
to deny that King Dardanus ever could have founded
Aeneas' line. Yet she dwells on it strangely at the end.

mortis: and so 'Aeneas' is her last thought, 'death' her
last word.

Virgil does not tell us of the kindling of the pyre (cf. note
on 498). We hear of it only from v. 3 ff. 'moenia respiciens,
quae iam infelicis Elissae/ conlucent flammis. quae tantum
accenderit ignem/ causa latet.'

663 f. dixerat . . . conlapsam: as she speaks, she falls. As Donatus remarked, Virgil does not describe her self-wounding; so
in xii. 603 f. we do not see Amata's fatal act, and in *G.* iv.
458 ff. we are left to infer Eurydice's death. Such reticence
is an integral part of Virgil's habit of mind; cf. 391.

663. atque: 'and suddenly' (see Page on i. 227).

ferro: probably 'upon the sword'; but it might be instrumental, 'from the blow of the sword' (so Henry, comparing
679). Cf. Soph. *Tr.* 930 f. ὁρῶμεν αὐτὴν ἀμφιπλῆγι φασγάνῳ / πλευρὰν
ὑφ' ἧπαρ καὶ φρένας πεπληγμένην.

664. conlapsam aspiciunt: note the elision, to show the horrifying moment of her falling.

664 f. ensemque . . . manus: 'and the sword in froth of blood,
and the limp-flung hands.' *Sparsas* could be taken with
cruore; but Henry makes a clear case for the meaning 'flung
wide', 'lying powerless' (Servius comments 'aut perfusas
sanguine aut morte resolutas'), for which he has a good
parallel from ps.-Quintil. *Declam. mai.* 8. 22 (a mother to her
dead son) 'sparsos artus amplexibus iunxi' (cf. note on 646).
Fanshawe has 'Here her maids saw her with spread hands
fall down / Upon the reeking blade', and Stanyhurst has
'hands outspreading'; Gavin Douglas has 'hir handis furth
sprent'.

665 ff. it clamor . . . deorum: 'a cry arises to the high halls'
roof; the city is stricken, as Rumour goes wantoning through
it; the palace is a maze of noise, wailing and moaning and
shrieks from women's lips, the ether an echoing mass of
lamentation. It is just as if a foreign foe has forced the
gates, and all Carthage were perishing, Carthage or Tyre of
old, and the wild flames rolling their way through dwellings of
men and gods alike.' See Henry's vivid note; and cf. xi. 37 f.
(the mourning for Pallas) 'ingentem gemitum tunsis ad sidera
tollunt/ pectoribus, maestoque immugit regia luctu'.

666. concussam: emphatic. *Fama* tells truth at last, rounding
off the tragedy that she had in her own way begun. For
bacchatur cf. 301.

667. A fine onomatopoeic line (note the interplay of all five
vowel-sounds). So in ix. 477 ff., Euryalus' mother 'evolat
infelix et femineo ululatu/ scissa comam muros amens atque
agmina cursu/ prima petit'. Observe the pattern of the line-
ending, like that of 215 (see note). But here there is hiatus
between *femineo* and *ululatu*, so that the *-o* is prolonged, as
it were, to coalesce only slowly with the following *-u-*
(OOOULULATU), like an actual sound of wailing. Norden
(*Aeneis VI*, p. 438) compares Ovid, *Met*. xi. 17 'tympanaque
et plausus et Bacchei ululatus', and suggests a Greek original
such as γυναικείῳ ὀλολυγμῷ (but *Bacchei* there gives a Greek
touch that is not present here).

ululatu: this cannot but recall another cry, that of the
Nymphs in 168. The word is used especially of women (cf. ii.
487 f. 'plangoribus aedes / femineis ululant'); the tidy Pliny
remarks (*Epp*. vi. 20. 14) 'audires ululatus feminarum, in-
fantium quiritatus, clamores virorum'.

668. fremunt: cf. 146; the word implies an indistinguishable
hum of sound; cf. xi. 296 ff. 'variusque per ora cucurrit/
Ausonidum turbata fremor: ceu saxa morantur/ cum rapidos
amnis, fit clauso gurgite murmur/ vicinaeque fremunt ripae
crepitantibus undis'.

669. It seemed as if the city were being sacked, the most
dreadful scene of horror that an ancient writer could imagine (cf. ii. 746 'aut quid in eversa vidi crudelius urbe?'
and such passages as Cic. *Verr*. iv. 52, Livy i. 29. 2). But it is
no mechanical comparison; the rhetoric has meaning. For
Dido's death means the death of her own Carthage, and it
foreshadows the ultimate destruction of the city; and the
sack of Troy is an ever-present memory.

670. Tyros: mentioned as the mother-city of Carthage. Wagner remarks (*Quaest. Virg*. iv.) that this is the only name
of a town for which Virgil uses the Greek termination
-os.

671. perque . . . perque: for the double *-que* see on 83; for the
postponed position of *per* with *culmina* cf. 257 (*ad*), and v.
663 'transtra per et remos'. The repetition shows the flames
rolling on, wave after wave, as Page remarks; cf. ii. 364 f.
'plurima perque vias sternuntur inertia passim/ corpora perque domos', vii. 499 'perque uterum sonitu perque ilia venit
harundo'.

672–92. *Anna hears the cry, and knows its meaning. She hurries
to Dido, and as she goes she reproaches her for such deception,
and herself for her own part in preparing the pyre. But when
she reaches Dido, she is filled with love and pity, and seeks to*

staunch the wound. Dido tries to lift her eyes, but cannot; she
falls back with a sharp sigh of agony.

Note the supreme art with which Anna is now brought into
the last scene of all, to witness something very different from
what she had thought to see: the book began with her presence, and ends with it.

672 ff. audiit . . . clamat: 'and her sister heard the cry, and was
faint with terror; and with dread upon her she ran trembling,
staining cheek with nail and bruising breast with clenched
hand; and she swept through the throng, and called upon
the dying by her name.'

672. exanimis: explained in *trepidoque exterrita cursu* (Mackail,
on v. 669, is surely mistaken in translating it 'breathless').
With sudden intuition, Anna knows at once what has happened, and she is 'dead' with fear.

673. unguibus . . . pugnis: cf. xi. 86 'pectora nunc foedans pugnis, nunc unguibus ora', and xii. 871 (a repetition of the present line). See note on 589 f., and the passages collected here
by Pease. North would have translated *foedans* by 'martyr-
ing'.

ora . . . pectora: a frequent 'poetic plural' with reference
to one individual (so too *terga, colla, corda*); classical prose
not only avoids such a plural altogether, but rarely has the
plural forms even where several persons are concerned. The
earliest certain examples of this poetic use occur in Cicero's
Aratea; in Virgil, the plural predominates in *terga, colla, ora*,
but the plurals *pectora* and *vultus* do not begin to predominate
over the singular until Ovid. Perhaps the usage developed
by analogy with such 'pluralia tantum' as *nares, fauces*. See
Maas, *ALL* xii, pp. 530 ff. for some interesting details, and
Löfstedt, *Synt.* i, pp. 30 f.

674. There is a formal caesura after *ac*, but its close connexion
with what follows blurs the pause, there is no fourth-foot
caesura, and the line falls into three groups of words in a
most unusual rhythm: *per medios ruit | ac morientem | nomine
clamat*; haste and breathlessness are well illustrated. Cf. vii.
119 'eripuit pater | ac stupefactus | numine pressit', where
surprise and haste are combined.

675 f. hoc illud . . . parabant?: '*this* it was then, my sister?
I--I deceived all this time, and by you? *This* it was that
that pyre of yours had in store for me, *this* those flames, and
this that altar?'

675 hoc illud: literally, 'this, then, was that', 'this is what it
meant', cf. Ter. *Andr.* 125 f. 'hoc illud est, / hinc illae lacru-
mae', Soph. *El.* 1115 f. τοῦτ' ἐκεῖν' ἤδη σαφές· / πρόχειρον ἄχθος,

ὡς ἔοικε, δέρκομαι (and somewhat similarly vii. 128 'haec erat illa fames').

me: both this and *fraude* are stressed, and the imperfect implies 'you were deceiving me all along'.

676. ignes araeque: a variation of *rogus*; so the *aram* of vi. 177 = the *pyram* of vi. 215; see Norden on vi. 177. Cf. Stat. *Th.* iv. 456 ff. (Tiresias sacrificing to bring up the ghosts), where *focus, agger, ara* are referred to as *pyras* (465) and *rogi* (472). For the plural *arae* see on 219.

677 f. quid . . . moriens?: 'you forsook me, and what first shall be my lament? I was the sister who shared your life, and have you scorned me in your dying hour?' Anna cannot tell what distresses her most, her own part in the tragedy, or the way that she was deceived, or the fact that her own *unanima soror*, to whom she has always been a *comes*, should have deceived her: hitherto, Dido has always needed her—now, Dido has thrust her away. *Comitem* is the emphatic word, like *me* above. *Moriens* shows that Anna has no doubt of what has happened.

678. vocasses: a past jussive, like *tulissem, implessem* in 604–5. The use of *eadem* here is very close to that of *eandem* in 124 (where see note).

679. idem . . . tulisset: 'that same sword-wrought agony, that very same hour should have taken us together.' *Ferro* is formally an instrumental ablative with *tulisset*, but it is so close to *dolor* that the two form a unit (cf. Mackail's Appendix A). *Tulisset* might be taken as an apodosis with suppressed protasis ('if you had sent for me, we should have perished together'), but it is much more probably another past jussive, as *idem . . . tulisset* is so clearly a variation of *eadem . . . vocasses*.

680 f. his etiam . . . abessem?: 'and—more—was it with these very hands that I built it, did I pray solemnly to our country's gods, only to be far away from you—O the cruelty of it—when you were laid so?'

680. struxi: sc. *pyram*. The omission would be strange, were it not that the pyre fills Anna's thoughts.

680 f. patriosque . . . deos: we are not told when Anna did this; cf. note on 498 (p. 149).

681. voce: practically equivalent to 'loudly'. The formula *voce vocare* is a type of pleonasm which goes back to Ennius (*Ann.* 44 'exim compellare pater me voce videtur') and beyond Ennius to Homer (*Il.* iii. 161 Ἑλένην ἐκαλέσσατο φωνῇ); Virgil uses it as an archaism in a formula of solemnity (so too iii. 68, vi. 247, 506, xii. 638); see Löfstedt, *Synt.* ii, p. 185. Cf. 'At the beginning of Morning Prayer the Minister shall read with a loud voice some one or more of these Sentences of the Scriptures that follow'.

sic: with *posita*; cf. ii. 644 'sic o sic positum adfati discedite corpus', xi. 30 f. 'corpus ubi exanimi positum Pallantis Acoetes/ servabat senior'. *Posita* recalls the words of Bishop King's *Exsequy*, 'So close the ground, and 'bout. her shade/ Black curtains draw: my bride is laid'.

ut: final, not consecutive; yet the clause is not an ordinary final, as it expresses not the purpose of Anna but that of Fate; cf. Tac. *H.* i. 48 'ipse diu exul, quadriduo Caesar, properata adoptione ad hoc tantum maiori fratri praelatus est ut prior occideretur': see R. G. Nisbet in *AJP* xliv, 1923, pp. 27 ff.

crudelis: this may be either nominative or vocative. Commentators have been divided from early times on the point; and as one thinks now of Anna, now of Dido, each without the other's comfort and confidence at such a moment, how can any sure decision be made, and why should it be made? It is a similar, but more important, ambiguity to that of 634. Heinze (op. cit., p. 144 note 1) well compares Soph. *Ai.* 908 ff. οἷος ἄρ' αἱμάχθης, / ἄφαρκτος φίλων· / ἐγὼ δ' ὁ πάντα κωφός, ὁ πάντ' ἄϊδρις, / κατημέλησα.

682 f. exstinxti . . . tuam: 'you have blotted out your life and mine too, my sister, yes, the State of Carthage and the city that was yours.' Dido has brought her whole proud creation down in ruins: Anna did not hear her words in 655, but she knew what Carthage meant to Dido and what Dido meant to Carthage.

682. populumque patresque: a typical example of the double *-que* in what amounts to a formula (cf. ix. 192, and see note on 83, Christensen in *ALL* xv, p. 203). The words imply the whole fabric of the city-state: for the *patres* cf. i. 426 'iura magistratusque legunt sanctumque senatum'. The phrase forms a single unit, like *te meque*, with *urbemque tuam* added as a third item. Henry succeeds in working into his note a reference to those of his contemporaries who 'lose themselves in admiration of the fantastic, tortured and torturing phraseology of *Hiawatha* and the *Idylls of the King*', a nice thought.

683 ff. date . . . legam: 'O help me bathe her wounds in water, and if any breath remaining strays to be her last, O let me catch it on my lips.' Anna's reproaches end abruptly, as she catches sight of her dying sister; cf. ix. 486 f., where Euryalus' mother cries 'nec te tua funera mater / produxi pressive oculos aut vulnera lavi'.

683. date: cf. vi. 883 f. 'manibus date lilia plenis, / purpureos

spargam flores', and see Mackail on both passages. It is possible, as Servius saw, either to supply an object (aquam) to
date, or to take date as equivalent to permittite, with abluam as
dependent jussive. For the latter construction cf. Plaut.
Curc. 313 'vin aquam?'—'si frustulenta est, da, opsecro
hercle, opsorbeam', Auson. Ephem. 2. 5 f. 'da rore fontano
abluam / manus et os et lumina' (see Thes. L. L. s.v. do, col.
1691. 10 ff.). The distinction seems academic: the thought in
the heart is clear. Date is a prayer, and we need not specify
to whom, God or man: Anna cries in her anguish, 'Let me be
able to help her and comfort her, let me not be too late.' I
should prefer to omit the comma after date, as Mackail and
Page do.

684. **abluam**: cf. 387, where the cretic *audiam* is similarly used,
involving a most unusual elision. Virgil does this very spar-
ingly, and with clear limitations. Parallel with this passage
and with 387 is xii. 569 'eruam et aequa solo fumantia culmina ponam': *et* follows the verb in all three, and the context of each is one of deep emotion. The form *Ilium* occurs
eight times (incidentally, never after the sixth book, although
Ilia tellus occurs in ix. 285, xi. 245); in seven of these lines *et*
follows the name, and in one the following word is *in*: if
Virgil had not allowed himself such an elision, he could not
have used the name at all. In i. 599 the line ends with *om-
nium egenos*, especially striking because an elision at this
place in the line is so rare: Norden (*Aeneis VI*, p. 372) suggests
that it is an Ennian phrase, used for archaic tone. In ii. 667
the line opens with *alterum in alterius*, a rhetorical juxtaposition which adds vividness in the context and would have
been impossible without elision. There remains one further
example: x. 514 'ardens limitem agit ferro, te, Turne, superbum', which Norden (op. cit., p. 454) thinks may also be an
Ennian reminiscence; it might also be explained by the
violence of the context. See Norden, op. cit., Anh. XI; Maas,
ALL xii, pp. 508 f.; Platnauer, op. cit., p. 73. Ovid has two
such elisions, both at the end of a line (*Am.* iii. 6. 101 'flumi-
num amores', *Met.* vi. 524 'virginem et unam').

extremus . . . errat: the last breath was so caught, that the
soul of the dying might be caught by the living kinsman; cf.
Cic. *Verr.* v. 118 'matresque miserae pernoctabant ad ostium
carceris ab extremo conspectu liberum exclusae; quae nihil
aliud orabant nisi ut filiorum suorum postremum spiritum
ore excipere liceret'. Pease has many illustrations from
literature and folklore; see also Henry's note, and his quota-
tion from St. Ambrose, *de exc. Sat.* 1. 19. Editors compare
Pope, *Eloisa to Abelard* 324 'Suck my last breath and catch

my dying soul', and Shelley, *Adonais* 44 f. 'O let thy breath flow from thy dying soul / Even to my mouth and heart, that I may suck', an interesting example of literary genealogy.

685 ff. sic . . . cruores: 'and as she spoke, she had passed all the stairs to the top, and caught to her heart her sister with life so nearly gone, and tried sobbingly to warm her and to dry the black gouts of blood with her dress.' Gavin Douglas translates:

> This sayand scho the bing ascendis anone,
> And gan embrace half dede hir sister germane,
> Culzeand in hir bosum, and murnand ay
> And with hir wympil wypit the blude away.

685. gradus . . . altos: all this time, Anna had been climbing the stairway to the tower or keep where the pyre was; they seem endless stairs (*altos*); *evaserat* marks the moment at which she first caught sight of Dido, when her tone changed from reproach to pity, and with *ore legam* she is at her sister's side. *Gradus* here is in place; contrast 645-6.

686. semianimem: the *i* of *sēmi-* has to be treated consonant-ally, as here, if such a word is to be used in a hexameter, so that a quadrisyllable results by synizesis ($\overline{semjanimem}$); cf. x. 396, 404, xi. 635, xii. 356; similarly $\overline{semihominis}$ (viii. 194), $\overline{parietibus}$ (ii. 442), $\overline{abietibus}$ (ix. 674). But the scansion $\overline{fluviorum}$ (as a trisyllable) in G. i. 482 is not quite parallel, since *flŭvĭorum* could stand elsewhere in the line without such treatment. Cf. Platnauer, op. cit., p. 68.

fovebat: probably conative (like *siccabat* below), though it might be the imperfect of repeated action. The word is full of emotion: Anna gives her sister the warmth of her body and the comfort and blessing of her heart, to ease her last moments on earth (cf. note on 193). Cf. x. 837 f. (of the wounded Mezentius) 'ipse aeger, anhelans/ colla fovet'; xii. 420 'fovit ea vulnus lympha longaevus Iapyx'. Heinze (op. cit., p. 137, note 2) well compares Soph. *Tr.* 938 f. ἀλλὰ πλευρόθεν / πλευρὰν παρεὶς ἔκειτο πόλλ' ἀναστένων.

687. cruores: Maas (*ALL* xii, p. 520) observes that this plural use, in the sense of 'drops of blood', is one of Virgil's inventions, which he does not use elsewhere; Horace has *cruoribus* in the same sense (*C.* ii. 1. 5). Ovid has *cruores* once only (= 'bloodshed'), *Met.* xiii. 482, and Lucan has *cruores* (vii. 636) and *cruoribus* (iii. 405), again meaning 'bloodshed'; Valerius Flaccus, Statius, and Silius use the plural fairly freely, in the sense in which Virgil has it here (see *Thes. L. L.*, s.v.). Virgil probably had the Greek use of αἵματα in mind; cf.

Eur. *El.* 1172 f. ἀλλ' οἵδε μητρὸς νεοφόνοις ἐν αἵμασι / πεφυρμένοι βαίνουσιν ἐξ οἴκων πόδα, and Denniston's note.

688 f. **illa . . . vulnus:** 'but Dido made an effort to raise her heavy eyes to meet her, and fell fainting; the wound, the deep-pierced wound, cried out beneath her breast.'

rursus: with *attollere*; as Anna looks down upon Dido, so Dido tries to look up at her 'in turn'; cf. Ovid, *Met.* xv. 607 ff. 'verba tamen vulgi vox eminet una "quis ille est?"/... rursus ad hos Cipus "quem poscitis" inquit "habetis"'.

689. **deficit:** the run-over word, and the pause, are eloquent.

infixum: note that this is said of the wound; Virgil does not mention a weapon, and it is the wound that cries aloud.

stridit: 'the word accurately expresses the whistling sound with which breath escapes from a pierced lung' (Mackail—see Irvine also).

The echo of 67, 'tacitum vivit sub pectore vulnus', may be unconscious, but the mind cannot help going back to it; but that other wound did not 'cry out'.

690 ff. **ter . . . reperta:** Dryden has

> Thrice Dido try'd to raise her drooping head,
> And fainting thrice, fell grov'ling on the bed.
> Thrice op'd her heavy eyes, and sought the light,
> But having found it, sicken'd at the sight:
> And clos'd her lids at last in endless night;

with which compare F. W. H. Myers (*Essays Classical*, p. 176),

> For thrice she turned, and thrice had fain dispread
> Her dying arms to lift her dying head;
> Thrice in high heaven, with dimmed eyes wand'ring wide,
> She sought the light, and found the light, and sighed.

Mark the slow spondees in *ter sese attollens* for her effort, the dactyls (691) as she falls back writhing, and again the spondees (692) as her dim eyes grope for the light.

691. **alto:** not otiose; the sky was so far above.

692. **lucem:** the *lux* that she had sought *quam primum abrumpere* (631). Note the beautiful elision in *lucem ingemuitque* (Virgil could have written *gemuitque* if he had wished), so suggestive of Dido's sigh, and of the failing of her strength, and of the emptiness of her quest. Catullus comes near it in his words at his brother's grave (101. 3 f.) 'ut te postremo donarem munere mortis/ et mutam nequiquam alloquerer cinerem', where the elision before the caesura in the pentameter has its own pathos.

ingemuit: 'she sighed deeply' (the intensive use of *in*). Henry comments:

'there is no so touching word in the whole *Aeneid* as this *ingemuit*, placing as it does before the mind capable of such sympathies the whole heart-rending history in a single retrospective glance'. One could find many others as touching, but Henry was right to say here what the word conveyed to him. Every reader will find his grief in his own way.

693–705. *And at last Juno took pity upon Dido, and sent Iris down from heaven to end her agony; and Iris cut off a lock of her golden hair for Dis; and Dido's spirit was released, and sought the shelter of the winds.*

After the unbearable climax, the book ends in tranquillity, like a Greek tragedy.

693. omnipotens : yet Juno the protectress of Carthage had neither power nor wish to prevent the pity and terror of Dido's tragic course. Is the epithet Virgil's own comment on the inscrutability of the will of God?

694. difficilisque obitus: 'and the hard travail of her death'. The word *obitus* for 'death' is rare in poetry, just as *obire* is rarely used for 'to die' (cf. Axelson, *Unpoetische Wörter*, p. 105, n. 27). Used in the plural, as here, of a single death, it is rarer still (cf. Prop. iii. 4. 12, Statius *Th*. ii. 118, vii. 693, Val. Flacc. i. 769, 810). It does not occur at all in Catullus, Horace, Tibullus, or Lucan, and Ovid has it (in the singular) twice only (*Met*. iii. 137, xv. 151); Lucretius, however, uses it before Virgil. Its occurrence here is striking, and Virgil has plainly made an innovation just as he did with *rogos* (646).

It is hard to believe that this plural has no nuance of meaning. In the only other line where Virgil has the word, he avoids the plural although that context would have made it quite natural (xii. 500 ff. 'quis carmine caedes/ diversas obitumque ducum . . . / expediat?'); similarly, Ovid avoids the plural in *Met*. iii. 136 f. 'dicique beatus/ ante obitum nemo supremaque funera debet', where the use of *funera* (cf. note on 500) might have suggested *obitus*. May the plural here not be 'intensive', marking the slow agony of Dido's death, the tortured moments one by one? There is an analogous use of θάνατοι in tragedy (see Jebb on Soph. *El*. 205 f., and cf. *O.T*. 497, *Tr*. 1276) where a violent death is implied; cf. W. Havers in *Festschrift für Paul Kretschmer*, pp. 44 f. Norden holds (*Aeneis VI*, p. 409) that Virgil has used the plural form to avoid hiatus, which is of course possible, and the same reason could be given for the plural in Stat. *Th*. ii. 118 and Val. Flacc. i. 769 (where a singular epithet could not stand) and in Stat. *Th*. vii. 693 (where a vowel follows *obitus*). But metrical necessity does not account for Val. Flacc. i.

810 'indecoresque obitus', where no vowel follows and where the epithet could have been singular. In Prop. iii. 4. 12 'ante meos obitus sit precor ille dies', it is open to argue that the plural is caused by the impossibility of *meum*; but why did Propertius not write 'ille dies obitum sit precor ante meum'? I doubt if metrical needs will wholly account for Virgil's use of this plural. However, a label such as 'intensive' is full of pitfalls, and is highly subjective in its application; see some cautious remarks by Löfstedt on the matter (*Synt.* i, pp. 53 f.). Perhaps the most to be said of either view is 'not proven'.

Irim: the Rainbow, messenger of Juno or Jupiter (cf. ix. 803, x. 38, etc., Ovid, *Met.* xi. 589 ff. 'induitur velamina mille colorum / Iris et arcuato caelum curvamine signans / tecta petit iussi sub nube latentia regis'), Homer's Ἶρις ἀελλόπος, Ἶρις χρυσόπτερος.

695. quae . . . artus: 'to loose her struggling soul and close-locked limbs'; the soul seems to wrestle with the body that holds it back. Henry takes *nexos artus* of the whole organism or *compages* of the body, its μελέων σύνδεσμα (Eur. *Hipp.* 199); but it is simpler to regard *nexos* as the counterpart of *luctantem*, *artus* of *animam*.

696. fato: equivalent to 'the fulfilment of time'; Dido's act cut short her allotted span. Henry compares Pliny, *Epp.* i. 12. 1 'decessit Corellius Rufus, et quidem sponte, quod dolorem meum exulcerat: est enim luctuosissimum genus mortis, quae non ex natura nec fatalis videtur'.

merita nec morte: 'nor by a death that was her desert'; for the postponed *nec* see on 33. Virgil's judgement here is explicit; and we must remember that when Aeneas meets Dido's ghost in the *lugentes campi* (vi. 442 ff.), she is among those who died for love, not among those who had killed themselves. See Norden, *Aeneis VI*, p. 12.

697. ante diem: as she herself had prayed that Aeneas might die (620).

698. In a sacrifice the hair of a victim was first removed and offered as a first-fruit; and when men die at the appointed time, Proserpina herself cuts off a lock of hair as a like first-fruit (cf. Hor. *C.* i. 28. 19 f., Stat. *S.* ii. 1. 146 f. 'et iam frigentia lumina torpent,/ iam complexa manu crinem tenet infera Iuno'): but she could not do this for the untimely dead, and so Iris is sent to do it, out of special compassion for Dido. See Bailey, *Religion in Virgil*, p. 246: he thinks that the conception of Proserpina's powerlessness in such a case is Virgil's own. Both Servius (on iii. 46) and Macrobius (*Sat.* v. 19. 2 ff.) refer to Eur. *Alc.* 74 ff., where Thanatos says στείχω

δ' ἐπ' αὐτήν, ὡς κατάρξωμαι ξίφει· | ἱερὸς γὰρ οὗτος τῶν κατὰ χθονὸς
θεῶν | ὅτου τόδ' ἔγχος κρατὸς ἁγνίσῃ τρίχα: cf. Heinze, op. cit.,
p. 246.

698 f. nondum . . . Orco: 'Proserpina had not yet taken to herself the golden tress from her head, in forfeit of her life to
Stygian Orcus.' The phrase appended by *-que* explains the
consequence of *abstulerat*. For the sense of *damnaverat* cf.
Mackail on xii. 727. The name Orcus is used as a synonym
for Dis or Pluto (cf. ii. 398 'multos Danaum demittimus
Orco'); Bailey remarks (op. cit., pp. 251 f.) that in Roman
usage Proserpina 'always remained a figure of legend and
mythology, and never faded, like Dis and Orcus, into a
symbol of the lower world'.

700 ff. ergo . . . recessit: 'and because of this, down across
heaven, with dew upon her saffron wings, came Iris skimming, trailing a thousand colours that glanced gay in the sun
as he met her; and she stood above Dido's head. "This tress,
consecrate to Dis, I take as I am bid; and so from your poor
body I give you release." So speaking, she cut the tress with
her right hand: and with it all the warmth melted away from
Dido's body, and her soul sought the shelter of the winds.'
Fanshawe has:

> So Iris her great mistress' will obeys,
> Descending to the earth immediately
> On curious wings, which the sun's oblique rays
> With water-colours painted variously:
> And standing right over her head, said she,
> 'As I am bid, these vowed locks I bear
> To Hell's black prince, and do pronounce thee free
> From body's bonds.' This said, cut off her hair;
> Heat left her, and th'uncaged soul flew through the air.

The beautiful picture of the Rainbow (the identification with
Iris goes back to Hesiod, not to Homer) heightens the bitter
contrast between the light that Dido had sought and the
darkness that she had found. Virgil has a like description
elsewhere (v. 88 f., 609), but not in so poignant a context.

701. varios: cf. 202 and note. There is a fascinating passage
on rainbows and their causes in Seneca, *NQ* i. 3; he explains
their *varietas* (§ 12) as due to the fact that 'pars coloris a sole
est, pars a nube illa; umor modo caeruleas lineas, modo virides,
modo purpureas similes et luteas aut igneas ducit, duobus
coloribus hanc varietatem efficientibus, remisso et intento',
etc. Virgil's *varius* implies the variety of the different colours,
their gay brightness, and their iridescence *adverso sole* (cf.
Sen. l.c. 11 'illud dubium esse nulli potest quin arcus imago

solis sit roscida et cava nube concepta. quod ex hoc tibi appareat: nunquam non adversa soli est').

702. The pause after *astitit*, so late in the line, is unusual and effective (cf. 13, 704); for the end-pattern *hunc ego Diti* cf. 336, 420.

703. sacrum: emphatic, both in its position and because it stands alone with no run-over to the second foot. *Isto* is said pityingly, by goddess to mortal.

    solvo: cf. xi. 828 f. (of Camilla) 'tum frigida toto/ paulatim exsolvit se corpore'.

704. The pause is in the same position as that in 702, but is less marked.

705. So when Lausus died (x. 819 f.) 'tum vita per auras / concessit maesta ad manis corpusque reliquit'; and at Turnus' death (xii. 952) 'vitaque cum gemitu fugit indignata sub umbras'. The rhythm should be noticed: the third-foot caesura is blurred by the elision of *atque* before *in*, and there is no fourth-foot caesura; the effect is one of a gradual commingling of word with word, spirit with air.

    Dido's bright day is done; and all the heat and fury of her tragedy is fallen to nothing, ending quietly and almost imperceptibly at the last. It is the end of the 'first act' of the *Aeneid* (cf. Mackail, p. 298). Henry's epilogue here should be read by all who (in his words) 'dare to feel that the exercise of their intellectual faculties in the ennobling, exalting, purifying contemplation of the grand, the beautiful and the pathetic, whether in the poetical, philosophical, or manuplastic creations of the master spirits of mankind, is not, cannot be, of the nature of sin.'

APPENDIX

OVID, *Heroides* VII

DIDO AENEAE

Sic ubi fata vocant, udis abiectus in herbis
    Ad vada Maeandri concinit albus olor.
Nec quia te nostra sperem prece posse moveri,
    Adloquor: adverso movimus ista deo.
5 Sed merita et famam corpusque animumque pudicum
    Cum male perdiderim, perdere verba leve est.
Certus es ire tamen miseramque relinquere Didon,
    Atque idem venti vela fidemque ferent?
Certus es, Aenea, cum foedere solvere naves,
10   Quaeque ubi sint nescis, Itala regna sequi?
Nec nova Carthago, nec te crescentia tangunt
    Moenia nec sceptro tradita summa tuo?
Facta fugis, facienda petis: quaerenda per orbem
    Altera, quaesita est altera terra tibi.
15 Ut terram invenias, quis eam tibi tradet habendam?
    Quis sua non notis arva tenenda dabit?
Alter habendus amor tibi restat et altera Dido:
    Quamque iterum fallas, altera danda fides.
Quando erit, ut condas instar Carthaginis urbem,
20   Et videas populos altus ab arce tuos?
Omnia ut eveniant, nec di tua vota morentur,
    Unde tibi, quae te sic amet, uxor erit?
Uror, ut inducto ceratae sulpure taedae:
26   Aenean animo noxque diesque refert.
Ille quidem male gratus et ad mea munera surdus
    Et quo, si non sim stulta, carere velim:
Non tamen Aenean, quamvis male cogitat, odi,
30   Sed queror infidum questaque peius amo.
Parce, Venus, nurui, durumque amplectere fratrem,
    Frater Amor; castris militet ille tuis.
Aut ego quem coepi, neque enim dedignor, amare,
    Materiam curae praebeat ille meae.
35 Fallor, et ista mihi falso iactatur imago:
    Matris ab ingenio dissidet ille suae.
Te lapis et montes innataque rupibus altis
    Robora, te saevae progenuere ferae,
Aut mare, quale vides agitari nunc quoque ventis,
40   Quo tamen adversis fluctibus ire paras.
Quo fugis? obstat hiemps: hiemis mihi gratia prosit.
    Aspice, ut eversas concitet Eurus aquas.

Quod tibi malueram, sine me debere procellis:
    Iustior est animo ventus et unda tuo.
45 Non ego sum tanti—quid non censeris inique?—
    Ut pereas, dum me per freta longa fugis.
Exerces pretiosa odia et constantia magno,
    Si, dum me careas, est tibi vile mori.
Iam venti ponent, strataque aequaliter unda
50   Caeruleis Triton per mare curret equis.
Tu quoque cum ventis utinam mutabilis esses!
    Et, nisi duritia robora vincis, eris.
Quid, si nescires, insana quid aequora possunt?
    Expertae totiens tam male credis aquae?
55 Ut pelago suadente etiam retinacula solvas,
    Multa tamen latus tristia pontus habet.
Nec violasse fidem temptantibus aequora prodest:
    Perfidiae poenas exigit ille locus.
Praecipue cum laesus amor, quia mater Amorum
60   Nuda Cytheriacis edita fertur aquis.
Perdita ne perdam, timeo, noceamve nocenti,
    Neu bibat aequoreas naufragus hostis aquas.
Vive precor: sic te melius quam funere perdam:
    Tu potius leti causa ferere mei.
65 Finge, age, te rapido (nullum sit in omine pondus)
    Turbine deprendi: quid tibi mentis erit?
Protinus occurrent falsae periuria linguae
    Et Phrygia Dido fraude coacta mori;
Coniugis ante oculos deceptae stabit imago
70   Tristis et effusis sanguinolenta comis.
Quid tanti est *ut* tum 'merui! concedite!' dicas,
    Quaeque cadent, in te fulmina missa putes?
Da breve saevitiae spatium pelagique tuaeque:
    Grande morae pretium tuta futura via est.
75 Nec mihi tu curae; puero parcatur Iulo:
    Te satis est titulum mortis habere meae.
Quid puer Ascanius, quid commeruere Penates?
    Ignibus ereptos obruet unda deos?
Sed neque fers tecum, nec, quae mihi, perfide, iactas,
80   Presserunt umeros sacra paterque tuos.
Omnia mentiris, neque enim tua fallere lingua
    Incipit a nobis, primaque plector ego.
Si quaeras, ubi sit formosi mater Iuli,
    Occidit a duro sola relicta viro.
85 Haec mihi narraras: at me movere: merentem
    Ure: minor culpa poena futura mea est.
Nec mihi mens dubia est, quin te tua numina damnent:
    Per mare, per terras septima iactat hiemps.

Fluctibus eiectum tuta statione recepi
90   Vixque bene audito nomine regna dedi.
His tamen officiis utinam contenta fuissem,
   Et mihi concubitus fama sepulta foret!
Illa dies nocuit, qua nos declive sub antrum
   Caeruleus subitis compulit imber aquis.
95 Audieram vocem: nymphas ululasse putavi;
   Eumenides fati signa dedere mei.
Exige, laese pudor, poenas violate† Sychaei . . .

*   *   *

Ad quas, me miseram, plena pudoris eo.
Est mihi marmorea sacratus in aede Sychaeus:
100   Oppositae frondes velleraque alba tegunt:
Hinc ego me sensi noto quater ore citari;
   Ipse sono tenui dixit 'Elissa, veni!'
Nulla mora est, venio; venio tibi debita coniunx;
   Sum tamen admissi tarda pudore mei.
105 Da veniam culpae: decepit idoneus auctor:
   Invidiam noxae detrahit ille meae.
Diva parens seniorque pater, pia sarcina nati,
   Spem mihi mansuri rite dedere viri.
Si fuit errandum, causas habet error honestas:
110   Adde fidem, nulla parte pigendus erit.
Durat in extremum vitaeque novissima nostrae
   Prosequitur fati, qui fuit ante, tenor.
Occidit internas coniunx mactatus ad aras,
   Et sceleris tanti praemia frater habet;
115 Exul agor cineresque viri patriamque relinquo
   Et feror in duras hoste sequente vias;
Adplicor ignotis fratrique elapsa fretoque
   Quod tibi donavi, perfide, litus emo.
Urbem constitui lateque patentia fixi
120   Moenia finitimis invidiosa locis.
Bella tument: bellis peregrina et femina temptor,
   Vixque rudis portas urbis et arma paro.
Mille procis placui, qui me coiere querentes
   Nescioquem thalamis praeposuisse suis.
125 Quid dubitas vinctam Gaetulo tradere Iarbae?
   Praebuerim sceleri bracchia nostra tuo.
Est etiam frater, cuius manus impia possit
   Respergi nostro, sparsa cruore viri.
Pone deos et quae tangendo sacra profanas:
130   Non bene caelestis impia dextra colit.
Si tu cultor eras elapsis igne futurus,
   Paenitet elapsos ignibus esse deos.

Forsitan et gravidam Didon, scelerate, relinquas,
    Parsque tui lateat corpore clausa meo.
135 Accedet fatis matris miserabilis infans,
    Et nondum nati funeris auctor eris,
Cumque parente sua frater morietur Iuli,
    Poenaque conexos auferet una duos.
'Sed iubet ire deus.' vellem, vetuisset adire,
140 Punica nec Teucris pressa fuisset humus.
Hoc duce nempe deo ventis agitaris iniquis
    Et teris in rapido tempora longa freto!
Pergama vix tanto tibi erant repetenda labore,
    Hectore si vivo quanta fuere forent.
145 Non patrium Simoenta petis, sed Thybridis undas:
    Nempe ut pervenias, quo cupis, hospes eris.
Utque latet vitatque tuas abstrusa carinas,
    Vix tibi continget terra petita seni.
Hos potius populos in dotem, ambage remissa,
150   Accipe et advectas Pygmalionis opes.
Ilion in Tyriam transfer felicius urbem,
    Resque loco regis sceptraque sacra tene.
Si tibi mens avida est belli, si quaerit Iulus,
    Unde suo partus Marte triumphus eat,
155 Quem superet, nequid desit, praebebimus hostem:
    Hic pacis leges, hic locus arma capit.
Tu modo, per matrem fraternaque tela, sagittas,
    Perque fugae comites, Dardana sacra, deos,
—Sic superent, quoscumque tua de gente reportat
160 Mars ferus, et damni sit modus ille tui,
Ascaniusque suos feliciter impleat annos,
    Et senis Anchisae molliter ossa cubent!—
Parce, precor, domui, quae se tibi tradit habendam:
    Quod crimen dicis praeter amasse meum?
165 Non ego sum Phthias magnisve oriunda Mycenis,
    Nec steterunt in te virque paterque meus.
Si pudet uxoris, non nupta, sed hospita dicar:
    Dum tua sit Dido quidlibet esse feret.
Nota mihi freta sunt Afrum frangentia litus:
170   Temporibus certis dantque negantque viam.
Cum dabit aura viam, praebebis carbasa ventis:
    Nunc levis eiectam continet alga ratem.
Tempus ut observem, manda mihi: serius ibis,
    Nec te, si cupies, ipsa manere sinam.
175 Et socii requiem poscunt, laniataque classis
    Postulat exiguas semirefecta moras.
Pro meritis et siqua tibi debebimus ultra,
    Pro spe coniugii tempora parva peto,

Dum freta mitescunt et amor, dum tempore et usu
180   Fortiter edisco tristia posse pati.
Si minus, est animus nobis effundere vitam:
    In me crudelis non potes esse diu.
Aspicias utinam, quae sit scribentis imago:
    Scribimus, et gremio Troicus ensis adest,
185 Perque genas lacrimae strictum labuntur in ensem,
    Qui iam pro lacrimis sanguine tinctus erit.
Quam bene conveniunt fato tua munera nostro!
    Instruis inpensa nostra sepulcra brevi.
Nec mea nunc primum feriuntur pectora telo:
190   Ille locus saevi vulnus amoris habet.
Anna soror, soror Anna, meae male conscia culpae,
    Iam dabis in cineres ultima dona meos.
Nec consumpta rogis inscribar ELISSA SYCHAEI,
    Hoc tamen in tumuli marmore carmen erit:
195 PRAEBVIT AENEAS ET CAVSAM MORTIS ET ENSEM;
    IPSA SVA DIDO CONCIDIT VSA MANV.

INDEX VERBORVM

INDEX NOMINVM ET RERVM